W9-ABN-283

VIETNAM

in

AMERICAN
LITERATURE

TWAYNE'S
LITERATURE
&
SOCIETY
SERIES

Leo Marx, General Editor
Massachusetts Institute of Technology

Warren French, Volume Editor
University of Wales, Swansea

VIETNAM

in

AMERICAN

LITERATURE

Philip H. Melling

University of Wales, Swansea

Twayne Publishers • Boston

A DIVISION OF G. K. HALL & CO.

Twayne's Literature and Society Series No. 1

Copyright 1990 by G. K. Hall & Co.
All rights reserved.
Published by Twayne Publishers
A division of G. K. Hall & Co.
70 Lincoln Street
Boston, Massachusetts 02111

Copyediting supervised by Barbara Sutton.
Book design and production by Janet Z. Reynolds.
Typeset in Primer by Crane Typesetting Service, West Barnstable, Massachusetts.

First published 1990.
10 9 8 7 6 5 4 3 2 1

The paper used in this publication meets the minimum requirements
of American National Standard for Information Sciences—Permanence
of Paper for Printed Library Materials, ANSI Z39.48-1984. ∞™

Printed and bound in the United States of America.

Library of Congress Cataloging-in-Publication Data

Melling, Philip H.
Vietnam in American literature / Philip H. Melling.
p.   cm.—(Twayne's literature & society series: #1)
Includes bibliographical references and index.
ISBN 0-8057-8850-6
1. American literature—20th century—History and criticism.
2. Vietnamese Conflict, 1961–1975—Literature and the conflict.
3. Puritans—New England—Influence.   4. War in literature.
I Title.   II. Series.
PS228.V5M45   1990
810.9′358—dc20   90-37718
                                                                 CIP

To my father

But this too, is true; stories can save us. Mostly, though, we had to make up our own. Often they were exaggerated, or blatant lies, but it was a way of bringing body and soul back together, or a way of making new bodies for the souls to inhabit.

—TIM O'BRIEN, "The Lives of the Dead"

CONTENTS

ACKNOWLEDGMENTS

I wish to express my gratitude to the British Council for providing me with a grant to visit the United States in 1984–85 and to Stephen Cooper and the Louisiana State University English Department for the support and encouragement they gave me during that visit. I am indebted to Jim Babin for the conversations we had about literature in general and to John Konopak, friend, neighbor, and scholar, whose concern and enthusiasm for the literature of Vietnam set me on the road to research.

I am grateful to Rick Sutton and the Office of International Programs, University of Wisconsin–La Crosse, for help at a crucial time in the writing of this book and for the facilities placed at my disposal in the summer of 1988.

I would also like to thank Jeff Walsh of Manchester Polytechnic for the interest he has shown in my research over the years and my colleague Jon Roper for his willingness to discuss the problems of Vietnam, whatever the hour. Thanks also to Paddy Griffiths at Sandhurst for his comments on military strategy and to the talents and energies of Paul Davies and Volcano Theatre for other interpretations.

Without the advice and generous support of Warren French, who first proposed the idea of a book on Vietnam, this project may never have been completed. My debt to Liz Fowler at Twayne is also considerable. Her faith in my efforts never flagged and her reading of the script was always meticulous.

Sharon, as ever, smiled her way through the scribbles. (Who else but her?) Most of all, thanks to Susan for finding the mistakes I couldn't. And, of course, for the million other things she has helped me with over the last five years.

INTRODUCTION

The "real key" to understanding the Vietnam War, writes David Halberstam, is that "it was all derivative of . . . history."[1] According to James C. Wilson, however, the United States "learned nothing" from history in Vietnam. "American officials did their best to deny history," he says, "and the news media simply ignored it. Similarly, very few Vietnam writers make use of this historical 'key' in their efforts to unlock the meaning of Vietnam." Wilson cites Michael Herr, Philip Caputo, and Ron Kovic as writers who "do not attempt to place the war in historical perspective." The personal narratives of these writers are "totally lacking a historical dimension" and only "present the war in terms of how it affects their protagonists personally."[2]

The assumption that personal narratives "dehistoricize" the war and its literature is misleading. Throughout the history of American literature personal narratives have served as a familiar means of addressing issues in public history. In the literature of Vietnam that tradition continues. Personal narratives restore to the reader the vitality of the past and the opportunity for self-discovery that is often available to those who retrieve it. Personal narratives reflect both the anguish and the joy of a colonial vision in a strange new world. They remind us, in particular, of the testimonies of spiritual experience delivered by the Puritans, in the gathered churches of New England, between the 1630s and the end of the seventeenth century.

In *The Puritan Conversion Narrative* Patricia Caldwell provides an illuminating analysis of the confessions given at the First Church of Cambridge, Massachusetts, between 1637 and 1645.[3] Her work illustrates a number of parallels that exist between those who journeyed to New England in the early years of the seventeenth century and those who went to Vietnam in the 1960s and 1970s. The common core of both experiences was the displacement of the individual from a familiar land. For soldiers and journalists the journey and period of exile in Vietnam involved a profound emotional and spiritual experience, one that in many ways reminds us of the Puritan colonial experience in New England. The expressions of personal faith and failure, so dramatically evoked in the conversion testimonies of the New England churches, bring to mind the confessions of the Vietnam writers, many of whom provide a vivid commentary on the comings and goings of individual soldiers and the extent of their involvement in this latter-day errand.

At its simplest the American literary response to Vietnam articulates the nature and purpose of a devout mission and the extent to which individual experience supports the philosophy of the state in making that mission. In the literature of Vietnam the veteran's need to reflect on the purpose of the errand often takes form as a testimony in which the writer expresses his faith, or the lack of it, in the morality of that errand. The quality of faith can vary from sober commitment to ruinous skepticism, from the anguish of a sinner in need of reassurance to a statement of loyalty from the chosen and elect. Writers may agree or disagree with the errand. The disagreement might involve a doctrinal rejection of the errand, or it may be no more than an argument over strategy—with means rather than results. Narratives that relate to strategic disagreements (such as Harry Summers's *On Strategy*) may be seen as jeremiads, sermons that combine a criticism of the current form of the errand and an affirmation of the correctness of its fundamental character. The vigilance required of the reader of war narratives also reminds us of the vigilance required of the Puritan congregation in New England, and the extent to which personal narratives satisfied the standards of witness and adjudication that were expected in matters of public faith and testimony.

In colonial New England spiritual autobiographies were immediate performances. In the literature of Vietnam they are reflections written or published, usually, in the aftermath of war. In both cases the narratives investigate, at a distance, the relationship between personal and public errand and the role of faith in the making of that errand.

To the Puritan, testimony was an integral feature of the experience of errand and a crucial determinant of the individual's right to membership in the church. The idea of making a private stand on a public mission—of testifying to one's own religious experience in front of others—was regarded as a spiritual duty. The alternative was spiritual death for, as Thomas Shepard preached, "a dead man is a speechless man" (Caldwell, 96). Signs of life were proved by signs of speech, attempted speech rather than colorful effusions or extraordinary statements of faith. The demonstrated willingness to speak for oneself and to do this before friend and foe, even allowing for the mystery and imprecision of verbal expression, was a basic requirement of church membership. To express publicly one's own experiences—one's feelings of guilt and joy and sinfulness—was seen as the beginning point of confession and a necessary preliminary to spiritual conversion.

The conversion narrative of New England, as Caldwell tells us, does not attempt to suppress complaint. There is always a core of disappointment and anguish that animates the narrative, much more so than any immediate expression of joyous rebirth and spiritual awakening. What is surprising about the New England Address, says Caldwell, is the extent to which it professes feelings of inadequacy, frustration, and spiritual incapacity and does not seek to hide them away. In these narratives, as in the narratives of the Vietnam War, anguish and disappointment are often the central characteristics of public speech. Experience is traumatic, and ocean crossing as a prelude to rebirth is endured only with the utmost pain and difficulty. As Caldwell tells us, many of the narratives express the problem of silent suffering and the difficulty of communicating one's thoughts in public on the posttraumatic stress of migration. "It is no discovery," she says, "that the emigration to America promises a change in people's spiritual and emotional lives, nor even that the land proved disturbingly different from their expectations" (119).

The problem of the disturbing journey recurs in Vietnam literature. Here the experience of disappointment exists in two locations, once in Vietnam during the war and again on returning to the United States at the completion of one's tour of duty. Personal narrative testifies to the problem of survival not only in the wilderness of Asia but in the uncaring world to which the narrator subsequently returns. In Vietnam literature the problem of expression relates, therefore, to two distinct experiences in two completely opposed environments, both of which are socially hostile and unsympathetic.

For the New England Puritan there was no going back, no returning to the home environment. For the Vietnam veteran going home is not only possible but inevitable in view of the failure of the mission. Yet to retrace one's steps is to regress spiritually, to re-enter a society that lacks the wisdom that comes with the errand. In the immediate aftermath of Vietnam the veteran must overcome the trauma of returning to a place in which frequently there is no longer an acknowledged or professed interest in the war. In such circumstances the veteran is obliged to offer the reader a narrative in which the concept of mission is renewed and personalized and to testify to the truth as he knows it.

In recognizing the nature of his disappointment with the errand and his consequent displacement—either as an expatriate or as an exile in the country of his birth—the veteran demonstrates his strength, and his narrative announces the arrival of vitality. Vietnam narratives are offered to the reader not merely as testimonies of disappointment but as visible symbols of triumph over the public suppression of truth. The acquired voice allows the veteran to overcome the anguish of a disappointing mission. The saving experience is the act of testimony, the culminating moment in a process of self-restoration.

For the Puritan colonists public testimony was only a beginning, a point of departure that allowed the sinner the opportunity to profess his disappointment or anguish. For most speakers, disappointment with New England rarely amounted to outright disobedience or separation from the colony. Most sinners overcame their disappointment by demonstrating, in due course, their renewed faith and commitment to the mission. The Puritans were not a defeatist people, and in most of their accounts the speakers manage "to survive the disappointments and eventually to experience, or claim to have experienced, conversion." In spite of the intense anxiety of the errand the Puritans in New England "knew how to visualise problems as opportunities" (Caldwell, 128).

For a reader of literature the "problems" of Vietnam may be seen as "opportunities" in the discovery of Puritanism. If a sense of errand underwrites Vietnam it also determines the way in which the writer recollects his perception of the war. The writer may reject the Puritan ideal as colonial doctrine. But he may well affirm the inspiration of Puritanism by exploiting the impulse and energies of its voice. Testimony can be a way of bargaining with history, an act of collaboration that allows the writer the opportunity to be critical of history while, at the same time, to be implicated in it. As "the screen through which we see reality and the mirror in which we see ourselves" Puritanism offers the writer "opportunities" to contemplate the experience of history without, necessarily, being supportive of it.[4]

Personal narratives are foundation stones in the renaissance of Vietnam writing in the late 1970s.[5] They are a point of departure for the reader in a journey back to colonial New England. They are also rooted in a journey that others have taken before, a journey of inward navigation in which the speaker testifies to the personal and public anguish of his life and the possibility of triumph in conditions of adversity. With the writers' testimony in place the reader is able to perceive the often unacknowledged intellectual structures that underpin Vietnam: the philosophy of Puritan colonial endeavor, the technology of mission, the expressions of Puritan vision and design.

This book was conceived in the hope of investigating the "opportunities" the Puritan inquiry provides us with. Such an approach traditionally has been resisted by literary critics, many of whom attempt to persuade their readers that the role of history in the Vietnam War is explained by events in the 1960s. Michael Herr's *Dispatches* (1977) is a classic example of a work that has received considerable attention on the basis of its willingness to venture into a terrain where traditional literary narrative no longer applies, to represent Vietnam in the forms generated by the social and psychic information of the war. *Dispatches* is commonly described as a work of postmodernist journal-

ism, one that limits the role of traditional history as a cultural resource for
the writer and his times. I have tried to indicate some of the dangers involved
in such an argument, and the problems posed by those critics who see Vietnam as an opportunity merely to reaffirm the exceptional nature of contemporary life and Western thought.

One problem has already been alluded to by Malcolm Bradbury, who
links the popularity of postmodern writing with an antihistorical tendency in
American culture. "The temptation to give canonical status to the postmodern," says Bradbury, "has not only sometimes limited the way in which some
of the best writers have been read, but narrowed the span of American fiction
and led to neglect of other important writers and tendencies."[6] This study,
in part, focuses on those literary works that have been neglected or narrowly
read, narratives whose sense of historical consciousness and composition has
not been properly acknowledged in the critical debate on the war. It does not
attempt to review all the literature of the war, much of which has been
adequately discussed.

The book is divided into two sections. The first, "The Narrative Voice,"
stresses the use and importance of personal narrative; it focuses on Ronald J.
Glasser's 365 Days (1971), Ron Kovic's Born on the Fourth of July (1976),
Philip Caputo's A Rumor of War (1977), and Michael Herr's Dispatches,
works that describe the anguish of the narrator in his journey of initiation
in Vietnam. Personal narratives may be regarded as either autobiographies
or fictionalizations. There is no validity in the argument put forward by Nancy
Anisfield that one is easier to write than the other.[7] Some writers prefer to
express themselves through confession, others through exemplary fables.
Although I have attempted to indicate distinctions between works of fiction
and nonfiction prose, these distinctions may, on occasion, seem blurred and
unclear. A problem may arise when the writer attempts to exaggerate his
experience or to fictionalize certain episodes in his work. This can also happen
in the narratives of those who pride themselves, as Philip Caputo does, on
renouncing the claims of the literary "imagination."

By way of contrast, the first section concludes with a study of Mark
Frankland's The Mother-of-Pearl Men (1985). This account, given to us by
someone who was once a resident of Saigon, shows us how personal narratives
can work when they originate in a source other than that of residual Puritanism. Frankland's perspective on Vietnam is suffused with a sense of history, and a sense of Asian history in particular; it lacks the feeling of social
enclosure often typical of literary works inspired by the Puritan imagination.
What Frankland tries to explore, I suggest, is not some definitive route to
understanding Vietnam, but the way in which Vietnamese history can be
made more available to the reader and the manner in which the war might
become much more accessible to those who have no experience of it.

The second section, "Errand in a Wilderness," continues the thesis and
seeks to illustrate how, in the literature, colonial history reveals itself through

traditional allegories of survival and errand. In Robert Mason's *Chickenhawk* (1983), Jack Fuller's *Fragments* (1984), and Mary McCarthy's *Vietnam* (1967), the Puritan colonial is observed in a state of self-enclosure, laying down the foundations of empire and pursuing his errand in military environments that are well protected but lacking in native or wilderness features. In discussing Stephen Wright's *Meditations in Green* (1984) and Bobbie Ann Mason's *In Country* (1985), I look at the way film is used to interpret difficult and visually obscure landscapes and its role as an agent of divine providence in a secular age. In my final chapter I discuss the importance of colonial errand in Robert Stone's *Dog Soldiers* (1973) and *A Flag For Sunrise* (1981), novels in which the idea of a cultural and economic mission is seen as a continuing theme in American experience. Stone warns us, in particular, against seeing the war in Asia as a closed book. His depiction of Latin America provides us with a view of American adventurism in the seventies and eighties and is central to an understanding of the literature of Vietnam in the aftermath of that war.

Here and elsewhere the book challenges the idea that we must look at Vietnam as a source of "new history." It invites the reader to be wary of the assumptions on which such a thesis rests. It also asks that we approach with some skepticism the arguments of those who see Vietnam as a place of exceptional strangeness.

The Vietnam war does not offer us a model of historical clarity. What it does provide us with is an opportunity to re-examine those styles of life and art which are a characteristic of Puritan New England. It also indicates that whatever the secret or fraternal nature of the war, the act of rediscovering the past has a real fascination for the American writer.

PART I

The Narrative Voice

1

American
Graffiti

THE VIETNAM WAR HAS BEEN DESCRIBED AS "FORMLESS."
Instead of decisive battles, crucial targets, or even a recognizable army that
the American military could engage and destroy, "the war in Vietnam drifted
in and out of human lives, taking them or sparing them like a headless,
berserk taxi hack, without evident cause, a war fought for uncertain reasons."[1]
The apparent absence of aim and purpose, the disparateness of the soldiers'
experience is reflected, it is said, in the discontinuity of the military logic
that governed the experience and the random manner in which the strategies
of war were implemented. The counterinsurgency activity of LURPs, SEALs,
Green Berets and Rangers, and the U.S. Marine Force Recon unit was opposed to a doctrine of "attrition" and the indiscriminate use of high-altitude
bombing and Rolling Thunder. The use of defoliating chemicals and herbicides appeared to be in direct contradiction to the close-up activities of Combined Action Platoons, the use of Special Forces units, and the civilian-run
CORDS. The strategic hamlets program gave way to policies of search-and-
destroy, while winning hearts and minds made little sense given the existence

of free-fire zones and harassment and interdiction. If Vietnamese resettle-ment was not a success, then neither were the policies of pacification and "destroying the village in order to save it."

= A Retreat from Meaning =

Many of our literary and social critics prefer to see what happened in Vietnam as a "retreat from meaning," a condition of "reality wholly other" than any the soldiers "had known or were prepared to meet." The military experience described by one commentator as "us looking for him looking for us looking for him, war on a Cracker Jack Box, repeated to diminishing returns," is commonly referred to as "absurd," and "the word absurdity figures prominently," we are told, "in the soldiers' lexicon."[2] In an environment where events happened without sequence and for no apparent reason, "conventional modes of understanding were discarded."[3] In his book *The Tainted War* Lloyd Lewis argues that Vietnam broke down or "de-objectified," as he puts it, many of those meanings we tend to associate with conventional warfare. Vietnam, he argues, was a war without shape or purpose, a war in which the soldier found it impossible to decipher a coherent logic in the encounter. "The soldiers' reliance on the term 'senseless' points specifically to their thwarted expectations," says Lewis. In this "fundamentally different kind of war" where there were no front lines, no desire for territory or for pieces of land to be won and held, "the war was perceived as formless, without order and purpose."[4]

Lewis's argument was supported by *Newsweek*. "Vietnam," it argued, "was an immensely complex war with nearly as many realities as there were participants: what you saw and what you could remember depended very largely on where you were and how you got there. South Vietnam was a country of 67,000 square miles, or about the size of Missouri; but the nature of the war varied enormously from place to place and from year to year."[5] Given its largely youthful army, the inhospitality of climate, culture, and terrain, the lack of decisive battle or crucial target, the American effort in Vietnam cannot be recognized through familiar logic nor can its literature be accounted for in ways that do not reflect the shock and horror of a dis-locating experience. Given the originality of its form and the spontaneity of its action, the war produced "a series of 'contacts' with the enemy—brief, ferocious, unpredictable—which, the soldiers agree, were pointless." Since the war "eviscerated" meaning and lay essentially outside of history we may, it is argued, disclaim all useful comparison with previous military conflict.[6]

In the apparently formless environment of Indochina, conventional wis-dom is said to have had no meaning, since a soldier's experience alternated between "expectant waiting" and "vicious manhunts."[7] In a war whose am-biguity defied standard literary methods of analysis, whose incoherence and looseness of form made it resistant to the rules of causality, the writer is obliged, says Lewis, to investigate the stability of his text and to experiment with its form. The duty of the writer, therefore, is to establish the war's dislocation as a governing principle, to subvert the tenuous identity of received values and to support the recurrency of a provincial wisdom. (By incorporating the illogicality of Vietnam into the structure of his work, the writer will provide the reader with a true demonstration of his artistic faith.) His work will inevitably disappoint and mystify and prove itself difficult in the simplest of ways—by being hard to read. If the act of writing, therefore, is an act of wounding, criticism is the process by which we observe disfigurement in the text. This argument, which denies the reader understanding, denies the writer the opportunity to separate himself, should he wish to do so, from the larger world of public disorder.

Lewis's argument is accepted by most literary critics. If "the randomness and aimlessness of the firefight and the sheer perversity of the search and destroy strategy caused a wholesale retreat from meaning," says Lewis, then the war cannot be said to have made sense; the contradictions of experience transform it into a self-referential, metafictional text. If "reality [is] simply no longer navigable using the old cognitive maps," then the reader is obliged to live like the soldier, "adrift in an alien universe in which the familiar . . . landmarks [have] disappeared." The writer's primary obligation is to offer the text as a paradigm of the war, to make the experience of writing and the recollection of fighting coterminous. Since the Vietnam War was all things to all people—and no one thing to any one person—the Vietnam writer must present the reader with a devastated text—a structure whose brokenness contains the idea that the motives of the government in going to Vietnam were as senseless as the attempt to interpret them by the military. The discontinuities of the text must exist to indicate what Lewis calls "wretched excessiveness on a regular basis."[8]

If the reader is made to experience the life of the soldier, the flak he gets will come from the writer's attempt to convey the impact of the grenade and ricochet, the sudden eruption of a violent event. The breakdown of a sensible point of view must enact or evoke a similar experience for the reader in the text. Since Vietnam is a thing of uncertain definition, it must be seen as postmodern, an event in which styles of action disagree and motives are aimless and disconnected from one another. Since Vietnam is a thing of "hypermodernity," its multiple discourses demand from the writer an act of psychotic playfulness, a sense of "late modern energy" and "cultural diversity," a representation of our eclectic nature and our inconclusive language.[9] The traditional means for rendering experience intelligible, therefore, are not available to the Vietnam writer. There can be no sense of closure.

According to current postmodernist criticism, the temptation to seek coherence must be resisted, and "anyone who claims to have an inside track on the truth about the Vietnam War is actually demonstrating only biased myopia."[10] If a "tradition of dying"[11] died in Vietnam, so did the traditional text with its master narrative. Since the experience is an insurgent one, our primary obligation is to select those writers who are best able to incorporate into the fabric of their work that sense of Vietnam as a place of unreliable partnership, that idea of immediate and unexpected encounter. For Herman Rapaport, we need to feel the disarticulated experience through our reading. For the soldier, "the violence and terror which occurred appeared illegitimate and ethically perverse, that sudden blitz out of nowhere, and the mysterious dissolution of the enemy. It was a violence which we could not experience as violence, for nothing really felt like it 'engaged' anything else. There is just catastrophe and then Medivac." For Rapaport the lack of linkage between the events of Vietnam rendered the experience of combat "somewhat obsolete, since it suggests a relation, an active fighting with or against someone." In combat the lack of sequential narrative emphasizes the soldier's separateness from an opponent whose world he is supposed to "engage."[12] The text, likewise, must not be granted immunity from attack. The subversive experience of the Vietnam War must engulf the text. Through a lack of orderliness and shifts in causal structure, literature must reflect a lack of coherent sequence in the field, a fracturing of sensible narrative pattern which an episodic conflict brought about. According to James C. Wilson, most American fiction about the war insists that the reader is powerless to understand Vietnam:

> The unspoken argument of these books would seem to be: government and the media accounts of the war were false, therefore we can never know the truth about it. Government maps were misleading, therefore the Vietnamese landscape and culture are forever mysterious and unknowable. Government histories of the war were distorted, therefore the war's origins will never be clear. Our stated reasons for being in Vietnam were absurd; therefore we can never know why we were there (the war just appeared insanely and arbitrarily, like a sniper on a downtown building). Beyond a doubt, making sense of Vietnam *is* difficult, as so many of the Vietnam writers emphasize. However, by implying that the war is impossible to understand, these writers simply play into the hands of all those who wanted (and still want) to keep the war a mystery.[13]

Wilson's statement anticipates some of the wish fulfillment and a good many of the extravagant obsessions that have afflicted literary criticism since the publication of his book in 1982 and, in particular, the largely uncontested idea—which has gained currency through the work of Mark Baker—that "Vietnam was a brutal Neverneverland, outside time and space, where little boys didn't have to grow up."[14] Critics have remained fascinated with the marvelousness of the war and its capacity to offer up mythical or fabulous characters, legends, epic events, allegoric and speculative texts, and folkloristic tales—few of which, incidentally, are Vietnamese in origin.

In addition, there is a general acceptance of the surface logic of contradiction and breakdown, of the idea that Vietnam as a war was vague and indeterminate, and that few of its soldiers, who became its writers, were able to perceive it as a coherent experience or believe that what they had done had any bearing on the war's outcome. Vietnam is accepted, therefore, as a thing of possibility, a creature of the imagination, a place in which social relationships do not reveal the manners of a culture but the intense disorder of a "land without places," a body "devoid of any real parts."[15]

= Vietnam and the Sixties =

The emphasis on crisis and contradiction and the retreat from empiricism are the tithes the Vietnam writer pays the critic if he wishes to be seen as worthy of relevance. For those critics who came to Vietnam by way of the 1960s, as Jerome Klinkowitz did, Vietnam is merely American graffiti. The context in which the most imaginative literature of the war is rooted, says Klinkowitz, is defined by the conflict between those who exercised power and those who resisted its abuse in the United States. Thus the imaginative resistance to the war was provided not by the Vietnamese—since their opposition was stoical and their language impenetrable—but by a youthful counterculture: that loose assembly of dissenters who playfully and creatively opposed the exercise of institutional and administrative power on the streets of America in the 1960s. The literature of Vietnam, says Klinkowitz, is a representation of the myths and images that sustained dissent and translated the war into a domestic encounter rather than an encounter with the Vietnamese. In the literature of Vietnam, he says, the war is best defined as a theatrical contest between those who subscribed to an elitist use of technological power and those who resisted the role of authority through the politics of gesture and the rude amateurism of free play. The redemptive quality of life in Vietnam—its "spiritual truth"—was provided by those who took with them into the wilderness the values of the counterculture, who made their mark on the country by leaving behind them, as *Dispatches* puts it, "a California corridor cut and bought and buried deep into Asia."[16] Vietnam and the sixties were indistinguishable: "The one reinforced the other, since the causes and consequences of each were similar. Khe Sanh and Woodstock the Tet Offensive and the Jimi Hendrix Experience shared the same transformative energy." The war was not "a distant experience" but a generational one. "Virtually every day of it was protested at home, in disruptions whose violence approached that of the war itself. The several marches on Washington, where hundreds of thousands filled the streets, may have been symbolic affairs. But Berkeley—1965, Madison—1967 and finally Kent State—1970 could be considered legitimate skirmishes and battles of the Vietnam war, complete with guerrilla forces (the students), government troops (the National Guard), and a small but unnerving list of casualties."[17]

In attempting to invent Vietnam as a civilian conflict (which is then exported to Vietnam as a military encounter), Klinkowitz stretches credulity to breaking point. For him, Vietnam is what America has made of it: an American surrogate, a rock 'n' roll war—not Vietnam, but Nam. The writer's obligation, says the critic, is to see Vietnam not as a place but as a state of mind: a war conceived in America, administered by America, resisted by America. Vietnam exists by courtesy of America: we give it our attention because of America, we consider its derangement because of America, we acknowledge that its suffering is caused by America and that those who resist the desire to impose it—those whom the writer of *Dispatches* refers to as the "young, apolitically radical, wigged-out crazies . . . an authentic subculture" (189)—are themselves American.

=== The Short-Timers ===

Creative writers have exposed the limitation of this point of view in various ways. In *The Short-Timers* (1979) Gustav Hasford shows us how easily a reader is seduced by the mystery that a "wigged-out" crazy can bring to a text. *The Short-Timers* is often seen as a novel narrated by a member of an "authentic subculture," a playmaker who is also a wise fool, a man whose sense of parody and the absurd imitates that of the "radical" crazy. But *The Short-Timers* is a novel of seduction: it tests the ability of a writer to undermine a text by inventing a narrator whose comic credentials disarm the reader and whose persuasive manner can exploit our craving for entertainment. *The Short-Timers* contains many of the surface qualities of a romance; it appears to direct our attention to the ambiguities of war and the fabulous fictionality of its character and strategy; it emphasizes action at the expense of character, the mystical power of modern technology, the imminence of death, and the allegorical unworldliness of the Vietnamese. But these are mere qualities of convenience for the narrator, Private Joker: underneath the penetrable surface of his narrative there lies a world of fragile appearances, in which melodramatic scenes and wish-fulfillment endings are used to advertise the power of performance in the creation of a text. The sole beneficiary of *The Short-Timers* is Joker, an authoritarian streetwise bully who plagiarizes the style of those he derides and who is never anything but wholly obsessed with his own linguistic charm and charisma.

Joker's laughter has a sinister ring. It is targeted against those who flaunt their skills in public with "conviction"[18] and against those who are the perceived enemies of intelligence and realism, like the Hollywood warrior John

Wayne. What Joker claims for himself is the role of the articulate man of feeling, the necessary cynic whose love affair is with words, not guns ("the love of guns" [38], he claims, is responsible for the production of the film *The Green Berets*), and whose job is to observe wittily and to undermine the insane intelligence of the military. But the words of Joker, as Takeshi Kaiko puts it, turn "to ash the minute they [are] written." What the novel announces is that "the age of shadow-boxing literature" in Vietnam writing has now begun.[19]

In *The Short-Timers* Joker is as preoccupied with master narratives as any of the villains he brings to our attention. For Joker, a villain is someone who can act better than he can, a rival performer who, in the course of the novel, he either kills or cleverly subdues. Joker's laugh-making manner belies a scheming intelligence. His reason for being a war correspondent—and for writing a book on Vietnam—is not to expose the absurdity of war but to exercise power and control over those he lives with and subsequently writes about. (As Joker tells the squad, " 'Well, I'm here in Viet Nam to entertain you' " [94].) His style of life and art is dominated by a lust for gainful impersonation, the memory of John Wayne's influence over others, and his parody of that influence is always pretentious. The approach is combative and unnerving, while the joke of the book is on those who approve of what Joker says but fail to appreciate the artfulness of the way he says it.

The Short-Timers exposes our complacent affiliations with literary language in order that Joker, as narrator, might work undercover and promote himself to an eminent position in the text. The text, therefore, is a work of ambush, a novel that exploits our sympathy for those who are playful in order to obscure their lust for glory. Joker's cleverness is that of a guerrilla and his motives are disguised, since what he has learned is that "the most important" resource of insurgency "is the art of camouflage."

Our job is to map out his strategy in the text, from the first moment at Parris Island, where Joker begins his training as a marine, and we, as readers, are encouraged to accept his stylish persona. Parris Island is the home of the enemy, the military mind, the drill instructors who live in "a swamp on an island, symmetrical but sinister like a suburban death camp" (3). We are told that Joker can survive his training and fake the toughness that is expected of him. "Years of high school drama classes have made me a mimic. I sound exactly like John Wayne as I say: 'I think I'm going to hate this movie' " (4). Yet Joker is the beneficiary of his own derision. John Wayne may be damned but he holds the key to Joker's success: the knowledge of how to control an audience. Like Ken Kesey's sixties hero Randall McMurphy, Joker knows that to be a hero you have to act a hero. Since strength can be simulated Joker chooses to base his strength, like Randall McMurphy, on the language of the screen. If you don't act tough, you can't be tough. Fakery is necessary in order to escape the weakness of those whose lives are supervised by others. Since being is acting, theater is the means by which power is exercised over those who are passive. It is a trusted formula and Joker uses it. He reinstates, through a hard-edged, aphoristic, tough-guy/good-guy style, the language of film in order to control the imagination of his audience. Under fire, he does impressions of Hollywood actors to test his ability to control an audience at a time of crisis. Cowboy's squad is Joker's drama class, an audience on whom he can practice impersonations of Bob Hope or John Wayne—the styles of those who are proficient in the manipulation of war audiences. Joker's graduation from that class and his elevation to the role of star performer and social controller is evident at the end of the text. His voice now carries a weight and authority that no one challenges: "I am their sergeant; they are my men . . . 'Saddle up,' I say, and the squad responds" (178).

If Wayne, the screen idol, is the supreme authoritarian, Sergeant Gerheim, the drill instructor at Parris Island, is a flawed poseur. Gerheim's style is terse and visceral. His intention is to create a theater of derision, one that does not liberate or entertain the individual but demeans him. Joker is aware that Gerheim is killed by Pyle, a grunt whom Gerheim abuses, because he presumes too much. As Gerheim is about to die, he loses control and ruins his theatrical manner with a string of obscenities. At Parris Island Gerheim invites his own destruction by describing the soldiers under his command as "maggots," "ladies," "shit."

By way of contrast Joker's exercise of authority is picaresque. It is premised on the belief that social control is more acceptable when qualified by an offbeat or comic manner. After Joker has killed Cowboy, the use of black humor adds to his newly acquired authority as leader of the squad. "I study their faces. Then I say, 'man-oh-man, Cowboy looks like a bag of leftovers from a V.F.W. barbecue. Of course, I've git nothing against dead people. Why some of my best friends are dead' " (179). Joker grants himself protection through the use of parody. His sense of the ridiculous and the scope of his derision are an attempt to remove any lingering suspicion that he has enjoyed getting rid of Cowboy. The reader is impressed with his sense of the grotesque and the lightness of his manner—as well as his nerve—at a moment of horror.

The narrative of *The Short-Timers* comes unstuck, however, in a schedule of violence that is too exhausting and in which the cinematic intentions of the text are graphically revealed. The steady piling up of grotesque details, the description of sadistic and violent acts, the imminence of death, are designed to encourage the reader to lend support to the liveliness of the dramatic action and to applaud the effort that is made by Joker to provide entertainment. But as we reach the conclusion, the orgiastic violence proves self-defeating and Joker's narrative self-destructs in a cartoon wipeout:

> Mother ignores me, watches Cowboy.
> Bang. Right leg.

Bang. Left leg. Cowboy falls.

Bang. The bullet rips open Cowboy's trousers at the crotch.

"No. . . ." Cowboy feels for his balls. He shits on himself.

Animal Mother takes a step.

Before I can make a move to stop Animal Mother a pistol pops in the clearing.

Bang.

Then: Bang

Donlon: HE KILLED DOC AND THE NEW GUY.

Cowboy shakes himself to stay conscious. Then he shoots Alice through the back of the head.

Bang. Alice's face is blown off by the forty-five calibre bullet. Alice flops as though electrocuted.

Cowboy raises the pistol and presses the huge barrel to his right temple.

Bang.

The pistol falls.

The sniper has put a bullet through the center of Cowboy's right hand. (176–77)

The street-wise language that joker uses exploits the idiom of the hard-boiled novel and is largely self serving. It exists merely to satisfy the reader whose approval Joker is driven to seek. As pulp literature it casts doubt on the quality of Joker's criticism of *The Green Berets*, a film that is said to be war obsessed and unrealistic.

The reader must hunt for tripwires in Hasford's novel. "Our survival hangs on our sniper bait's reflexes and judgment." We must "detect . . . tiny . . . fragments" of "debris," signs that reveal the presence of enemy "equipment" and activity. We must not "be diverted off the trail" by men like Joker, a predatory entertainer, one of that "shrewd race of men who fight for survival" without "scruples" (153). *The Short-Timers* is one of Joker's "booby traps . . . designed so that the victim" becomes "his own executioner" (152). If the reader accepts the marvelous progression of his tale, he, and not the narrator, will self-destruct on the tripwire of violence. Joker's authority, therefore, must be resisted; we must be neither subdued nor impressed by his wish fulfillment. We must not be cowed like "the Lusthog Squad" whose watchful silence allows Joker to feel "so alive" (178, 179).

The pacification of others through violent action is affirmed as a social achievement in the concluding line of the book. As the squad moves out, Joker gives us his final one-liner: "I wave my hand and Mother takes the point" (179). Joker takes his leave of us with a cinematic and elitist gesture. Animal Mother, the only remaining threat to Joker's authority, accepts his brief. Whether the reader will follow suit—walk "the point" because he has been directed to—or whether he will take "the point" in some other way will determine whether Hasford has been successful. The conclusion is ingenious. Joker's flourish takes us back to the concluding line in Howard Hawks's film *Red River*. "I wave my hand" . . . is a video replay of John Wayne's "Take 'em to Missouri, Matt." The power and appeal of the American western—as Joker realizes—is as fresh today as it always was.

In accepting the need for a strong resolution, readers are tempted to take the same route Joan Didion took at eight years of age in Peterson Fields, Colorado. There, in the hot summer of 1943, alone in the cinema she heard John Wayne, in *War of the Wildcats*, tell his girlfriend that he would build her a house "at the bend in the river where the cottonwoods grow"—heard it and was never quite the same girl again. Whether any of us grow up to be heroines in westerns or whether we build our houses where the cottonwoods grow is beside the point. In the illusory world we live in, each of us seeks that affirmative promise that we yearn to give or yearn to hear. What Joker emulates is the manner of the man who lives in a world of one-liners, lines that inspire a fantasy of obedience. Joker's understanding is the same as Didion's:

> When John Wayne spoke, there was no mistaking his intentions; he had a sexual authority so strong that even a child could perceive it. And in a world we understood early to be characterized by venality and doubt and paralyzing ambiguities, he suggested another world, one which may or may not have existed ever but in any case existed no more: a place where a man could move free, could make his own code and live by it; a world in which, if a man did what he had to do, he could one day take the girl and go riding through the draw to find himself home free, not in a hospital with something going wrong inside, not in a high bed with the flowers and the drugs and the forced smiles, but there at the bend in the bright river, the cottonwoods shimmering in the early morning sun.[20]

Joker may tell us, remembering Michael Herr, "that Vietnam was what we had instead of happy childhoods," but nothing could ever be further from the truth. The loss of one's childhood is evoked only as a pretense that masks his campaign for social control.

═ "The Fate of the Absurd" ═

Postmodernist speculation and a vision of the absurd dominate literary criticism of the Vietnam War. The belief that the breadth of a writer's achievement should be judged by the range of his inquiry into matters of contemporary American concern still prevails and rules out consideration of the work of accomplished novelists like Donald McQuinn, Takeshi Kaiko, and Tran

Van Dinh. On Jerome Klinkowitz's own admission, the literature of Vietnam ought to concern itself not with the country of Vietnam but with the struggle to understand what America did there at a particular moment in time. "The aesthetic truth of the war," says Klinkowitz, "is the works conceived in the sixties, not the seventies (when subtle falsifications begin)."[21]

To ask what the other side—the Vietnamese people—were doing in the war is thus considered irrelevant. If the logic of the sixties is correctly applied, then presumably the Viet Cong received its inspiration from the Avalon Ballroom in San Francisco and for much of the war tuned in, turned on, and tripped out on one of Uncle Ho's acid-rock light shows, while in hot pursuit, the North Vietnamese army ghetto-blasted its way down the Ho Chi Minh Trail to the latest Jimi Hendrix tape cassette. In "a war which defied reason itself," what else could have happened? In Vietnam, "operations were conducted high on grass to the tune of transistorized rock and roll; barracks yielded to apartments or hootches with black light and stereo. . . . Nothing from previous wars seemed to apply." In Vietnam, "conventional modes of understanding were discarded." What Klinkowitz describes as a literature of "truth" is a literature that reveals the "mystification" of moral experience and "the general lack of seriousness" with which the war was observed by the recruits. Since the definitive experience of Vietnam is "the unexplainable" phenomenon, then the task of the novelist is "to find a structure for this apparently structureless world" in which "everything that happens resists identification with reality."

Since the Vietnam War "defies the stereotypes of previous wars," everything of relevance that happens in fiction, according to Klinkowitz, is both formless and absurd. Black facts imply black fictions. Individual experience, once supposed to make the individual mature, whole, self-directing, becomes a source of cynicism and disenchantment. In Vietnam one's fate is determined by good or bad luck, not by the exercise of military logic. The novelist Josiah Bunting, in *The Lionheads* (1972), confirms the idea of "an absurd war" and is said to have created "an absurdist structure" that enables him to make "an informative statement on the style of Vietnam." For Klinkowitz, the requirement for writing the "great American novel"—seriousness, firmness of moral and political purpose—does not obtain in Vietnam, as it does not obtain in the work of Joseph Heller or Kurt Vonnegut. The antiwar novels of the 1960s, in other words, provide us with an original and "formative" mode for understanding Vietnam. Unable to take the world's pretensions seriously, the absurd novel lapses into farce and the streetwise theater of underground play. In William Pelfrey's *The Big V* (1972), William Crawford Woods's *The Killing Zone* (1970), and William Eastlake's *The Bamboo Bed* (1969) we are given a history "from the wars' hot phase," "innovative fiction" in which characters form themselves into two-dimensional caricatures and pop-art gestures are assigned to every act. Here we encounter a zone of consciousness in which fantastic events may be not just capturing the truths of the human heart but rendering the actual texture of human experience.[22] Here the dissenting activism of Heller's Yossarian lives on in Vietnam where the American army and, by implication, the United States is seen as a colossal ship of fools, an absurdist enterprise, made operational by its vast and ridiculous sense of mission. Here we are reminded of Saul Bellow's account of the poet Von Humboldt Fleisher in *Humboldt's Gift*: "The noble idea of being an American poet certainly made Humboldt feel at times like a card, a boy, a comic, a fool. Maybe America didn't need art and inner miracles. It had so many outer ones. The U.S.A. was a big operation, very big. The more it, the less we. So Humboldt behaved like an eccentric and comic subject."[23]

In order to acknowledge the importance of the theater of the absurd the critic is inclined to trace the roots of writing in Vietnam to *Catch-22*. The view is that because the tone of Vietnam is one of eccentricity, *Catch-22* is "innovatively accurate."[24] The argument, however, does not get us very far in dealing with the literature of the postwar years unless, of course, we are prepared to accept the view that an essential task for all Vietnam writers is to convey "the awful sense of absurdity and futility" and the idea that the world is in the grip of a "stoned despair."[25] But Vietnam writing no longer resigns itself to such absolute "despair." It extends itself into areas that are remote from military training and physical combat. It increasingly prefers to illustrate, as Paul Fussell puts it, "the way the dynamics and iconography" of war "have proved crucial, political, rhetorical, and artistic determinants on subsequent life."[26]

Even in the combat narratives the American writer of the 1980s has appeared far less willing than perhaps he once was to express himself through an absurdist testimony. Robert Mason's *Chickenhawk*—an account of a helicopter pilot in the Air Cavalry—is revealing. Toward the end of the book Mason is told that he will not, after all, serve out his remaining few days flying safe administrative missions (in spite of what he has been promised), but will continue with combat missions. The jauntiness and nonchalance of Mason's narrative gives way to a mood of defiance. Mason loses interest in his helicopter unit, "The Prospectors," who relieve the tension by throwing absurd parties in which the guest of honor is a Viet Cong skull. As he says to Doc Da Vinci:

> It's not that I'm skinny, it's why I am skinny. I'm worn out, I'm frayed. I want to fly admin flights like hundreds of other pilots do every day. . . . I'm not afraid to fly, I just don't think I or Gary or any short-timer should have to fly combat assaults anymore. We have each flown more than a thousand missions already. Isn't that enough?
>
> Gary and I sat at a table watching the Prospectors whoop it up at the party that night. Neither of us could join in. The laughing skull was no longer funny.[27]

As a character in Mark Baker's *Nam* puts it, "There are things and there are things, but your life is your life and you try to save it. It ain't a laughing matter."[28]

═ The Puritan Vision ═

The American writer in Vietnam affirms his attachment to history in a way that acknowledges, but also transcends, the influence of the sixties. The roots of writing cannot be found in the language of rock and roll, in jive and profanity, but in the ancient energies and assumptions of mission on to which jive and profanity have been grafted. If we wish to see the war, as Loren Baritz suggests, as a representation of the American self—an expression of the way in which the "culture thinks of itself and the world"—we cannot adequately do so in a language whose folklore is rooted in the recent past. Vietnam was an affirmation of an American way of life and an "American way of war"; it was a war invented, if not fought, as Baritz contends, "in ways our culture required."[29] It provided an opportunity for the country to reaffirm its belief in the cause of mission and to surround itself with the myth and ritual of a medieval past. It inspired a vision of righteousness in a world overrun with atheistic sin. And, in the war's aftermath, it provided the opportunity for a style of art in which the narrative resources of colonial life in New England were able to play a crucial role in shaping the writer's response to history.

The Vietnam War emphasizes the importance of cultural memory in American life. It reminds us that Puritanism is neither a spent force nor a dead religion but a complex philosophy that continues to provide guidance for principles and activities in our social, cultural, and political life. Puritanism is about the way selected people *live* in the world and the structures they create to make their world a safe and habitable place. It is about the way people *see* the world, their sense of Godliness, and the enemies that exist within it. Puritanism is about the way people *talk* about themselves in the world and convey their sense of faith to one another.

In New England the Puritans proposed an organic Christian corporation or community. Belief was expressed in good works and faith; faith was fortified by structure and plantation; duty was determined by errand and errand translated as mission. In literature, faith and grace were publicly professed and providences observed in the act of "seeing"; righteousness was demonstrated by good works and the rooting out of sin.

In its conduct and faith, if not its ultimate failure of will, the American experience in Vietnam resurrects the Puritan experience in New England.[30] Vietnam harks back to the original errand; it predates the return of a "lost frontier," and its literature is much more intense and enclosed than the literature of Western expansion with which it is often vigorously compared.[31]

The American writer interprets that errand as an act of spiritual faith and adventure; in his use of personal narrative he employs a mode of address that itself is historically conscious and refers us back to the colonial testimonies of New England. In Vietnam literature the writer reminds himself of history in the act of retrieving the history of the self. In so doing he is able to avoid the dead end of absurdity and the postmodern faith of a surrender to fragments.

2

The Puritan Imprint:
The Military,
The Militant,
and the Cultural Mind

IN HIS THOUGHTFUL ANALYSIS OF WILLIAM LEDERER AND
Eugene Burdick's *The Ugly American* (1958) John Hellmann attributes the
book's success, and its "pervasive" influence on the American imagination,
to its ability to retrieve at a time of cold war tensions the forgotten wisdoms
of the Puritan jeremiad.[1] In setting their fiction in Southeast Asia, the authors
Lederer and Burdick, says Hellmann, "told Americans that they were failing
in their world mission miserably" (15) and presented a critique of contemporary political mission in which the United States was seen as "too 'soft,'
immoral, and greedy to survive the Soviets' dedicated pursuit of world communism" (19). The ugly Americans are seen, says Hellmann, as decadent
Westerners, the secular priests of a narrow and materialistic society—"narrow
careerists in the diplomatic service, pleasure-seeking staff members," do-
nators of " 'big' foreign-aid projects which confer wealth and status on the
native elite without actually helping the people" (24). As a political sermon
that relies heavily on the Puritan ethos of rooting out the sinfulness that has
come to afflict a chosen elite, the book combines "a criticism of contemporary

errors and vision of future disaster with an affirmation of the correctness of the traditional character and purpose of the American 'errand' " (21). *The Ugly American* is a work of orthodox Puritan doctrine, says Hellmann, which demands that those who answer His Calling on their errand in the wilderness do so by affirming the spirituality of that errand rather than by cherishing the exported values of conformity and affluence.

For Hellmann the notion of mission is fundamentally one of expansion and westward movement. The Puritans, he says, "conceived of their 'errand into the wilderness' as the journey of a Chosen People," a "redeemer nation" predestined to lead "the Forces of Light" against "the Forces of Darkness," the "agents of Satan" (6). As a jeremiad *The Ugly American* demands that those who journey in search of monsters to destroy return to the way of the fathers and rededicate themselves to the special mission of the culture. The book "points its accusing finger at the loss of frontier values in postwar society" (24). It condemns the American abroad as a moral traitor to the cause of that original errand, as one who forsakes the "heroic ancestors' journey into a frontier, instead seeking the comforts and securities associated with Europe." Those who refuse "to go out into the countryside" to convert the inhabitants of the forest huddle instead within the secret fraternity of "enclaves" in the city (25). They offend against the spirit of mission and have turned their backs "on the frontier" (26). They have lost, for the most part, "the traits of self-reliance, democratic idealism, homespun practicality, adaptability and ingenuity," virtues we traditionally associate with "the American mythical-historical past," the ideal of service and the folklore of Puritan mission (27).

Hellmann's thesis is grounded in the notion of a fluent and mobile colonial destiny, "the march westward of American progress" (33), an open landscape of challenge and possibility, and a place in which an emergent nation can generate and "regenerate its traditional virtues while serving future progress" (36). *The Ugly American* is perceived as a definitive text, one that announces the coming colonial experiment in Vietnam and the political slogans of Kennedy's New Frontier. It anticipates the arrival in Vietnam of the Special Forces such as the Green Berets who became a leading symbol of the New Frontier and the doctrine of individualism which Kennedy contrasted with the perceived complacency of the 1950s. "As a single hero representing," says Hellmann, "the ideal answer of the New Frontier to the calls for renewal, the Green Beret of the periodical press occupied in a single timeless moment the whole of American myth" (47). The New Frontier and Green Berets were logical consequences of the calls for action and mythic renewal in the Puritan jeremiads of the 1950s. Books like *The Ugly American* provide a critical commentary on the unrighteous and a vision of future disaster, but they are expansionist and exhilarating in their commitment to the idea of an American errand. *The Ugly American* is seen to define this errand through a mythology of self-determination and an emphasis on the values of the American West. In its uncultivated and unregenerate state, Vietnam becomes a symbolic frontier, possessed of a rural geography in which Americans, as chosen people, can perceive themselves achieving their identity and working out their special destiny against the Forces of Darkness. On this symbolic landscape, what Vietnam offers the American Puritan is a "self-image of limitless possibility, mastery over nature, democratic equality, self-reliant individualism, and special communal mission" (8).

The naïveté of these messianic beliefs, says Hellmann, is fully exposed in the literature of the Vietnam War in which the yearning to commune with that ancient landscape inhabited by the fathers is seen to create an experiential hell. In war literature there is a dark regression of the soul in Vietnam, one that repudiates the idea of a calling in the wilderness and testifies against the validity of accepted American myth. "The landscape is an awful inversion of American assumptions and values, a nightmare version of the landscapes of previous American myth." Underlying the works of Vietnam writing "is a common allegory, an ironic antimyth in which an archetypal warrior-representative of the culture embarks on a quest that dissolves into an utter chaos of dark revelation!" (102). The knowledge that is gained from living on an "antifrontier" is the antithesis, says Hellmann, of those public testimonies of faith in the West, those notions of errand and adventure that characterize Puritan narratives and that underpin American frontier jeremiads in the 1950s (165).

= The Puritan Enclosure =

Hellmann's thesis points us to a composite mythology in which the Puritan errand in colonial New England is able to regenerate itself on a number of American historical frontiers, one of which is Vietnam. Just as the backwoodsman with his bowie knife and Winchester rifle—the solitary romantic at home in the wilderness—becomes the definitive American hero, so the appearance of the Green Beret allows us to interpret the war in Vietnam as a mythic experience. For the Westerners who visit Vietnam, says Hellmann, Puritanism is invigorated by the wilderness and by those keen to subdue it. Puritanism is identified, therefore, not as a formal structure of belief whose attitude to growth is highly ambiguous but as an inspirational theory for those who travel to a newfound land and commit themselves to frontier pursuits. In the literature of the Vietnam War, says Hellmann, American writers either confirm their belief in the appeal of the western (47) or they invent a substantial body of "antimyth" with which to repudiate it. A good example of a work that repudiates the western myth, says Hellmann, is Ron Kovic's *Born on the Fourth of July*. Kovic's anger, says Hellmann, is a revolt against the soldier's desire to "emulate the 'true' fathers" of his "mythic heritage," the Puritan adventurers of old, and a repudiation of the youthful desire to seek "communion . . . through ritualistic play" with a world of "open" landscapes (147, 148).

In Hellmann's analysis, Kovic rejects both the Puritan way of seeing the world and the Puritan way of discussing it. Disagreement with the errand appears to include—not preclude—a disagreement with the mode of address the Puritans used to explain their errand. But here is the difficulty. For if Kovic provides the reader with a critique of Puritanism he does so in a language that attests to the importance of testimony and mission. Kovic's narrative is redolent with that mixture of fervor and disappointment that we find in the Puritan conversion narrative; it also partakes of the emotional vigor that was a necessary part of the Puritan sermon. Kovic is willing to profess his faith, to extol the virtue of a personal calling. But he does so in order to challenge the notion of public mission and to question the righteous basis of the errand. Personal adventure prevails over public doctrine. Kovic rejects the orthodox wisdom of the elect who have ordained the mission, but he professes his faith, and the salvation he has experienced, in the company of those who are obliged reluctantly to carry it out. The autobiography Kovic gives us, therefore, validates the moral and empirical basis of Puritan writing—a sense of mission—but it also crucially supports the need to dispute the Puritan faith. Kovic's testimony is meant not to affirm the great glory of God's errand in Vietnam but to illustrate the knowledge of the experiential self and the sins of those who have fallen from grace.

One danger in employing Puritanism as a blueprint is the tendency to define its legacy purely as a territorial one. In so doing we limit our understanding of the range and reference of Puritanism and the narrative opportunities that the form provides. Thus, in *Born on the Fourth of July*, Kovic is concerned to reject the political implications of the Puritan mission but is keen to explore its meaning in the narrative voice of one who bears witness for the benefit of others. Kovic is committed to a personal calling but lacks the devotion of those who believe in state activity.

We ought to avoid the tendency to see Puritanism as an unambiguous point of reference in Vietnam, a style of life and of art that the writer's work clearly confirms or repudiates, The Puritan past clings to the writer in curious ways in the literature of Vietnam. Those who want to liberate themselves from the publicly mandated errand also struggle with the predicament of having spent their lives in a confined intellectual space. But the errand of the state is not easily overcome. Nativist suspicion persists. It threatens the writer's sense of charity and underlines the difficulty he has in sharing his newfound cultural freedom with the Vietnamese. In a large number of autobiographies and novels, especially those written by Vietnam War veterans, the writer self-consciously restricts himself to observing the American predicament. He also notes the extent to which the Americanness of the mission—an Americanness that perhaps persists in him—inhibits the idea of an outward-looking, cultural crusade. In war writing the land remains an ambiguous force and the native inhabitants an ambiguous and socially difficult people. A fear of wilderness, of "Indian" captivity even, occasionally refers the writer back into the camp of those from whom he wishes to be dissociated. The memory of captivity and its narrative legacy in American culture is a popular refrain for writers and politicians. President Johnson set the tone for the debate early in the war when he described Vietnam as a place "of unparalleled brutality" in which "simple farmers are the targets of assassination and kidnapping. Women and children are strangled in the night because their men are loyal to the government. And helpless villages are ravaged by sneak attacks."[2]

The importance of personal protection—brought about by land cultivation and the destruction of wilderness—was a mainstay of American military thinking in Vietnam. Soldiers found it hard to experience the Vietnamese hinterland unless they were living in an approved location within it. Just as the enclaves of church, plantation, covenant, and garrison were necessary to the Puritan experiment in New England as a means of resisting the wiles and temptations of a libidinous countryside, so in Vietnam the role of the protective enclosure—in combat, defense, hospitalization, entertainment— restricted the soldiers' knowledge of grass-roots Vietnamese life. What Andrew Krepinevich calls "the enclave strategy" in Vietnam—massive firepower and technological attrition—refers us back to the "walled garden" of early New England and the Puritan belief in fortified settlements. This strategy, says Krepinevich, arose from the army's fundamental impatience and its inability to appreciate the nature of counterinsurgency. This strategy, which often posited "rapid airmobile sweeps through enemy territory, followed by a quick return to the unit firebase, created . . . a garrison mentality" and "was dubbed 'firebase psychosis.' " It created in the soldier a psychological dependency on familiar surroundings and the kind of tools he was provided with in order to survive. A production culture spawned a production mentality that, in turn, induced a horror of the physical deprivation threatened by the wilderness.[3]

Those who entered the kingdom of the devil voluntarily or relied on their expertise with primitive tools often posed a direct threat to orthodox military codes in Vietnam. President Kennedy's "constant battle" with the Regular Army over the introduction of the Special Forces units in Vietnam was soon resolved in the army's favor when Johnson took office. The pacification programs instituted by the Green Berets in the early years of the 1960s were eventually terminated because the army came to regard them as too irregular and self-determining. Whereas Kennedy regarded the Green Berets as a virile symbol of wilderness individualism and self-reliance, the army preferred to subsume the Special Forces within a bureaucratic hierarchy, to make them "shine their buckles and keep the base lawns tidy rather than to let them hone their wilderness skills and devise innovative new tactics" (Hellmann, 45).

His decision illustrates the contrast between good and bad Puritanism, good "enclaves" and bad "enclaves" (74), a contrast that reappears in the film *Apocalypse Now*. Colonel Kurtz is menacing precisely because he has established a bad enclave and has incorporated into that enclave too many of the nativist features the American military associate with the enemy. Kurtz's encampment is remote and camouflaged; it is redolent with wilderness energies and pagan ritual; it flourishes in spite of orthodox political and military belief; it pays no heed to the conventions of the garrison; and it disputes the compelling commission from God to build a visible city on a hill. The encampment, therefore, is a threat to Puritan order and stability. In an era of machine dreams and technological change Kurtz stands as the exemplary primitive. He disobeys the energy of his culture and brings to mind the memory of Puritan Massachusetts when individuals were refused the right to leave the colony of their own accord and settle in the wilderness. In New England, as Loren Baritz tells us, each individual had pledged himself as a Christian to a covenant that could not be broken by private or solitary pursuits.

> The law of the colony made it illegal for an individual to live alone; everyone had to be or to become a member of a household or family. The Daniel Boone type was considered as dangerous to the organic community as were mavericks like Roger Williams and mystics like Mistress Anne Hutchinson. The nation was made of a series of covenants, ascending from the basic and essential covenant between a man and God, to the family, church, and state, and an uncovenanted or otherwise exotic individual would be a threat to the entire structure.[4]

In keeping with the Puritan idea that moral watch had to be kept over everyone, Johnson preferred a strategy that limited the soldier's knowledge of the wilderness and distanced him, as much as possible, from the enemy or object he sought to attack. Johnson advocated a strategy "of cold technological aggression" and "attrition" that relied on a massive infusion of American weaponry into South Vietnam and the relegation of the Special Forces—the symbols of American frontier individualism—to a secondary role. Johnson's perception of Vietnam, in other words, was reminiscent of the attitude of the Puritans at the time of the Great Swamp Fight of 1675 when an English expedition wiped out a concentration of Narrangansett Indians. Joseph Slotkin has described the Swamp Fight of 1675 as a "seventeenth-century My Lai," a moment when the Puritans went berserk in punishing those who did not bow down to their mission. In Puritan literature it was reported as a triumph of purity and diligence:

> Capt. Henchman and the Plimouth forces kept a diligent Eye upon the Enemy, but were not willing to run into the mire and Dirt after

them in a Dark Swamp, being taught by Experience how dangerous it is to fight in such dismal Woods, when their Eyes would be muffled with the Leaves, and their Arms pinioned with the thick Boughs of the trees, as their Feet were continually shackled with the Roots spreading every Way in those Boggy Woods. It is ill fighting with a Beast in his own Den. They resolved therefore to starve them out of the Swamp. . . . To that end they began to build a Fort, as it were to beleaguer the Enemy.[5]

This picture of the eternal presence of the native people of the woods, dark of skin and seemingly dark of mind—mysterious, cruel, devil-worshiping, and trapped in original sin—has implications for the soldier in Vietnam, faced with the prospect of encountering the North Vietnamese Army, an enemy whose weapon is camouflage and whose traditional stronghold is the rural hinterland. The parallel with New England should be borne in mind since the colonial principle was not to adapt to native ways but to erect structures in spite of them. For the colonial magistrates and divines, the errand in the wilderness demanded utmost vigilance. He who entered and became lost was, according to William Bradford:

in continual danger of the savage people, who are cruel, barbarous and most treacherous, being most furious in their rage and merciless where they overcome; not being content only to take away life, but delight to torment men in the most bloody manner that may be; flaying some alive with the shells of fishes, cutting off the members and joints of others by piecemeal and broiling on the coals, eat the collops of their flesh in their sight whilst they live with other cruelties too horrible to be related.[6]

The Massachusetts government in the seventeenth century viewed the limitation of movement to the frontier as a key to the maintenance of moral and social order in the coastal towns, and the establishment of a stable, limited New England as essential to the fulfillment of their mission. Antinomians, such as John Underhill, who spoke about establishing new, independent settlements in the wilderness were disfranchised. The magistrates of the General Court disapproved of the expansion of coastal settlements into the deeper wilderness without strong supervision by men of proven orthodoxy and social position.

= Protection and Talisman =

The Puritan experiment in the colonies was possessed of a characteristic ambivalence, and many of the features of that vision—enthusiasm and paranoia, commitment to the spiritual errand and reluctance to expand its physical boundaries—reappear in the literature of the Vietnam War. Few American soldiers, whatever their view of the nature of America's errand, are able to accept the native conditions of life in Vietnam. Whatever their sympathy for the Vietnamese people, few are able to escape the belief that the wilderness is a wasteland and that it functions as an analogue of the human mind, redolent with the possibilities of good and evil. It is as if the American soldier in Vietnam is haunted with the memory of the darkness the Indians once flitted through, "like the secret Enemy of Christ or like the evil thoughts that plague the mind on the edge of consciousness."[7] In the literature most of the soldiers who go to Vietnam are not encouraged to use the wilderness for their own protection, and counterinsurgency has little appeal.

The problem once again echoes New England history. Only on rare occasions did the colonial community, in its skirmishes with the Indians, turn the wilderness to its own advantage. The Apostle John Eliot described how, in the Pequot Wars of 1677, settlers learned the art of camouflage and hid themselves behind rocks and tree trunks during an Indian attack. But camouflage was rarely an accepted practice. It smacked of the duplicity of the "skulking" heathen whose ways were those of the forest and who would not wage war during clear weather or in open fields.[8] To counteract this the Puritans created militia systems and mass fortifications—formal structures of organized defense—that anticipate the fire bases in Vietnam. Since survival "made a strong military posture necessary to resist inroads by hostile outsiders,"[9] the happiest time for the earliest settlers in New England, as Joseph Doddridge informs us, were the winter months when the harvest was gathered and the trees were stripped bare and "owing to the severity of the weather, the Indians were unable to make their excursions into the settlements."[10]

In the literature of Vietnam the forest gives strength and assistance to the enemy. The paranoia reaches its most extreme state in Stephen Wright's *Meditations in Green* where an entire American military intelligence unit is devoted to locating the hiding place of an NVA regiment somewhere in the jungle. In a world where "the Bush was reaching in" and "the company's nerves had thinned to wire" the mission is regarded, by the unit's commanding officer, as the raison d'être of the military intelligence facility in Vietnam. A network of computer terminals and data programmers is geared up to the task of defoliating the wilderness in order to reveal the enemy. Only technology and American business efficiency will achieve this task: "The General went on to speak of the virtues of systems analysis, the sanctity of the data base, the effective utilization of common sense, he talked about the program, getting with it, he elaborated on progress, the correct tallying of figures, the latest consensus upon which everyone should clamber aboard or be left at the dock with the gooks."[11]

There is a tendency in reading novels like *Meditations in Green* to associate such thinking with a military elite. But the dependency on technology is not just a feature of military orthodoxy or an American faith in scientific gadgetry. It is also a characteristic of the survival needs of many of the wayward and uncommitted, those whose narratives contain within them much of that disobedient energy we have come to associate with "grunt" literature. Even in a text like Robert Mason's *Chickenhawk*—in which the narrator's life can hardly be described as conformist or supportive of the military establishment—there is a strong dependency on talismanic structures that enclose the individual or protect him from the ravages of unfriendly fire. Mason buys a double-barreled derringer in the States and has a holster made for it from "a couple dozen folding P.38 can openers from our C rations." As an article of war the finished product is more like a handmade tool in a frontier settlement than an effective implement of self-protection in a dangerous war zone. "A leather ring on my left shoulder had the holster sewn on near the bottom. I slipped the heavy derringer into the holster while the mate watched proudly. With the weight of the gun, the holster slid comfortably and invisibly under my arm. Maybe it would save my life; maybe I would use it to kill myself if I was captured. I really didn't know why I wanted it" (51). The presence of an American artifact provides reassurance and assuages loneliness. The flak jacket that he wears does not stop bullets. "As a matter of fact," he admits, "it won't even slow them down" (198), but it is symbolically important as a protective shield to deflect the energies of the enemy on the ground. So too his wristwatch which he considers "a charm" (387). Most important is the Huey helicopter, a machine that Mason controls with grace and skill and through which he filters his entire understanding of the world outside. Since that world is alien to him the helicopter becomes his refuge, an "island" (242) in a sea of horror that threatens "to overrun" (182) him whenever he lands.

It is only through the idiom of the tool as a symbol of cultural form that Mason can begin to make sense of Vietnam. Through his empathy for engineering he reaches out to a culture that demonstrates, historically, its high regard for construction skills. The existence of a waterwheel—"as efficient as any device our engineers could produce"—is important because "the knowledge that built it was being systematically destroyed" (251–52). The master carpenter's box of tools that he discovers is an extension of a world he knows and can respect; because of these tools and their quality, he can relate to a people who are not unlike him, a race of individuals who "were definitely not savages." Prejudice is momentarily overcome through the "enlightening symbol" of technological proficiency. "I had never heard of a gook or a slope-head or a slant-eye or a dink who did anything but eat rice and shit and fight unending wars. These tools and that waterwheel convinced me that there was a successful way of life going on around us" (261–62).

In a world where safety is at best provisional such insights are of little practical benefit, however. The tragedy of *Chickenhawk* is that the simple delights of American culture are difficult to resist. On R & R Mason visits a bar in Saigon. It lacks intrigue but its luxuriance is familiar and it proves irresistible. "The bar served any drink you could name, made with American booze for a quarter. . . . As the bourbon flowed into my bloodstream, I began to warm to the occasion. Drunk enough to relax and be hungry, Riker and I got a table overlooking the city. We had rare sirloin and baked potatoes with sour cream served with a huge tossed salad of crispy fresh lettuce and juicy tomatoes that might have been grown on a farm near my home-town in Florida" (127). In a navy PX depot Mason is seduced by a glittering array of consumer durables; the variety of products on display overrides any of the concerns he might have about their relevance. "The Saigon warriors had a complete department store. The stuff for sale here was actually better and cheaper than the merchandise sold at PXs in America—Nikon cameras for $150. A Roberts tape recorder cost $120. There were clothes, tools, canned food, books, even cases of Kotex" (127). As he leaves Vietnam the seduction is complete. Cocooned inside the sanitized cabin of a 707, Mason is grateful for the comforts that await him in a familiar world: "Sitting in the soft airline seat, I savored the air-conditioned crispness of the air and breathed in the scents of the passing stewardesses. I had a grin on my face that wouldn't quit. . . . [I was] aboard a chartered Pan American 707 going to the land of the big PX" (387).

There are few correlations in American prose writing between a soldier's disagreement with the war and a long-term affiliation with things Vietnamese. The enclave or garrison mentality underpins not only the errand itself but also the beliefs of those who oppose it. Even the airspace is a spiritual condition affording protection because of its remoteness from things on the ground. The higher reaches of space are places of retreat: "We flew at 5000 feet, where the air was cool and the bullets couldn't reach," says Mason, "a beautiful two-and-a-half-hour flight" (124).

A common perception of the Vietnamese is that they wish to seduce the Americans onto the land and, in so doing, deny the security that space provides. As Ronald J. Glasser suggests, to make Vietnam into "a close-up war" induces unease.[12] For others the land is dangerous and to wander onto it is to risk contamination. The purpose of defoliant is not to pollute the land but to decontaminate it, to make the wilderness no longer toxic. To lose one's way without the approved resources is to risk—as in the Puritan captivity narrative—death, torture, a loss of moral autonomy.

= A Sexual Wilderness =

In *Meditations in Green* spiritual catastrophe is signified by the physical dismemberment of the downed helicopter's crew and its passengers whom Griffin searches for in the jungle. When Griffin finds them they are hanging from the trees. "Their unbuttoned unzipped pants dropped in folds about their ankles. Groins and thighs were black with stale blood, alive with insect movement. Protruding between the lips of each mouth was a small grey mushroom, the severed remains of each man's penis" (279). The helicopter crewmen have suffered the fate that Robert Mason dreads: they are "overrun" and rendered sexually impotent by the perverse libidinous energies of the forest. Castration is an act that reminds us of the symbolic horror of the Indian menace in the Puritan wilderness of New England. For the Puritans sexual freedom was "synonymous with the sin of lust." For the Indian, on the other hand, "sexual freedom . . . was an assumed right . . . [and] was deemed essential to the health of both individual and tribe, besides consti- tuting a pleasurable and at times sacred source of personal gratification."[13] In Wright's novel the Vietnamese deny the right of sexual health and grat- ification in a language that retrieves the castration myths of the Puritans. The sexual energy of the wilderness attracts and ruins the helicopter crew- men who are downed in a world of abundant greenery. Griffin responds to the riotous procreative energy of this world with the "indignant" urge of the magistrate. "The whole stinking forest should have been sprayed long ago, hosed down, drenched in Orange, leaves blackened, branches denuded, un- dergrowth dried into brittle paper. . . . Who permitted these outrages, where was the technology when you needed it?" (278).

Those who go into the wilderness of their own volition, or because they are sent there alone, are regarded with extreme suspicion and risk chastise- ment. Those who celebrate the rural life-style of the Vietnamese and associate with them, like Mary McCarthy, are liable to be denounced as treacherous, for they revive the memory of what Slotkin calls "intimacy with the Indians" and have become "tainted."[14] In the Puritan mythology of Vietnam, the most tainted of all Americans was Bobby Garwood who, as a nineteen-year-old marine, was wounded and captured by the Viet Cong. Fourteen years later he returned to the United States, shoeless and chattering in Vietnamese, to face a court-martial for desertion. He had learned how to cook rats and appeared to the military to have abandoned his desire to live in the United States. A "marked man" to the marines, Garwood was referred to as the "White Cong" and conjured up fantasies of men who go AWOL for the love of adventure. The venom that was directed his way, the accusations of de- sertion, call forth an old fear of antinomian anarchy and unbridled nativism, a paranoia of the American colonial soul that was first demonstrated at the time of the Great Swamp Fight when an Englishman turned up who was living and fighting with the Indians. Garwood stirred memories of Indian revelers and paganists like Thomas Morton and Indian apologists like John Underhill whom the seventeenth-century Puritans severely punished for their enthusiasm for the natives. Garwood's disappearance resurrected, too, the memory of the Indian belief in "wilderness life," in which boys were sent on initiation rites into the wilderness to dwell in free solitude until their voices had changed to men's voices. One of the horrors evoked by Garwood when he was picked up and at his court-martial was that his voice had changed—he spoke Vietnamese.[15]

It is worth noting that in Ronald J. Glasser's 365 *Days* it is deemed acceptable for teenage soldiers to accept an ambush assignment at night in the bush providing they demonstrate, upon their return, that they have not been transformed or contaminated by the experience. This is done in "No Fucken Cornflakes" when a teenage killer berates a cook for having run out of cereal. The fact that the soldier is psychopathic is not relevant in the army. What is important is that he signifies his need for nourishment in a familiar and trusted language. In so doing he reestablishes his identity and admits his dependency on a breakfast cereal. This makes clear what he really is: an American consumer.

Without that signification—or without a recognition of its existence—the soldier's individualism is potentially alarming. This is apparent in the testimonies of those who were assigned to a remote rural posting, such as David Donovan who became an adviser to the Vietnamese in the MeKong Delta and testifies to the great suspicion his work aroused in the Regular Army. Although the U.S. Army LURPs (Long Range Reconnaissance Patrol), the U.S. Navy SEALs (Sea, Air, and Land), and U.S. Marine Force Recon (Reconaissance) units proved adept at counterinsurgency warfare, they were hampered by a military strategy that failed to acknowledge the realities of waging an unconventional war. The problem with Special Forces strike teams and the use of Combined Action Platoons—which, as Robert Thompson noted, was probably "the best idea I have seen in Vietnam, and it worked superbly" (Krepinevich, 174)—was that the marines could never sell the idea to the American army. Instead, the army preferred to rely on its "technological and logistical strong suits" and preferred to use "sensors, infrared photography, helicopters, and a host of technological wonders to find the enemy, and firepower and mobility to destroy him" (Krepinevich, 177).

The insularity and suspicion aroused by nativist encounters remains the most disturbing legacy of the American experience in Vietnam, especially since writers have been unable, and perhaps unwilling, to examine the problem in any great detail. Surface impressions of the Vietnamese have proven as satisfactory to the contemporary liberal imagination as they were to militarists like Gen. William Westmoreland who eschewed the use of Combined Action Platoons and the establishment of strong social relationships with the Vietnamese. America's Vietnam, as Rick Berg has said, has "always been more a war than a country." Although America "lost the war in 1973," it lost "the country in 1975" and hasn't recovered it since.[16] The Puritan legacy of Indian treachery remains a dominant imprint in film and fiction, and in American literature the Viet Cong nightmare becomes a repeat of the Indian terror. We see the Vietnamese as a race of people who remind us of John Eliot's "skulking Indian"—he who can never be trusted and who "kills indiscriminately." It is the Indian, now, who has moved through time and space to dog the American mission in Vietnam. His "sneak attacks, irregular warfare and unexpected and unheralded tactics" are the stock-in-trade of primitive people who do not obey the "laws of war" and oppose Christian virtues.[17] In New England "the Indian was omnipresent; he struck without warning and was a nightly terror in the remote silence of backwoods cabins." This refrain is constantly heard in the literature of Vietnam. In *Chickenhawk*, Robert Mason's nights get "harder to bear." One night in the bush when he lacks "protection" Mason finds himself awakened from his sleep, "sitting upright but not understanding," as the Viet Cong attack his unit. Although the helicopters "are invisible in the moonless night" (238), the Viet Cong are able to pick them out and then melt away into the jungle.

= Pollution =

In the city the contours of reality appear equally vague; fundamental distinctions between the Vietnamese are made only with difficulty by American soldiers, if at all. Since the Viet Cong wear no recognizable uniform, there is, according to Tim O'Brien, "no reliable criterion by which to distinguish a pretty Vietnamese girl from a deadly enemy: often they were one and the same person." The Vietnamese are all "gooks." Their duplicity is proven by the different identities they assume during the course of a day. The problem for the soldier is one of cognitive definition. As one critic has said, "The differences between 'regular' gooks, local gooks, 'foreign' (North Vietnamese) gooks, hostile gooks, and so on are open to sudden and unpredictable permutation and therefore cannot serve as sound premises upon which to base judgment and action."[18]

Although the problems for the American soldier were genuine enough, few writers have been willing to investigate them or to reveal the more complex features of Vietnamese life. For the poet and journalist James Fenton, in his article "The Fall of Saigon" (1985), corruption is endemic in South Vietnam and the writer is obliged to provide his reader with physical evidence through images of filth and pollution.[19] The South, to Fenton, has offered no resistance to foreign intervention; it is the prey of all patriotisms, willing to accept both communist and capitalist systems of belief. Fenton's Saigon is so contaminated it lacks any claim to self-determination or spiritual purity and has suffered a complete breakdown in its immune system. Fenton remembers Saigon as an "addicted city," hooked on the drug of American vanity and consumer wealth. There is nothing to see beyond "the corruption of children, the mutilation of young men, the prostitution of women, the humiliation of the old, the division of the family, the division of the country— it had all been done in our name." In its mission to convert the Vietnamese to the righteous beliefs of America and the West the United States has inflicted disease and spiritual despair. As the American forces leave there is "a desperate edge to life" and it is "impossible to relax for a moment." Filth is everywhere, the excremental residue of the secular and profane. The coffee at breakfast tastes "of diarrhoea," the street urchins beg for money and pretend to "eat shit." On their faces the young bear "thirty years of degeneration and misery" and spend what money they can beg on the streets to get high. Women drug their babies and lay them on the "pavement," "repulsive" figures of pity to the passerby. The landscape is "miserable," the inhabitants speak with "terror" in their voice, and the observer is "disgusted" at what he sees. Puritan feelings of censure prevail in a world that Puritanism, even to a non-American, has failed to redeem. "It was impossible in Saigon to be the passive observer. Saigon cast you, inevitably, into the role of the American."[20]

Fenton's picture is that of a voyeur, created to demonstrate to the reader the sordid fatality of capitalism's decline. His work displays the tendency of the political tourist who is unable to see beneath the surface appearance of life in Saigon. Like one of Hawthorne's "uninstructed multitude" that "attempts to see with its eyes,"[21] Fenton is concerned only to paint his visual impressions of Saigon in the "predominant colourings" of "melancholy and gloom." What is lacking in Fenton's essay are those very qualities that make Mark Frankland's *The Mother-of-Pearl Men*, a novel set in Saigon at roughly the same time, so culturally persuasive and informed. Frankland is one of the few writers who are prepared to dig down beneath the obvious sordidness the West has brought to Vietnam in order to uncover something of the historical structure of the underworld that survives there—whether criminal or guerrilla, rural or revolutionary—and its changeable and complex attitude toward history. Fenton lacks the desire to look beneath the screen of corruption the country throws up, and his squeamishness prevents him from acknowledging the syncretic nature of Vietnamese history. Fenton's approach tends to be one of moral outrage, something that is missing not only in Frankland's novel but in another neglected work of Vietnam scholarship, *Vietnam: The Unheard Voices* (1969) by Don Luce and John Sommer.[22]

Luce and Sommer were members of International Voluntary Services and spent many years in Vietnam working directly with the people on socioeconomic aid projects in the 1960s. In *The Unheard Voices* Luce and Sommer reject the moral absolutism of Fenton. For them "it is surprising that the ravages of war have not affected Vietnamese society more than they have." They argue that to those who are unfamiliar with Vietnam it might seem that the war has "left practically no facet of life untouched or unmarred. Yet the pillars of Vietnamese cultural values persist, their strength proved further by the awful stresses." The writers are aware that "American visitors are sometimes repelled by certain practices that they take to be natural to the Vietnamese people. Corruption is one such practice, and though it should not be condoned, it is, to a large extent, one method by which individuals adjust to the uncertainties of economic life in a war-torn country." Luce and

Sommer also refer to "the fantastic proliferation of prostitution, of the 'bar society,' and of the rather nefarious activities which seem to glut and downgrade the once fashionable city streets." Yet, as the writers reveal, the act of giving oneself up to prostitution in order to help one's family is "a sacrifice exalted in Vietnamese literature." The noble heroine of the nineteenth-century *Kim Van Kieu*, Vietnam's greatest literary masterpiece, they point out, sold herself in order to earn enough money to help her father and brother survive in difficult circumstances.[23] This theme is also developed by the Vietnamese writer Minh Duc Hoai Trinh in her novel *This Side . . . The Other Side* (1980).

= Stick Figures =

In spite of the arguments put forward by Luce and Sommer over twenty years ago, few American writers have considered it politic to regard the Vietnamese as an accessible subject. With the exception of such writers as Victor Kolpacoff, Robert Roth, John Balaban, Mark Frankland, and Donald McQuinn, the Vietnamese people are still represented in Western fiction as withdrawn and remote, figures of negligible cultural importance. As "Americans pre-empted the war in reality," says David Gelman, so "in most of the books and films, they seem to pre-empt the suffering and heartbreak of the war."[24] Gelman's comment was made in 1978 and it still remains substantially correct. As Peter Marin has said, the Vietnamese have rarely been portrayed "as anything more than stick-figures in an American dream."[25] Writers, on the whole, have not made the effort to get to know Vietnam because, one suspects, the subject is not regarded as marketable. The American writer still believes his obligation is to look at Vietnam as a place of war and to write about the war as an American event in a way that is familiar to the American people. The writer's low opinion of the Vietnamese is often signified by his attempt to represent them through the prism of their corruption—their lack of solidarity and their loss of culture. One thinks, for example, of the Hollywood decadence of Lieutenant Phan in *Meditations in Green*.

Elsewhere, writers have a tendency to patronise the Vietnamese and to make them recognizable through Western intellectual and linguistic structures. In John M. Del Vecchio's *The 13th Valley* the Vietnamese scout, Minh, is not only voluble and articulate; he has lost all trace of his native speech and colloquial heritage. Although Del Vecchio tells us, in the words of a black American soldier, that "words are important" (501), the words spoken by Minh have become so Westernized that the cultural values he claims to represent have lost their meaning. In *The 13th Valley* the Vietnamese with whom we are most familiar are verbally proficient, well able to communicate their thoughts in superb English. But the enemy are still the dark ones in the jungle, the unseen menace both speechless and obscure. As he waits for the NVA to attack, Minh stares up through his poncho and discusses the merits of Western intellectual thought. His conversation with the American soldiers consists of a block of speeches that show little other than a potential for philosophical posturing. Minh lectures Brooks: "All you really have is a systematic format on which to pose [your] questions. Your religion has no more meaning, no more real answers, that the Tao did twenty-five hundred years ago. And the Tao did not then and does not now have a rigid format or a firm construction, so its answers were not and are not conceived in the asking. Do you understand, Sir?" (503). *The 13th Valley* is a thoughtful work and one of the few epic novels of ideas that the war has inspired, but in its perception of native culture and character the achievement is limited.

In most American novels the Vietnamese are bit-part players, movie extras who provide the fiction with vernacular support and local color. Few writers, as Ross McGregor has said, have found it useful to learn the Vietnamese language or to acquaint themselves with Vietnamese culture or to "create complex characters capable of reflecting the tragedy in other than American terms." As a result, "characterisation of the Vietnamese to a point where they can hold their own amongst Americans is rare." The Vietnamese remain "little more than impressions,"[26] figures of darkness and obscurity who live on the wrong side of history, the bearers of a primitive and fallible wisdom who have fallen prey to an atheistic mission and a communist myth. In this respect the Vietnamese have been culturally undermined in American autobiography and fiction. Peter Marin made this point as far back as 1980 when he argued that American writers have not been willing "to confront . . . the war . . . from the Vietnamese point of view—in terms of their suffering rather than ours. The same cultural bias that has traditionally marked our attitude towards other races seems to be still at work."[27]

Literary critics do little, if anything, to rectify the prejudice of American writers. To a book like *Dispatches*, which pays no attention to the Vietnamese except to look at them as a corrupt and morally degenerate people, critics have given unqualified support. Even the revisionist critic Peter Rollins describes *Dispatches* as "one of the finest books to come out of the war," and Peter McInerney says that *Dispatches* offers "the finest example of facts about the American experience in Vietnam."[28] If books about Vietnam can truly be regarded as books about America and if, in the process, they can successfully legitimize the act of displacing Vietnam from the cultural agenda with a view of the American scene, then *Dispatches* is indeed a fine book. C. D. B. Bryan also describes *Dispatches* as "the best book to have been written about the Vietnam war,"[29] yet it contains not one Vietnamese character of note. In the narrative Saigon is a place of unquestionable corruption. The "air" is like Los Angeles "on short plumbing"; the streets are "intense with bad feeling: despair, impacted rage, impotent gnawing resentment." The narrator detects nothing beyond foulness and clutter in a world unwilling to collaborate with him or conform to his expectations. He talks constantly like a spoiled tourist, and his bark is that of the closet authoritarian. "You can't get these people to do a fucking thing, you can't get these people to do a fucking thing" (38).

= "Excrement and Sacrament" =

In Takeshi Kaiko's *Into a Black Sun* (1968) the level of commitment to Vietnam and the quality of observation is much improved. *Into a Black Sun* is the personal narrative of a Japanese poet and journalist. It describes the writer's picaresque wanderings in Vietnam between 1964 and 1965. Kaiko's vision takes in the junk and clutter of the country as well as the fragile beauty of its fields and forests. For the narrator Vietnam reveals itself only to those who observe its slow metamorphosis under the sun. All life is subsumed within nature. On the edge of the Iron Triangle he takes in the dawn: "Until a few minutes ago, buses passing on the highway had seemed like a deep-sea fish blinking red and blue lights; now the sun was up to the treetops. The sky was suffused with saffron, and two or three streaks of vermilion streamed out between the clouds and trees. It was a time when I could read the lines on my palm. A time when the new leaves on a tree stood out from the old" (33).

When he is not observing the American camp on the edge of the jungle the narrator exposes himself to the airless world of the Saigon streets. He explores the excremental filth, the urban decay, the daily life of the Saigon alleys. He accepts contamination, infection, sluggishness, nausea, "glare" (102), not as one would a disability, but as a preliminary state of creativity which guarantees the writer some immunity from the sanctified dream of protection rackets in American sectors.

Illness and hangover are signs of involvement which Kaiko's reader comes to expect in his meeting with the "common scum." Like E. E. Cummings's *The Enormous Room*, the novel manipulates the images of the erotic, the urinary, and the excremental to symbolize the precious mysteries of brotherhood. Kaiko's Saigon reeks of emission: sweat, excrement, sexual discharge, pus from festering wounds; these are fluids that rise to the surface of the body in visible illustrations of feeling. From the stench of defecation and the high-voltage smell of sexual encounter the air of Saigon is a high-octane gas of "oxygen, nitrogen and Tet" (54). The smell of Vietnam does nothing to contaminate the American soldier in his sanitized parlors and glamorous bars with their "licked-tin taste" of air conditioning. Yet filth and understanding are interdependent, and the smell of "fetid and nutritious" air, which so disgusts the sensibility of the West, is "characteristically Asian" (64). In the city, where "the war had receded, was being fought elsewhere, on another continent, in some hinterland beyond my reach" (110), pollution gives way to sexual fertility. Inside Vietnam there is always the "reek of sweat and betel" (97), "the smell of urine and sex" (106), things overripe and overcrowded, fluids leaked, spilled, discarded: urine, semen, sweat, tears. Ducts and channels are never blocked for long with unspent emotions. Spillage and release is always available and "sorrow and passion" (143) are always liable. The interior world affords no protection from the splashes of filth and fetid air. In the places where "a wizened rump . . . suddenly splashed urine" (145) privacy is abolished. In the "cluttered alley" behind the Ginh Dinh district market, where the Americans do not wander, there is work and camaraderie. "At the mouth of one dark alley, men were cleaning pigs' intestines in a large metal tub of hot water in the middle of the passage, drawing through their fists as though wringing silk sashes. Blood, fat, and feces—the giddying odor filled the air. The critic guided me into a small adobe house on the riverbank" (126). Inside the house the wrinkled body of Vietnam is laid bare in the bronzed and writhing body of a Tamil, her "fleshy labia" (127) and twitching rectum opened wide for investigation. In the city's sweat and stench, people dream "behind grimy walls, panting in the heat" (79), seeking their release in social lives that overcome the claustrophobia. In a city of no exclusion zones, the reader moves at an eager pace from shelter to hovel, breathing in the suffocating odor of a pungent and colorful world, as if to be alive on a "fetid street" is to smell "like an unwashed crotch" (185). To capture that smell is the writer's mission. As the narrator says to Captain Wain, "The essence of any object is its smell. Sweat smells of sweat, and papaya of papaya. I know papaya doesn't smell of anything much, but its odour doesn't die out, and it doesn't change. I want to write about smells that don't fade" (76).

The journeyman seeks Vietnam in its entrails; he ingests and emits the sought-for correlatives of the natural world: "The vodka smouldering in my body flared up from time to time, blue flames flickering, and my swollen tongue felt hairy. The sun went swiftly down and the hibiscus in the garden faded" (108). Whether he is hungover or merely hungry, the flare of sensations sought within his body evokes the flair of an illuminated world: "Biting off bits of a vinegary red-hot pepper, I'd slurp the noodles up and soon my mouth would be on fire, but hot spices go well with tropical mornings" (64 –65). The narrator ranges in pursuit of the sensations of exotic energy within the body of the country and the wound and the suffering that body has encountered in a civil war. Those who must know the body must become the body, must feast on its wounds. After witnessing an execution, the writer contemplates eating Vietnam. "When I first drew my knife across the rare meat, fragrant with garlic, a puddle of pale red blood oozed out. I put my fork down and stared at the red liquid spreading over the white plate. The pink cross section with its blackish crust was exactly like a wound—a wound where flies would swarm, sucking, feasting, fucking on some peasant's body found abandoned in high grass. I speared a piece of meat and chewed it slowly. It was succulent, delicious. There was no physical revulsion. No resistance on the way down" (136).

American tastes are largely sacramental. As the two-man ambush teams in Glasser's *365 Days* stand in line outside the mess tent after a night's "work" in the bush, Truex points to Johnson's hand as he holds his weapon, a bicycle chain.

> "That you?" Truex asked, pointing down at Johnson's bloody hand.
> Johnson looked thoughtfully at his hand. He seemed suddenly subdued, almost awed. "No," he said, "that's him."
> "Yeah, I know. I got some of mine on me, too," Truex said. "Took him down from behind. Must have got an artery right off. Jesus! I mean I even got some in my mouth." (121)

When Truex says "I got some of mine on me, too," he doesn't refer to his own blood but to his kill, that of the enemy he has just murdered. The syntax is a way of uniting a captured object with a loved object, a reference that has its origins in the homoerotic brotherhood of killing. The same is true for Cram: "Suddenly another form appeared. The figure seemed to hesitate and was about to turn back when Cram leaped up and got home. For a moment, as Cram worked in his knife, it looked as if they were embracing, then quietly Cram lowered the body to the ground" (117). To deliver one's enemy from a state of evil, to save him from the torment of his heathen ways, is an act of love or "embracing." The man of ambush—who takes on the appearance of the devil in the bush, who goes out "clean" (113) and comes back "filthy" (120)—is a purifying minister, a merciful Christian. When the severed artery of a "gook" spurts blood into the mouth of Truex, what Truex ends is the torment of a soul blighted by communism; when he swallows the blood, what his body ingests is the plasma that occasions human bonding. There is closeness in death, a warmth of feeling. The act of tasting the blood of one's enemy is an act of communion. If "him" is me and "him" has got inside "my mouth," then what has occurred is transubstantiation in reverse, the blood and body of the evil gook turned into wine in the body of his saviour. The war that has bred a terrible hunger is satisfied in death, a state of being that for Truex is tantamount to godliness. Truex wishes to kill or be killed in order to achieve the immortality of the divine. Like the cause he serves, Truex is obsessed with delivering others from their evil ways. He is severed not from America but from that very humanity America purports to serve. In these circumstances the horror of what a soldier will do to act like God and what a country will do in the name of God are one and the same.

For Kaiko's narrator the reverse is true. To explore Vietnam is to lose protection, to penetrate a membrane without a sheath, to accept the risk of disease and infection that comes from wandering the streets with neither aim nor invitation. Kaiko's narrator tramples through the strewn, heaped-up rubbish of the alleys, the mush and excrement of those who find the fastidious manner of the West distasteful. Vietnam celebrates itself through its filth, through the waste and sickness of its suffering, the rotting detritus the American presence creates and a corrupt regime tolerates. To find Vietnam in a wasteful world is to find the waste with which the city surrounds itself in spite of its afflictions. To wander "down an alley littered with bits of vegetable refuse, fish entrails and papaya rinds" (83) is to come across a city littered with waste but not yet wasted, a city that fashions something of itself through its filth.

= Savage Cleansing =

Kaiko's suggestion is that filth is adversarial to a childish country. Those who cannot understand filth are far "too young to understand" Vietnam (87). In Graham Greene's *The Quiet American* (1955) the adolescent Puritan Alden Pyle wishes to cleanse his lover, Phuong, by taking her to America to redeem her body in a Christian church. The act of "protection" through marriage is a proper gesture for the American visitor to Vietnam. Pyle abhors the native ways which are filthy and suggest contamination. The sight of blood on his shoe from the bombing of the milk bar, for which he is responsible, repels him.

> "Pyle said, "It's awful." He looked at the wet on his shoes and said in a sick voice, "What's that?"
> "Blood," I said. "Haven't you ever seen it before?"
> He said, "I must get them cleaned before I see the Minister."[30]

Pyle is an intruder, a spiritual tourist who comes for a glimpse and goes back home with his trophies and his treasures. Marriage eliminates the foreignness of the object of possession by providing it with a status and a fixed identity that makes that object culturally neutral. This need to corral and supervise the native energy of a potential aggressor is reminiscent of the forced resettlement of the Vietnamese villagers to strategically safe, "Westernized" hamlets in the 1960s, a policy of the Diem regime which the American government helped implement. While the strategic hamlets policy was designed to halt the flow of recruits to the enemy, it also served to emphasize the lack of trust the American Army had for the rural populace of South Vietnam. The policy was thus a manifestation of the curious way in which the legacy of Puritanism survived in Vietnam.

The dispersal of the villagers in the South and the acquisition of native land remind us of Puritan attitudes toward the Indian's right to title in New

England. For William Bradford the Indian could not be left to wander at will through the forest. The wilderness was a place of "savage and brutish men who range up and down, little otherwise than the wild beasts of the same."[31] The pressure of demographic expansion, coupled with the psychological fear of acculturation, moved the Puritans toward a policy of reducing the Indian to a semicaptive status on reservations which were called at the time "praying towns." Since the Indian could not be left to his own devices, he was, wherever possible, converted to Christianity. In this context the digging of moats and the erection of stockades around the strategic hamlet settlements of South Vietnam may be looked upon as an act of rededication to the Puritan principle of garrison and enclosure.[32]

What happens in Vietnam is relevant to the Puritan experiment in New England. In both locations the creation of enclaves and their fortification offers protection from attack and the opportunity for self-reformation. During the middle years of the seventeenth century, aided by the missionary work of the Apostle John Eliot, some four thousand converts—"Praying Indians"—chose a European way of life and lived in or close to Puritan settlements. By 1663 colonial printers had already issued over a thousand copies of Eliot's famous translation of the Bible "into the Indian tongue." The principle of establishing a relationship with the Indian, therefore, was based not on a policy of native accommodation but on conversion, tuition, and reform.[33]

The Indian's savagery and his capacity for evil, as Eliot testified in King Philip's War, was never taken for granted in New England. Although the Puritans were concerned with Christianizing the Indian in the seventeenth century, they often acted without compassion in defense of their own interests. After years of conflict it became increasingly clear, for example, that the Indians would never entirely convert to Christianity. And, as the seventeenth century progressed, the "puritan missionary spirit," says Richard Slotkin, "gave way to the military spirit." As a result the Puritans "came to define their relationship to the New World in terms of violence and warfare."[34] To Indian sympathizers like Thomas Morton, the Puritans were guilty of withholding "their hearts and their persons from the Indians and the wilderness, seeking only the corruption and destruction of both for their own gain." Thus in King Philip's War of 1675–76, when New England experienced the horrors of large-scale Indian massacre, the Indians were regarded as dogs to be hunted down "because they did not," as it was argued, "manage their war fairly."[35]

One is reminded here of the assessment of the Viet Cong that McGeorge Bundy provided to President Johnson in a memorandum: "The energy and persistence of the Viet Cong are astonishing. They can appear anywhere— at almost any time. They have accepted extraordinary losses and they come back for more. They show skill in their sneak attacks and ferocity when cornered. Yet the weary country does not want them to win."[36]

= An American World of Hurt =

As an expression of historical memory, the American response to Vietnam in literature tends to be introverted and self-obsessed. Ross McGregor describes it as a "turning inward to examine a selfhood under threat, often leading to painful admissions, but confined to the boundaries of that self. The war remains an American 'world of hurt.' "[37] Given the constraints the American military imposed in Vietnam, and the kind of training the American soldiers received, the condition of "selfhood" is hardly surprising.

The military experience of the soldier in Vietnam often prevented him from gaining a view of those he was living among and the enemy he was supposed to be fighting against. "Theoretically," says McGregor, "there should have been excellent opportunities for developing cultural contact with the Vietnamese," but "in practice, the regular troops had little chance to mix with the Vietnamese on anything other than a specific level." American "needs" were defined through American service industries that "sprang up in response to American purchasing power" but did nothing to stimulate "cultural interchange" and a genuine knowledge of the Vietnamese people.[38] The American government self-consciously created an enclosed world, redolent with historical meaning but lacking in social and cultural awareness. As Peter Marin says, "Few of the men who fought in Vietnam were ever really there, ever really saw the place and their enemies. They were locked, still, in our classrooms, in our national dreams, in our old Hollywood films living out, almost like robots, the pervasive national myths of virtue, prowess and power."[39] Locked up in his own world and shut off from the Vietnamese world, the soldier defined the conflict according to the logic of colonial garrison and enclosure.

Those soldiers who became writers and wished to repudiate the logic of enclosure were limited in both knowledge and opportunity. The problem of social readjustment undoubtedly held up the development of Vietnam writing and, in some senses, deprived it of a generous and neighborly disposition. The need to examine the "American world of hurt" was much more protracted than it would have been had circumstances in the United States been different and had the reception of the veteran been more humane. Many of the veterans who returned from Vietnam experienced a feeling of betrayal, of being "stabbed in the back" by a country that refused to discuss the war publicly or to commemorate the soldier's achievement in it.[40] In the later years of the war many of the veterans were shunned as losers or publicly vilified for the atrocities others had committed. Worst of all the country turned its back on the veterans, many of whom "carried a burden of guilt unrelieved by the customary rites of absolution, by the parades, the welcome home, the collective embrace that gathers a soldier back into the fold of the community after he has been sent out to commit the inevitable horrors of a war that his elders told him was necessary."[41] As one soldier puts it in James Webb's *Fields of Fire*, "We been abandoned, Lieutenant. We been kicked off the edge of the goddamned cliff. They don't know how to fight it, and they don't know how to stop fighting it. And back home it's too complicated, so they forget about it and do their rooting at football games. Well, fuck 'em. They ain't worth dying for."[42] The veteran became a victim of two wars: one against an enemy he didn't recognize (the Vietnamese), and the other against an enemy that didn't recognize him (the American public). His experience of enemies, both visible and invisible, forced him to struggle with the aesthetics of combat. In a world of booby traps Vietnam veterans often kept quiet and bided their time.[43]

Much of the literature of Vietnam must be seen against this background of enforced silence in the 1960s and 1970s. The release from that silence, when it came about, was highly dramatic. One of the ironies of Vietnam is that the Puritanism that helped define the war as both subject and structure also provided the soldier with a way of explaining it to others. Puritan instruction and exegetical address came to the Vietnam veteran's assistance. It gave him a voice and provided him with the opportunity to testify to what he had seen and personally witnessed. The Puritanism that had contained the soldier in Vietnam—garrisoned him in with enclaves and enclosures—now provided the means by which he could realize his freedom. Slotkin describes the original conditions that determined the importance of personal testimony:

> Since the "community of Saints" was made up by the gathering together of converted individuals, the Puritan emigrants paid careful attention to the religious experiences of individual members of the transplanted community in order to discern the positive and negative effects of emigration. This concern created a view of the individual experience as community experience in microcosm; and the community's development in the New World was seen primarily . . . in terms of a psychological and spiritual quest.[44]

In the later years of the 1970s the veteran's compulsion to testify at last met the community's need to hear that testimony. There emerged an awareness that the Vietnam veteran had fulfilled the role of the emigrant in history, a man whose errand had made him a part of a "transplanted community." The belief that the veteran, because of "emigration," might now be the bearer of a special kind of wisdom and that through his experience of trial and hardship in an inhospitable environment he had gained a deeper awareness of life accorded well with the Puritan belief in "converted individuals." In the course of time what was once a handicap ("I paid my own way to school. I didn't want to get my G.I. benefits because I didn't want nobody to know I was a vet. I was ashamed because everybody in the U.S. hated GIs for being in the Nam. I was trying to hide myself")[45] became for the veteran an act of necessary testimony ("There's still a lot of things that I'm real close to in there. . . . But the people I know say, 'Steve, forget it. It's over.'. . . . People want me to bury it. I can't bury it. I did learn something and I'm not sure what. But I know it affected me a whole lot").[46] The emotional primacy of the affecting experience, the need to declare one's faith in public and to make one's narrative a dramatic event, recall the conditions of the conversion narrative and the diaries and journals of the sinners in New England. Those who went to Vietnam partook in a redemptive mission inherited from the Puritans, an errand in which the personal testimony of the soldier-as-witness was an essential means of dramatizing the truth.

The guideline is provided by what happened in colonial New England. There, subjective experience was not valued for its own sake but was used "for evidence or instruction." In New England the private often became public and the individual was located in relation to the community as an exemplar. "Conversion as regeneration was taken very literally as a cohesive device, a re-birthing, the taking on of an identity as a visible saint."[47]

In Vietnam testimony the conversion narrative may be identified as a simple affirmation of the public mission. Such an affirmation is often provided for us in air raid stories, narratives of capture, and in the accounts of heroic platoon leaders and Green Beret warriors. But there is also a literature of opposed conviction, a literature that does not subscribe to the doctrine of intervention, that reveals the errand as a thing of misplaced idealism. Here conversion takes place as a process of ironic reconstruction, and the self is distanced from the strategy and intention of a virtuous mission. The rebirth that is offered is not an exemplary commitment to mission but a separation from mission; it is rooted in an intensely private understanding of the limitations of mission on the basis of personal experience; it partakes of the idea of "ocean-crossing as a spiritual rebirth" (Caldwell, 133) but distances the witnessing self from those who subsume individual commitment within the identity of a corporate errand. If the "equation of new life with New World, and of baptism with the Atlantic as a greater Red Sea, becomes a staple of colonial autobiography,"[48] then in the literature of Vietnam the born-again experience that derives from the war involves a disagreement with orthodox thought. In many of the Vietnam autobiographies the emphasis on a faith that is private is absolute, and the need to investigate the disparities between public errand and personal experience function as climactic moments on the road to conversion. The Puritan narrative of self-transformation undergoes a "dark revision" in Vietnam literature. The experience of personal shock is so resonant that it provides the dominant imprint on creative expression. "Urgent in tone, autobiographical in content," many of these works "seem to have provided their authors with an emotional catharsis. This need to testify to what one has witnessed and somehow to make sense of it through words" is represented in the narrative of a 'true-to-life' fiction."[49]

= The Disobedience of a Sinner =

At the core of Puritan culture has always been the crucial problem of how to identify the "chosen" and how to determine which individuals ought to be accepted into the fraternity of the elect. In New England the question of which testimonies were truthful was keenly debated. Those who claimed to have gone through a special converting experience were aware that the adjudication of their case was determined by the extent to which the congregation accepted that grace had been conferred and sin humbly confessed.

The parallels with Vietnam testimonies ought not to be ignored. The disobedient or "separatist" quality of renegade testimonies by Anne Hutchinson or Roger Williams is also characteristic of a narrative style that appeared in the later years of the 1970s, particularly in a small number of often-forgotten personal narratives that were written during the war and were largely ignored at the time. These earlier works appeared out of step with the age in which they were published. Writers like Martha Gellhorn, Mary McCarthy, and Ronald J. Glasser testified to a surviving belief in the efficacy of Puritan testimony but rejected the orthodox wisdom of the errand. In an era when the Vietnam veteran as autobiographer kept his own counsel, Gellhorn, McCarthy, and Glasser were alert for every symbolic moment and sign that might, in the future, grant their work "justification." The problem of interpreting those signs correctly finds expression in the rhetoric of proper "seeing": the desire, as Thomas Shepard wrote, "that no man's Spectacles may deceive him."[50]

Martha Gellhorn was one of the first American journalists who desired to "see" Vietnam in her own way—and was punished for it. "I went to Vietnam," she says, "because I had to learn for myself, since I could not learn from anyone else, what was happening to the voiceless Vietnamese people." Gellhorn had to see for herself because Americans are blind, they "do not notice the military activities of their government." This is confirmed after her visit to Vietnam when she asks a taxi driver, "Do people talk much about Vietnam?" The driver replies "No."[51] Reflecting on her experiences in the late 1960s, Gellhorn directs her anger against those who refused her the right to return to Vietnam, the American official who put her name on a secret blacklist and prevented her from seeing and witnessing and testifying to what she observed as the criminality of the American war effort. "I wanted only to return to Vietnam, stay longer, learn more and place my reports wherever I could, but I was exiled." The American conspiracy against the truth ruined, for Gellhorn, the promise of an errand of original truth. The effect was traumatic. She left her country behind her and devised "a life which seemed to me good because it was harmless, behind high garden walls."[52]

The need to see things as they are in a "concrete" way also underlines the disobedient energy of Mary McCarthy and her missionary witness to the truth in Vietnam. As she says in *The Seventeenth Degree* (1974), "I could not write about our involvement in Vietnam unless I went there."[53] McCarthy's publications, *Vietnam* (1967), *Hanoi* (1968), and *Medina* (1972), indicate her refusal to accept the constraints of an unsympathetic liberal press and a largely indifferent public. McCarthy's commitment to the North Vietnamese, if somewhat naive, is always rooted in a general belief that wherever one goes "there is truth, and that it's knowable."[54] Lying about the truth, public deception on matters of great humanitarian concern, is something McCarthy is unable to tolerate—hence her attack on Lillian Hellman, a writer who, according to McCarthy, fraudulently testified to a moral involvement in the antifascist movement of the 1930s in her three autobiographies, *An Unfinished Woman* (1969), *Pentimento* (1973), and *Scoundrel Time* (1976). In accusing Hellman of deceit, McCarthy was at pains to open up her own work, and her emphasis on the truth, to close and immediate inspection. For this reason McCarthy attaches great importance to the purity of plain speech. The legacy of autobiography is for her the saving remnant of plain-speaking testimony, a Puritan style that is now practiced by the communist people. Understanding language and understanding mission amount to the same thing; as Ky, "the orator,"[55] is a tool of America, so is his language. Not surprisingly, Ky's Saigon is the center of false information, what Gellhorn calls "the cheer syndrome,"[56] a style of propaganda "which optimistically falsifies the conditions of Vietnamese civil life." But McCarthy sees little to worry about in the North. Underneath "the forbidding rhetoric" there lies something else, something more dependable than the "slippery Aesopian language of the American politico"; it is a need by "the North Vietnamese, in their stiff phraseology, [to] persist in speaking quite plainly." For McCarthy, "although we complain of the monotony, the truth, renamed by us 'propaganda,' has shifted to the other side."[57]

Much of what Norman Podhoretz calls the "acerbic" quality of McCarthy's writing on Vietnam—her plainness of style, her unpretentious and astringent honesty—was out of step with the age in which it was written.[58] The fate McCarthy's work suffered revealed much of the underlying paranoia in American life toward a person who argued, from a position of conscience, for the self-determination of the Vietnamese people. What is interesting about McCarthy is that her work was given, as she says, "the silent treatment" not merely by the right-wing journalists who refused to review her but by "practically the whole liberal establishment"[59] that turned its back on the political issues her work raised. McCarthy's essay on this subject in *The Seventeenth Degree* illustrates the extent to which her books were implicitly censored as a result of the freedoms she willingly extended toward the North Vietnamese and the voice she gave them. In the 1960s McCarthy violated Puritan orthodoxy when she went unsupervised to Vietnam and, as "the first American novelist to descend at Hanoi airport,"[60] observed for herself the Vietnamese people in their own world.

McCarthy's beliefs remind us of the nativist piety of Roger Williams and the continuing dilemma of those who violate their Puritan heritage by culturally affiliating themselves with the enemy. Just as the banishment of Williams in 1635 was a consequence of his belief in freedom of worship and the redistribution of land to the Indian tribes, so the hostility shown toward McCarthy's work was directly the result of the interest she had shown in the Vietnamese. Her antinomian interest in Vietnamese culture makes her, in the words of Benjamin DeMott, one of the "most original and readable Puritans this country has produced."[61] She sees the Vietnamese (as Roger Williams saw the Indians) as a people who have fulfilled the legacy of Israel and are able to avoid, by their openness, the mistaken features of the Puritan mission. For McCarthy, the North Vietnamese are destined for an errand in sacred history because they are openly committed to accepting the conversion of the unregenerate and the redemption of the disobedient. The landscape of the North is a spiritual garden; it satisfies her "dream of a New Jerusalem,"[62] a land that repudiates America's belief in a divine appointment and a singular mission. Here again she reminds us of Roger Williams who, in his *Key to the Language of America*, regarded the Indians as descendants of the Jews, the ten lost tribes of Israel whom the Puritan colonists were actively dispossessing in the Canaan of New England. For McCarthy the act of dispossession in the Canaan of Hanoi is manifested in the saturation bombing of the North and the offenses committed against those who put their trust in nature.

The spirituality of the Vietnamese faith in an unfenced garden is a threat to the notion of American cultivation and enclosure. As the people are nourished energetically in their lives through the transcendental world of nature[63] so, for Roger Williams, the Indians were superior in their natural state to the pious and obedient Christians of New England. Williams desired to talk to the Indians, and his conversion to their cause in the obscure settlement where he lived in New England anticipated McCarthy's need to converse with the Vietnamese people in Hanoi. The retribution and censure both these separatists experienced, and their vigorous opposition to the Puritan crusade and to those who believed in "the bringing of wild men, wild passions, and wild nature under the check of order," brought about their spiritual exile.[64]

Conversations with the enemy made little headway during the war, and visits to Vietnam by David Dellinger, Daniel Berrigan, Susan Sontag, Jane Fonda, and Ramsey Clark provoked hostile reactions in the American press. Like Bobby Garwood, those who pursued unmonitored conversations were accused of indulging in maverick activities that undermined the interests of the American people. In Vietnam, as in New England, the existence of unilateralist plantations or "arbitrary"[65] forms of self-expression was severely discouraged and seen to constitute a direct challenge to the authority of the organic corporation.

Martha Gellhorn, Mary McCarthy, and Ronald J. Glasser are writers who anticipated the importance of personal witness long before that mode of address was approved as a legitimate expression for Vietnam narratives. These writers were not willing to bide their time in criticizing the war effort, and each suffered the fate of testifying to the truth in an unsympathetic age. To our detriment their work is still largely ignored and is not easily accommodated by the approved literary and critical procedures.

= A Language of Local Objects =

Ronald J. Glasser testified about his long tour of duty in Vietnam in an age that had not yet declared itself willing to approve the honest pursuit of a personal calling. Feelings of discomfort and censure underlie *365 Days*, a work of semifictional autobiography that recalls his experiences in the 1960s on a burns unit in Zama, Japan. As a doctor, Glasser's commitment to his work is total. Yet, as a writer, he has nothing solid in which to root his work or with which to explain his knowledge—neither a mood receptive to testimony nor an inner belief in the morality of the American presence in South Vietnam. He wishes to dissociate himself from "the confusion and the politics" and to have "something else . . . remembered" (ix) other than the wrangling. He wants to "explain" what he has really "seen" (xi), to break, if necessary, his covenant with those who subscribe to orthodox military and medical belief and to replace it with a vision that is based on his knowledge of the wounded and the terminally ill.

Glasser's work emphasizes the importance of the eyewitness account, that worm's-eye view of things he has had as a surgeon. The act of peeling away the burned layers of flesh, of controlling the fear and trauma of the wounded, evokes an immediate parallel in the writing: the removal of obfuscation, the paring down of extravagant rhetoric, the avoidance of emotional proclamation. The decisions the writer must make about language to prevent the reader from losing his way are those of the medic who struggles to keep his patient steady in the face of excess. Glasser's "plain style" is a prophylactic in a world where, in Valéry's words, "there are too many facts" and "all . . . results speak at once."[66] The core of his belief is that death and distress have earned him the right, in an uncaring world, to testify to what he has seen. "I certainly did not see it all," says Glasser, "and in truth I have dealt with only a small part, but I saw enough, more than enough. . . . Sooner or later they all came to us at Zama" (xii). Yet the book also expresses, like most of the early works of colonial autobiography, his feeling of "inadequacy," for Glasser shares "the pain" his patients endure in their own spiritual wilderness, a pain "that can be neither fully expressed nor suppressed, neither exorcised nor denied, and that constitutes the core of the real expressive challenge" of the war (Caldwell, 141). Although Glasser aspires to the membership of a church, at the time of writing he has no one to address, no congregation. Glasser's ministry is a tentative one.

365 Days was published during the dark days of the war, at a time when the Vietnam veteran lacked a congregation and could not "speak to [his] neighbors" (Caldwell, 137). In spite of the silence Glasser sets things down on behalf of those who are incapacitated, the soldiers who cannot write or speak and whom the world would not listen to even if they could. Glasser gives expression to those who cannot articulate and who are, as he puts it, "all saying the same things—without quite saying them." In the absence of a sympathetic and humane environment in which the veteran is encouraged to discuss his problems openly with others, Glasser demands the right to be listened to.

> They were worried, every one of them, not about the big things, not about survival, but about how they would explain away their lost legs or the weakness in their right arms. Would they embarrass their families? Would they be able to make it at parties where guys were still whole? Could they go to the beach and would their scars darken in the sun and offend the girls? Would they be able to get special cars? Above all, and underlying all their cares, would anybody love them when they got back? (xi)

The book is written in defiance of those conditions of silence in a world that extends no charity to the veteran and afflicts him with its ignorance and neglect. "I would leave the head wounds with the frightening thought that some day someone might ask them what had happened to their faces." It is important to Glasser that the reader be aware that "the stories . . . are true," for if truth is a statement of personal experience, then the book is a record of his witness to that experience: "I would have liked to disbelieve some of them, and at first I did, but I was there long enough to hear the same stories again and again, and then to see part of it myself" (xi). Testimony is the essence of truthful literary ambition: "to tell what I was seeing and being told" (xi); it is an act of giving form and voice to the stories of "these kids" in "a brutal time." The extent of that brutality is conveyed in the narrative of David Jensen, a boy who has suffered burns to 80 percent of his body and who (because of his disfigurement) is afraid to go home. The story ends as Jensen, dying and afraid of rejection, asks the medic to accompany him so that when he lies in the casket he will not have gone back to America "alone." This is the route to Glasser's "conversion," an expression of faith in the need to accompany those who are rejected. Glasser's conversion occurs in the company of the disfigured and dying, in the affliction of others, an "affliction that [is] terrible but also comprehensible and expressible." It is an affliction that is rooted in what America has done and in the "ever-deepening inability of men to admit their failure" (Caldwell, 162).

In *365 Days* Glasser confronts the American people with their failure of moral understanding. As he says, "There are no veterans' clubs for this war, no unit reunions, no pictures on the walls. For those who haven't been there, or are too old to go, it's as if it doesn't count. For those who've been there, and managed to get out, it's like it never happened. Only the eighteen-, nineteen-, and twenty-year-olds have to worry, and since no one listens to them, it doesn't matter" (5). Alongside the acute physical pain endured by the blind, the burned, the paraplegic is the emotional distress of wondering how to cope in an uncaring world. The shabbiness of Vietnam is reflected in the careless attitude of those who "embarrass" (xi) the veteran and burden him with guilt. Those who bear the heaviest burden are least able to withstand it. "I soon realized," says Glasser, "that the troopers they were pulling off those medical choppers were only children themselves" (x).

What America abandons is its youthfulness, its capacity for hope. To turn one's back on one's own children "is really to lose the whole thing" (x), the whole moral purpose of the mission. What remains is the dignity of those who stay in Vietnam in spite of that loss. For Glasser, suffering and sacrifice are not the prerogatives of the elect. One of the most disturbing stories, "Joan," describes a tour of duty of an American nurse with the 312th. The hospital in which she works has been mortared five times. "There was nothing to do except to endure the heat and discomfort. There was no privacy and never any place to go" (216). Joan, who has "gathered her courage," receives no privileges, with the hospital bombed and the ward overrun by the NVA. Her world of work is a "shambles," bodies are "sprawled all over the floor" (223), and she is "lying where she'd been thrown, crying, her left leg folded grotesquely under her" (224). Neither the horror of the war nor the effort to combat its futility is denied. For Glasser, "everybody pays" (32).

Glasser's writing, like William Bradford's *Of Plimouth Plantation*, glows with a sense of rightness that is never self-righteous. Glasser is "the common man discovering his potential in direct confrontation with his own nature."[67] He commits himself to a particular discipline and sets things down in spite of the war that, for most of the time, seemed so "foolish, so hopeless" (x). Alfred Kazin has described autobiographical writing as the attempt "to make a home for oneself, on paper," not only to tell the truth but also to find the "line, pattern, the form, that will articulate the truth."[68] Like Hemingway, Glasser is "trying to write, commencing with the simplest things, and one of the simplest things of all and the most fundamental is violent death." Glasser's intention is to be "definite" and to avoid the "blur" that often afflicts those who write about violent death in an emotional or abstract way.[69] This involves avoiding sentimental, overwrought vocabulary and the language of critics like Raymond Olderman who recommend that the writer concern himself, in the early years of the 1970s, with the constant "blur" of fact and fiction and the "mystery" that lies behind "a new kind of helplessness" in modern society.[70] Glasser pursues the naked object, the experience in itself, without decoration or adjectival flourish. The resonance of the writing is often located in the actual procedure that the medic adopts, the sequence of motion and fact that is an integral part of the saving of life:

> Pierson wrestled him quiet. While the rest of the squad hurried by, he took out his knife and, grabbing the protruding piece of jaw bone, forced back the soldier's head and calmly cut open his throat, then punched a hole into the windpipe. A sputtering of blood and foam came out through the incision, and as his breathing eased, the soldier quieted.
>
> There was another explosion up ahead and the rattling of small arms fire. Taking an endotracheal tube out of his kit, Pierson slipped it in through the incision and threaded it down into the soldier's lungs, listened for the normal inward and outward hiss of air, then reached for the morphine. One of the troopers who had come up from a trailing squad was checking the other bodies. "Hey, Doc," he said, "those two are dead." Without looking up, Pierson shoved the needle deep into the soldier's arm and drove the plunger smoothly down the barrel of the syringe. (50)

The anesthetics, ventricular shunts, craniotomies, and enuncleations that the medic performs are the ordering points, the objective correlatives that reduce the associational value of language and provide the writing with a technical correctness and a motive for achieving dramatic control. Wary of the bogus emotion and the bogus damage that a facile writer can generate by a too uncritical use of language, Glasser moves in the direction of those who believe that art must rid itself of romanticism and become impersonal and hard.

If the enemy of understanding is excessive emotion, the account in "Final Pathological Diagnosis" offers a corrective. The diagnostic history of an un-named black soldier blown up by a chicom mine, the precise record of the soldier's wounds and their treatment, the telling of the soldier's attempted suicide, remind us of Hemingway's account of Litri's death in *Death in the Afternoon*. Glasser's language is clinical yet observational, and it stresses concrete noun and verb in order to avoid mystification. In a landscape dominated by the destructive character of experience Glasser keeps his emotional distance and his eyes hard on the sequence of motion and fact that records the death of the mutilated soldier. The account emphasizes the use of blood and antibiotics, the extent of secondary infection and the injuries sustained, the provision of surgical dressings, operation and autopsy. The writing provides "a decent view" of the practical activity that is necessary to acquaint the reader with an essential task and the need to sustain emotional control. For Glasser, the technique of surgery and the craft of writing are controlled by the pace at which things happen, the use of objects that correlate activity and inhibit misleading speculation.

365 Days offers the reader a fragmented text, a set of unfinished "sketches" that, together, lack overall resolution and ideological soundness. The intention is not to create meanings that resolve disputes through "doctrine or polemics" but to achieve some small moment of understanding or healing. The meaning of Vietnam is the meaning the medic is able to give to the lives of those on the ward and the quality of feeling he is able to experience to aid recovery. In the tumbling world to which he is posted, the mental and physical damage the war has created demands an imaginative response. To discover the extent of a patient's injuries is to discover the anatomy of the war itself, the body of Vietnam that the war has dismembered. Those who remain imprisoned in "doctrine" offer no remedies.

Glasser's Vietnam is a land of uncertain values, yet informed with complex meanings. The struggle to write about the war and the work of the medic cannot be seen as an "effort" with "little value," in which "death" is a "purely physical event, bereft of larger import." Glasser sees the dead but not the dead end. His book is the testimony of a man changed by the suffering of the soldiers and the effort he has made to save their lives. It is because of these "kids" that meanings can be assigned to one's work. As the dying soldier Grant Edwards says in a letter to his brother, "For the first time in my life, everything seems to count" (265).

Glasser opposes those who translate casualties into statistics, rendering death mere terminology. If the priority of Vietnam is the perception of "wretched excessiveness"—as it seems to be for the critic Lloyd Lewis[71]— then what we have done is replace the fact of death with a euphemism that denies its meaning. Where death does not deserve our recognition, we write it off as a military dilemma, "a wastage rate—a series of contrapuntal numbers, which seems to make it all not only acceptable, but strangely palatable as well" (5).

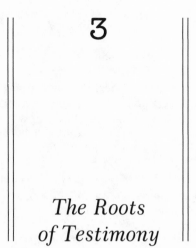

3

The Roots of Testimony

ELLMAN CRASNOW MAINTAINS THAT "PURITANISM WAS THE most important formative influence on American culture."[1] As a cause célèbre of the anticommunist crusade, Vietnam reconfirmed the special errand of that culture and rededicated the people to a belief in moral and spiritual mission. Yet it was only in the aftermath of war that the legacy of the American mission to Vietnam was fully appreciated and assessed by those who had fought there. It was only, furthermore, in the later years of the 1970s that the Vietnam veteran came to be regarded as a genuine witness whose right to testify publicly was seen as a worthwhile calling, an approved literary vocation. With the exception of Mary McCarthy's and Ronald J. Glasser's personal narratives, which were published during the war years, the work of self-examination and testimony was delayed. It was not until the moral awakening of the American people had become an issue of public debate and a born-again Christian was elected president that the autobiographies of Vietnam veterans gained in status and public recognition.

= The Rejection of the Veteran =

In the early seventies the Vietnam veteran was the object rather than the agent of censure—the problem rather than the victim of the war. In the period 1970–74 he was regarded as public enemy number one in the nation's media, "the psychotic who would go off at the sound of a backfire." As Adi Wimmer has said, "Even within the V.A. [Veterans Administration] the 'prevailing attitude,' in the words of its chief administrator Max Cleland, was that the Viet vet was a 'social misfit.' On T.V. he was a hired killer in 'Columbo,' a drug dealer and sadist in 'Mannix,' and a terrorist on 'Hawaii Five-O.' " By a process of extension the veteran was rejected along with the war in which he had served. The problem of rejection both by the media and by the antiwar movement came to animate much of the writing by Vietnam veterans in the later 1970s.[2]

The roots of rejection, as Rick Berg and Adi Wimmer have suggested, lie in the My Lai massacre and the use it was put to by Hollywood and the peace movement. The massacre, more than any other event, "subverted" the image of the Vietnam veteran. Although Lt. William Calley's lawyers emphasized that their client's "normalcy before the war" had been ruined by his military experiences, they also insinuated "that any veteran might have behaved like Calley, or indeed, might still go on to demonstrate such behavior after his return home."[3]

In this atmosphere the Vietnam veteran was seen to carry the war around within him. In films like *The Losers* (1970), and *Welcome Home, Soldier Boys* (1972), he was portrayed as an "outlaw," a member of a "marginal and irreconcilable counter-culture." In Elia Kazan's *The Visitors* (1972) the vet was pictured as an "ominous threat" who was "irrepressibly uncivilized" and who violated "the sanctuary" of the American home.[4] In *The Stone Killer* (1973) and *Dead of Night* (1972) he was a frustrated killer and a schizophrenic. In these and other films the veteran of the early 1970s was repeatedly seen as a sadistic killer and a sociopathic menace to society, a person who, as Rick Berg says, was "infected spiritually and mentally—never politically —by the senseless genocide in Vietnam."[5]

As a symbol of American disgrace the Vietnam veteran—like the gangster before him in the 1930s—was the nation's favorite cultural scapegoat during the war years. Few people, it appeared, had any sympathy for his plight, and those who did not publicly abuse the veteran turned their back on him. For "a long period in the 70s, the nation indulged in a remarkable exercise of recoil and denial and amnesia about Viet Nam."[6]

= Moral Reformation =

One group that appeared to be at the opposite end of the moral spectrum to the Vietnam veteran was the New Right, a loose assembly of conservative religious groups whose gradual emergence in the 1970s "signalled a return into public life of traditional moral forces that had gone underground after the public defeat of the fundamentalists in the 1920s" (the specific catalyst for change, says Raymond J. Bakke, was the Supreme Court ruling in *Rowe v. Wade* in 1973, which legalized abortion nationally on demand).[7] The campaign of the New Right aimed at preserving the traditional moral ideas of the Republic by providing an "unequivocal alignment of Christian zeal and political conservatism." At an obvious distance from the veteran the New Right was supremely patriotic and much of its evangelical theology was jingoistic and reactionary. In the moral crusade to redeem the world, religious leaders like Jerry Falwell, Oral Roberts, and Pat Robertson celebrated the supremacy of American power and "resuscitated a theme from earlier eras by looking upon America as God's New Israel providentially designated for moral leadership in the world."[8]

The desire to recapture a fading Christian culture in a secular age appears, on the face of it, to have little in common with the anti-institutional inclinations of the veteran. Yet for all their apparent differences the religious conservatives and the Vietnam veterans found themselves to be in agreement in one important respect. In the aftermath of Vietnam and Watergate, the United States looked to be in a state of moral collapse. In such an environment the quest to articulate the reason for collapse could best be achieved through public testimony and moral witness. During the 1970s, the appeal of the evangelical movement and the search for personal authority, which "the Moral Majority" movement inspired, had a dramatic effect on the public persona of the Vietnam veteran. That the veteran (as one who had received a special converting experience) should come to benefit from the energies of a movement whose taproot was conservative and fervently pro-American is one of the great ironies of the period. Nonetheless, during the seventies, the individualistic and empiricist energies of the veterans' movement cross-fertilized with the righteous energies of the evangelical movement to strengthen the case of the spokesman-as-witness and the experiential self.

Testimonies of knowledge underpinned the faith—the moral pentecostalism—of both groups and reaffirmed the legacy of what Patricia Caldwell terms "the Puritan conversion narrative." To be struck down in conflict or singled out by God gave both the veteran and the evangelical the feeling that they were distinctive and had been marked out for a higher calling. This sense of distinctiveness accorded well with the Puritan belief in the wisdom of the elect, the conviction that insight was granted only to those with a particular experience of grace and a personal knowledge of temptation and sin. The cult of "piety" based on the notion of "insight" emphasized the principle "that faith must be personal" and authoritarian. In the 1970s the notion of the "powerful and talented" individual "appealed to what was best and worst in evangelicalism" and placed an emphasis on resourcefulness and personal initiative. If "confidence that bureaucratic structures and government programs could solve the country's most pressing problems had plummeted," then individualism could become the key to "recovery."[9] In the 1970s the American people came to accept, says Claude-Jean Bertrand, an evangelical approach of plain speaking and proselytizing. In an age when everyone appeared to be looking to his "own welfare rather than to the fate of others," the person who professed his faith in public talked "to the individual." In what Bertrand calls "an intensely nostalgic time," the evangelical reached back "to the eternal verities," and offered the nation "a guide to life."[10]

═ Born Again ═

With the emergence of a national and increasingly classless congregation of born-again Christians, a chastened press, prodded by the Gallup polls, began to realize that the phenomenon of evangelical renewal reflected a major loss of confidence in institutional and public morality in the United States. In 1976 a Gallup poll revealed that 51 percent of Protestants and 18 percent of Roman Catholics claimed to have experienced spiritual rebirth. This same poll revealed not only that 56 percent of the population considered that religion played a large part in their lives but also that 50 million adults—including Eldridge Cleaver and Bob Dylan—looked upon themselves as born-again Christians. It is estimated that in the 1970s as many as 14 million of those in the National Council of Churches, whose membership totaled 42 million, were evangelical and that denominations such as the Southern Baptist Convention were dominated by evangelical interests. The year Jimmy Carter was elected president, 1976, was quickly declared by the press to be "the Year of the Evangelical" because Carter—a daily Bible reader, Sunday school teacher, and unabashed Christian witness—was so forthright about his spiritual beliefs.[11]

Insofar as he stressed the importance of personal morality as a redemptive force, Jimmy Carter was instrumental in the rehabilitation of the Vietnam veteran. Like the veteran, Carter, as Peter Carroll has said, was "an 'outsider' at a time when Washington politics were inherently suspect."[12] In a period of institutional corruption Carter represented the moral significance of the grass-roots community and the ethical virtues of the small-town past. The moral imperatives of his campaign rhetoric emphasized the need for personal honesty and the need to bear witness to the truth in public. Announcing his presidential candidacy, he promised "to restore in our country what has been lost," and in his campaign autobiography he declared that "there is no need for lying," thereby touching on the rawest of public nerves: the loss of faith in institutional morality that followed the Watergate scandal. As a national opinion poll of 1975 showed, 69 percent of those interviewed felt that "over the last ten years, this country's leaders have consistently lied to the people."[13] At a time when the moral authority of government was in question Carter appeared to refer his followers to the language of old-fashioned virtue and not the virtue of expediency. What Carter provided was an impetus that made the language of personal faith an accepted form of social narrative. As the father of a Vietnam veteran who could talk with feeling about his son's humiliation on returning home, Carter was a political figure with the "standing to be a healer."[14] In a country where Vietnam literature had consistently failed to ignite the public imagination, Carter directed the energies of investigation both downward and inward in order to create a climate that favored the writing of autobiography.

As a small-town planter from Plains, Georgia, Carter argued the case, in advance of the veteran, for the moral authority of the common man. In this way the people could establish "a solid base" under their lives and a shared understanding of the vitality of "faith." In describing the Vietnam veterans as "the great unsung heroes,"[15] Carter offered complicity between those who aspired to high office and those who had been the victims of high office, a partnership in which the leaders received their strength from the led. As he proclaimed in his 1977 inaugural address, "Your strength can compensate for my weakness and your wisdom can help to minimize my mistakes." In the first week of his presidency Carter declared a full, complete, and unconditional pardon for those who had evaded or resisted the draft. In so doing he symbolically welcomed back to America not only the draft resisters but also the larger community of veterans who had spent their years in spiritual exile in the country of their birth, an excluded group whose "wisdom" the country had chosen to ignore.[16] Almost immediately the diaries, journals, and autobiographies of "born-again"—repatriated—veterans began to find their way into print, as if the credentials of the veteran had somehow been granted legitimacy in the eyes of commercial publishers and the book-buying public by the endorsement they had received from a born-again president.

What happened in America after 1976 was that a mood of born-again spirituality was grafted onto a set of values that were secular and humanistic. Born-again religion and the events of Watergate, combined with a mounting anti-institutional fervor, directly contributed to the legitimacy of personal narrative and the literary exploration of public history. Exposing the moral hypocrisy of power allowed the Vietnam veteran to assume the role of an investigative writer and to speak with increasing conviction. In an age when public institutions were either corrupt or inept the hard experience of the man who spoke at a worm's-eye level and publicly committed himself to a frank and intimate disclosure of the truth was worthy of attention. Just as the American public had been deceived at home, so the American veteran had been deceived by scandal on foreign soil. As a man who had witnessed the hypocrisy of power at first hand—and had suffered for it—the veteran was admirably placed to proclaim, in public, his knowledge of events and perception of the truth. Self-testimony was a duty. If patient investigation and public witness had solved a riddle as enormous as Watergate, then it was an even bet it could solve the mystery surrounding Vietnam.

Watergate opened a window of opportunity for autobiography. As society began to break away from the constraints of unbridled executive power symbolized by the presidential ability to prosecute an undeclared war, to "manage" the news, and to undermine political opposition by "dirty tricks," autobiography came to be seen as a realization of the spirit of the times, an expression of democratic conviction, an assertion that everyman's experience was of potential interest. Where de Tocqueville once noted that a democrat is empowered to seek the reason of things for himself and in himself alone, autobiography provided such a means of expression.

In the personal narratives of Vietnam writers this sense of self-discovery is strong. "I got back to the World," says a soldier in *Nam*, "but this wasn't the World that I had left. I was born again. Like the Christians say, 'Be born again.' "[17] Personal narrative was an act of revelation and duty, a way of speaking out against those forces in society that locked the individual within a prison of silence. It also made clear that the writer's conversion to the truth, and his knowledge of the truth, had been attained at great personal cost. Conversion was achieved through self-examination and a public demonstration of one's own failings. This process of redemption through suffering is often reflected in the titles of Vietnam narratives: *Out of the Night: The Spiritual Journey of Vietnam Vets* (William Mahedy), *Touched with Fire: The Future of the Vietnam Generation* (John Wheeler), *Vietnam: Curse or Blessing* (John Steer), *Vietnam: What a Soldier Gives* (David L. Hartline), *Testify* (Marvin Rhodes).

= A Search for Narratives =

There were other influences at work in the culture. The uncertainties of the age helped give the seventies, as Malcolm Bradbury has said, "a character all their own."[18] As outward certainties were shattered, the time seemed ripe for new pathways to inner certainty. The search for self-knowledge attained the status of a conventional wisdom. Self-examination as well as social examination—personal as well as public history—were the order of the day. The unprecedented success of Alex Haley's genealogical exploration in *Roots*, which was published on the eve of the 1976 presidential election —and the plethora of oral histories the book gave rise to—confirmed the belief that the maintenance of history was not "the exclusive province of the elite." *Roots* gave accreditation and impetus to the investigation of those "social groups traditionally excluded from the natural chronicles of greatness," especially ethnic and racial minorities; it also provided other "dispossessed groups," like the Vietnam veterans, with the confidence to seek out a "historical legacy to affirm their contemporary identity." If the histories and experiences of the dispossessed and marginal could stir the American public imagination, so could the grass-roots histories of the war. Thus the passion for oral testimony—a characteristic of American culture in the later years of the 1970s—proved to be of enormous benefit to the Vietnam veteran. It not only revealed a new respect for the spoken word in American culture but also "reduced the process of historical inquiry to its simplest form: the acquisition of raw experience."[19] By reflecting on the nature of "experience" the American people were encouraged to "discover" who they were and to provide themselves with a sense of direction. For the Vietnam veteran the war could provide that sense of direction; at a time of public and national crisis the war could become an anchoring point.

The public "enthusiasm for the past" and a burgeoning enthusiasm for American history and the historical environment[20] gave the veteran the opportunity to transform himself, to redeem himself in the eyes of the American public. No longer the moral outcast of America the veteran could now become its moral tutor and, in some respects, its moral scourge; he could act the part of the visible saint who has had a conversion and undergone a sea change in the journey to Vietnam. As Richard E. Ogden puts it in *Green Knight, Red Mourning* (1985): "Our country was not proud of itself; therefore it was unwilling, if not crippled, in showing us any pride or compassion. . . . Be proud you served and grateful you survived. You know more about life than anyone else around you."[21]

Not all Vietnam veterans by any means were able to demonstrate this sense of authority or to affirm publicly a facility for speech. Larry Heinemann's *Paco's Story* (1986) and Bobbie Ann Mason's *In Country* chronicle the tragic life of the Vietnam veteran as social misfit and American pariah, a relic who cannot adjust to life, even in the Reagan years. In Mason's novel the incidence of public amnesia lives on longer than it ought to and the veteran's life retains that quality of secrecy and repression perhaps more typical of the 1970s. Yet even here, the assertion of authority by the Vietnam veteran is only delayed, not denied. The novel concludes when the problem of language and articulation is overcome and the veteran is able to discover a social voice. Mason's Emmett Hughes gains in stature the moment he is able to discuss publicly, or without fear of embarrassment, his memories of Vietnam. Emmett's action, which lacks dramatic credibility, nevertheless provides a crucial moment of resolution. In a world congested with cinematic reference Emmett becomes a highly charged, dynamic performer. In taking his family on a visit to the Vietnam Memorial in Washington, he is described as a spiritual guide, a secular priest who leads his people to the tablets of stone. Emmett appears "so definite" about the plan that he is like "an executive making a big decision that would mean millions of dollars for his company." His niece Sam is "powerless" to oppose and has "never seen him swing into action" like this before. Emmett uses words "confidently" and appears to his family to have finally "come to his senses."[22]

= Born on the Fourth of July =

The quest for strength and authority is crucial if the veteran is to over-come the attempt to emasculate him in civilian and military life. Public speech and public narrative are the means by which authority is sought for and expressed. In one of the earliest Vietnam autobiographies, Ron Kovic's *Born on the Fourth of July*, a paraplegic is able to tap a source of inner strength in order to defeat the inertia of the country and his own despair. Kovic refers to himself in the third person: "He had to rise up out of this deep dark prison. . . . he knew the power he had . . . the power to make people remember, to make them as angry as he was every day of his life."[23] The war is a mistake; but what is also important—and what the American people must be made to realize—is that the war made possible the discovery of understanding. Whatever the war's status as public history its experience as private history is a thing of value, for it is only in the process of recollecting the conditions of personal learning that the writer reveals his authority.

The relationship between knowledge and experience is a way of restating a Puritan text, in which grace through errand and regeneration through suffering are exemplary forms of conduct. At a recent conference Kovic explained the affliction of paralysis as a means of attaining spiritual insight. "The bullet that hit my shoulder went through my lung and it severed my spinal cord, paralyzing me for life. It's taken me almost eighteen years to come to terms with my paralysis. I'm paralyzed from my mid-chest down— I can't feel or move anything from my chest down. I will never be able to walk again, or to make love. But I'm not complaining to you. I'm telling you that I'm strong and that I have my life together now. I feel a wholeness that I never believed in 1968 I would ever be able to feel."

What Thomas Couser calls "the prophetic autobiography" is a genre the Vietnam veteran favors, one that is "at once a record of the opportunities and the burdens of being American" and that becomes "a way of measuring individual achievement against cultural standards."[24] Strong elements of this approach appear in the work of Kovic and Frederick Downs, autobiographies that illustrate the shortcomings of the military and call the American government to account for the sins it has committed. Morality is a stick with which to beat a recalcitrant public. "All he had tried to do was tell the truth about the war," says Kovic. "He had never been anything but a thing to them, a thing to put a uniform on and train to kill, a young thing to run through the meat-grinder, a cheap small nothing to make mincemeat out of" (166).

Kovic infiltrates the Republican convention hall in Miami and accuses Richard Nixon of "lying to all of us about the war." The machinery of state is rotten if it is prepared to send innocent young boys to "fight and get crippled and come home to a government and leaders who could care less about the same boys they sent over" (178–79).

There is a raw, untutored energy in the way Kovic writes; the book is a public crusade against the immorality of high office and Richard Nixon's dishonesty. As he says at Miami: "The man who will accept the nomination tonight is a liar!" (179). When Kovic is manhandled out of the convention center by security guards for having, as he sees it, spoken the truth, he regards his mission as an overwhelming success. "If you can't believe the veteran who fought the war and was wounded in the war, who can you believe?" (180). The basis of Kovic's testimony is rooted in a desire to explain the war through narrative performance, to share his experience in a dramatic way with those who are "waiting to hear me speak" (149).

Kovic's intuition is correct. The book sells in large numbers and the language of the narrative has a major impact on the troubled conscience of the nation. *Born on the Fourth of July* is a wide-awake book. It takes you the full fifteen rounds in prose that is sharp and invigorating, reminiscent of the horror that Dalton Trumbo conveys in *Johnny Got His Gun*. Kovic remembers the advice of another thirties writer, Nathanael West, in the magazine *Contempo*: "Forget the epic, the master work . . . leave slow growth to the book reviewers, you only have time to explode. . . . A novelist can afford to be everything but dull."[25] Kovic explodes: the overall effect is that of urgency and directness: The material is stripped almost bald, and there is little digression from the central intention to awaken the reader to the horror of war. Kovic's language throughout is blunt, muscular, and compressed, emotional but not bathetic, the poetic vision savage and intense. "Every chance I had to get my broken body on the tube or in front of an audience I went hog wild. Yes, let them have a good look at me. Let them be reminded of what they'd done when they sent my generation off to war. One look would be enough—worth more than a thousand speeches" (150).

Each of the veterans' autobiographies in the 1970s has a touch of disaster in it, a sense of the high emotional cost of rescuing the world for truth and democracy. In the act of defining himself the veteran is compelled to risk his sanity, to plunge into the melee of social experience as if the claims of consciousness and the responsibilities of the human condition demand a confrontational approach. "In one big bang they have taken it all from me, in one clean sweep. . . . I have given my dead swinging dick for America. I have given my numb young dick for democracy. It is gone and numb, lost somewhere out there by the river where the artillery is screaming. . . . Oh God Oh God I want it back" (38, 112).

Kovic, who is born on the fourth of July, is reborn through the ruin of his sexual loss, the memory of a wound that can never be healed. Kovic's conversion takes place, ironically, outside of church—which is now associated with dispossession. Institutional religion, which tells him "he is a hero and a patriot in the eyes of God," makes him throw up "in the parking lot" (108). Kovic's faith, "born" (132) in a world of hurt and ridicule, is a testimony to the endurance of the spirit and the suffering inflicted by those who attack him for proclaiming his belief. Kovic's body provides the evidence of what has been done by the faithless ones; it becomes a reminder of the innocent "dead" who were sent to Vietnam, betrayed by lies. Kovic's body is used to convert the people into life and faith. The conversion of those who do not know Vietnam is achieved through the dispossession of one who does. In the act of exposure the burden of pain is shared by others. "One look is enough" (150) to prove his loss and inspire our faith.

= The Urge to Explain =

The need to "look" and see and hear and feel, the belief in the living power of testimony, brings with it a greater emphasis on realism. It also encourages a belief that the writer, as William Dean Howells argued, has a moral obligation to tell the truth. In the literature of the post-Nixon era it is this concern with the moral impetus of a work—and the morality of meaning—that displaces a tendency in the earlier fiction to regard the war as an absurd adventure. This is particularly true of the literature of women veterans, many of whom worked as nurses, Red Cross volunteers, low-ranking officers, and intelligence and language specialists, and whose contribution in Vietnam, until recently, has gone unrecognized. Although women were long excluded from the mythology of Vietnam, they experienced its horror and observed its suffering at close quarters and experienced severe problems of emotional adjustment on returning to civilian life. In recent works of oral history, autobiography, and memoir, such as Kathryn Marshall's *In the Combat Zone* (1987) and Myra MacPherson's *Long Time Passing* (1984), the witness and testimony of personal and group narratives disprove the claim that what women have to say is not a legitimate part of the war's history. In the work of writers like Kate Webb (*On the Other Side*, 1972) we encounter, says Jeff Walsh, "a profound concern to recover women's history" and the "authentic experience" that women had in Vietnam, as well as a realistic attempt to show that the war affected women as much as it did men. The interest that women writers have shown in the people of Vietnam, and its casualties, also illustrates what Walsh calls "the internationalist and feminist trajectory"[26] of Vietnam war writing. The recent work of Arlene Eisen on Asian women (*Women and Revolution in Vietnam*, 1984) and the collaborative venture of Wendy Larsen and Tran Thi Nga (*Shallow Graves: Two Women and Vietnam*, 1986) suggest that women may, through their own efforts, benefit from the attempt to rehabilitate those veterans who have lacked both a spokesman and a literary voice and whom male writers have frequently considered marginal.

The combat novel also experiences a change of emphasis in the 1980s. In John Del Vecchio's *The 13th Valley* (1982) the obligation to explain the war in a truthful and discursive manner—its psychological motives, its social meanings—becomes a moral imperative for the writer. *The 13th Valley* is a novel of ideas in which the narrative constantly gives way to autobiography. Sometimes the plot is dispensed with altogether as the writer insists on a relentless examination of the war's purpose and meaning. The psychoanalytical and sociological origins of American involvement in Vietnam are doggedly pursued by Del Vecchio. Speeches and lectures are given by the soldiers on patrol in a preacherly manner. Chapters are concluded with situation reports as if military shorthand adds weight and density to the realism of the text. Hardly the stuff of realism. And yet, in a sense, one can well understand Del Vecchio's intention. *The 13th Valley* seeks to explore the origins of conflict rather than simply to abandon the analysis to a self-referential or metafictional debate. The centering point of *The 13th Valley* is the desire to provide the reader with argument and analysis, and in spite of the war's unpredictability, to demystify both its social life and military mind. In the words of John Carlos Rowe, *The 13th Valley* is set up as an alternative "to the conduct of the war; the very form of the work itself, with its claim to coherence and understanding, is set against either the mystifications of Press and Government or the misconduct of the Pentagon."[27]

Autobiography in the post-Nixon era is concerned to retrieve the war, to reconstruct the war's history, and to redeem the memory of those who fought in it. Texts are often angry, shrill, affirmative, and confident—and, like Michael Herr's *Dispatches*, full of guile. But invariably they itemize the damage of war in Vietnam and attempt to make sense of the conflict as best they can, even if they have formed their argument on the assumption that sense is unobtainable.

In this light it is difficult to accept unreservedly the methodology provided for us by John Clark Pratt when he identifies one of the major themes of Vietnam War writing as "the inability, regardless of political, moral, or even religious beliefs, for American novelists to make sense out of the madness that creates wars such as Vietnam in the modern, 'civilised' world."[28] Although Pratt is referring us to fiction rather than to autobiography, he does identify those books published after 1972 as works that "contain strong themes of the modern American's inability to comprehend reality itself." Pratt's approach is unequivocal: "in actuality correct assessment is impossible"; the finest works "have at their centers, no matter how 'realistic' they appear, the inability of Americans to comprehend and understand the Vietnam experience they are able to see with their own eyes."[29]

To accept this argument in its entirety is to ignore a number of works that are driven by an opposing impulse, especially the desire to testify to what the writer has observed as an essential truth. When Pratt defines the writing on the war as "a metaphor" for a peculiarly American senselessness—a condition, says Pratt, to which all the best Vietnam novels subscribe—he dehistoricizes the literature and confirms the mistaken interpretation of Vietnam as an expression of random action and belief. If we accept this thesis unconditionally, we have no grounds on which to evaluate literature other than to stress its bizarre complexities and capacity for contradiction. But for many Vietnam writers the primary task is one of explanation. For them the text exists as an occasion for personal and public scrutiny, a place where the self can be taken to pieces and reassembled for the benefit of the reader. On these occasions the writer's hostility toward his subject is no longer absolute.

This is a far cry from the sexual and narrative discharge that confronts the reader in Norman Mailer's *Why Are We in Vietnam?* (1967). Here the autobiographer is the self-proclaimed genius of the sixties, D.J., an affluent Texas adolescent with the confidence to explain the origins of Vietnam on the basis of an experience he has had hunting caribou, wolves, and grizzly bears in the Brooks Range wilderness of Alaska. It is the supercharged landscape of the Arctic Circle that gives D.J. his authority and "power," not the wilderness zones of Vietnam in which he has yet to set foot. It is the brutal, adolescent exercise of that power, the electromagnetic "mosaic" of his energy, on which the reader vibrates. D.J.'s narrative is charged with aggression and intimidatory energy—white Negro jive, Texas tall talk, the braggadocio of the old frontiersman, the psychobabble of a radio disc jockey. In a journey through the wilderness of the American soul, Mailer's D.J. discovers his own priestly capacity as well as an undifferentiated passion to destroy. As the narrative degenerates into a welter of "fever and fuck lust" the reader is slowly suffocated. Like some "wandering troubadour" of the wavebands D.J. creates a work that suffers from "overlap on the frequencies." As interference increases and the magnetism fades, we come to realize that it's not just the "grizzers" that have "gone ape" but the writing as well.[30]

= A Rumor of War =

In the later years of the 1970s Vietnam writing changes dramatically. The autobiographer sees himself as the first generation of a new condition of modernity in American life, a person who has come from the world of the past and lives in the world of the future, an experimental landscape on the other side of some essential line drawn across human experience. Those who have survived that experience and come to maturity because of it are the bearers of a special kind of knowledge that an older generation—and a civilian readership—do not possess. The autobiographies of the Vietnam veteran are statements of revelation, often supported by a formal glossary of terms—a soldier's dictionary. With this dictionary a soldier may explain to his reader that in order to make "history"[31] come alive the principal qualification for writing is not talent, necessarily, but, as Hamlin Garland once said, the knowledge that comes from a direct contact with life. John Carlos Rowe talks about the "special privilege" that is "claimed" by those writers whose "credentials" are rooted in the world of "direct experience."[32] Feelings of reduction, the sense of individual powerlessness, the loss of personal authority— all these are offset by declarations of knowledge from those who have lived "in country." At its worst what we encounter is a masculine vérité school of conviction: "I am the man, I suffered, I was there," which can lead to an appalling emphasis on credentialism. Elsewhere, there is a genuine sense of social undertaking, as in the emphasis that Vietnam veterans like Robert Muller or Ron Kovic or Al Santoli have placed on public debate and testimony over the last few years.

Publishers have not been slow to seize upon the commercial possibilities of those who bear witness to the truth. "The war's remains," says Rick Berg, "have been resurrected and, like Frankenstein's monster, given new life. Fifteen years after Saigon's fall and liberation, Vietnam has become, if not a commodity, then a resource for the American culture industry. Publishers and producers are working it for all it is worth. Books on Vietnam, once almost impossible to find in any major chain, now are almost impossible to avoid."[33] A Bantam edition of Gustav Hasford's *The Short-Timers* flaunts the energies of crusade and resistance with an initial page of excerpts from articles that point up the "savage, unforgiving" honesty of the book. A 1984 edition of Philip Caputo's *A Rumor of War* is introduced with a series of reviews in which the phrases "troubled conscience," "truthfully," "thick of things," "cruelly honest," appeal to our current sense of what is appropriate to a war narrative.

Caputo lends himself to this kind of packaging. In an age of dirty politics he speaks on behalf of the misinformed, "those children," like him, who have grown "old" in a "land of endless dying" (319). In *A Rumor of War* Caputo takes us on a tour of the war's underworld; he is the "honest" (xvi) proletarian who shows us the fraud and deceit of the military, the moral detective who cleans up the mess in Vietnam, the "gulf that divides the facts from the truth" (312). In the purgatorial hell of the jungle Caputo is the evangelical private eye who has been tried and tested and born again. The epigraph to his text is from Matthew 24:6–13, a passage that describes the affliction of war as the death of self and the salvation of those whose souls endure. Caputo claims to have "saved" himself by the honesty of his vision, the refusal to compromise with his own sinfulness and the sinfulness that exists in all men. Court-martialed for the killing of two innocent Vietnamese, Caputo regards his crime as endemic to Vietnam: "If the charges were proved, it would prove no one was guaranteed immunity against the moral bacteria spawned by the war. If such cruelty existed in ordinary men like us, then it logically existed in the others, and they would have to face the truth that they, too, harbored a capacity for evil. But no one wanted to make that recognition. No one wanted to confront his devil" (313).

Caputo, who is "a moral casualty" (314) of the war, is prepared to face the devil within, to confess his crime in an intimate way. "Something evil had been in me that night" of the killing, he says. "I had wanted them dead. There was murder in my heart, and . . . I had transmitted my inner violence to the men" (309). Caputo is the vulnerable sinner who endures the war in order to testify publicly against it. "I would not break. I would endure and accept whatever happened with grace. For enduring seemed to me an act of penance, an inadequate one to be sure, but I felt the need to atone in some way for the deaths I had caused" (315). Like the condemned man at the Puritan gallows, Caputo delivers a "passionate and eloquent" sermon in which he calls on "the criminal," the American government, "to repent" while there is yet time, and then begs "the congregation," his readers, "to profit by this example."[34] It is important, therefore, that we accept his testimony not as "a work of the imagination" but as "true." Parables of fiction are unnecessary for a writer who has "tried to describe accurately what the dominant event in the life of my generation, the Vietnam war, was like for the men who fought in it." For this reason he has resisted—so he says—"the veteran's inclination to remember things the way he would like them to have been rather than the way they were" (xx–xxi). The authenticity of the information is determined by the nature of the involvement; in spite of the absence of "rules and ethics" (218), the experience has put him at a crucial advantage in providing a credible testimony.

A Rumor of War is a text of reckoning that makes Vietnam the responsibility of those who invented it. Although the veteran cannot be absolved from guilt, the burden of what he shouldered on behalf of the American public—and the dreams and "illusions" (xiv) that the public projected onto him—should now be recognized. *A Rumor of War* is neither "a grand gesture of personal protest" nor an attempt to reinstate, as he sees it, the "futile" critique of the sixties. The text demonstrates the veteran's need to set things down in some kind of order, to provide a purposeful chronology, a need which undercuts the claim that the dramatic focus of the narrative has been damaged beyond "recall" (24).

Realism isn't simply a means of getting down the brute fact and accumulated detail of Vietnam nor is it just a matter of telling the truth with an artless or slice-of-life commentary on events. However much the writer tries to think of himself as an initiate in art, however much he tries to desubstantiate the language, or to prove his truth by his wounds, realism is still an aesthetic proceeding. For the reader of *A Rumor of War*, realism isn't simply a question of discerning the truth but of looking at the way the truth is told, of observing the way Caputo chooses to discharge his obligation to be honest. In *A Rumor of War* the quality of that obligation is revealed only when we look beneath the various claims Caputo makes in his crusade for truthfulness.

The problem with Caputo's realism is that it is sometimes spoiled by an extravagant desire to rescue the reader from moral and emotional complacency. Caputo has a tendency to overcome lavishly "the problem of expression" that, according to Patricia Caldwell, was attendant upon the personal narratives of the saints in New England. Puritan conversion narratives, says Caldwell, were bedeviled by a lack of words and often the speakers were "unable to do full justice to their feeling." Caputo strives to avoid this fate. His text suffers from a surfeit of literacy, a desire to compensate for a personal and "overwhelming awareness of sin."

Caputo is determined to overcome the problem of communication, for if, like the saints, he "cannot speak" to his "neighbors" he can at least speak to his readers. As a result his vigorous evangelism, on occasion, resembles a sales pitch for the truth. Although he claims to speak on behalf of the marines only, Caputo extrapolates from the particular to the general on numerous occasions. One of the most repeated expressions in the book is "Other veterans I knew confessed to the same emotion" (xvi). His "charms and spells" remind us of the rhetoric of the New Frontier, the words of "witchdoctors" (315) like John F. Kennedy whose emotional language we are asked to condemn by a writer whose style is perhaps unwittingly imitative. The one "aspect of the Vietnam war that distinguished it from other American conflicts," we are told, was "its absolute savagery." Life in Vietnam is unethical and uncivilized. "It was the dawn of creation in the Indochina bush, an ethical as well as a geographical wilderness" (xx). The scale of the chaos is epic and intense: "The very ugliness of the war, the sordidness of our daily lives, the degradation of having to take part in body counts made us draw closer to one another" (xviii). Vietnam is a wasteland where pigs eat "napalm-charred corpses" and men sink into a brutish state. This level of expression renders Caputo's Vietnam bleak yet wearisome, a place fit only for overwrought melodrama, where even the rain leaks "from the swollen sky like pus from a festering wound" (228).

The need to portray the horror of Vietnam as exceptional and unprecedented limits the writer's capacity for realism as well as his sense of restraint. Caputo's weakness is a tendency to overstate the brutality and adventurism of Vietnam. He invites the reader to assess his work as a not unromantic moral tragedy. The tendency is common among veterans who are first-time writers. Many autobiographies are ruined by their role as cathartic therapy for war veterans who wallow in violence and the narcissism of individual experience. This tendency achieves a demented climax in the recent pamphlets from Jo-Ely Publishing Company that advertise Harvey D. Fletcher's three-volume study, *Visions of Nam* (1988), in this way: "It is not the war of the politicians, generals, reporters, T.V. cameramen, professors, protestors or official historians. It is the war of the men and women who went through it all. Felt it all. Saw it all. And now . . . one man tells it as it was never supposed to be told. The immediacy of oral history . . . the murder, atrocity and the unalloyed pleasure that war affords . . . relentless horror!"[35]

With his "blood-and-guts" (128) prose Caputo tends to shout too loud and too often to make himself heard. But the sin is one of enthusiasm, not one of calculation, and it ought perhaps to be kept in perspective, especially since, for Caputo, the true aesthetic of literature is morality. *A Rumor of War* announces a search for the forms and places in which the moral life and moral brotherhood of man might be invigorated. Caputo constantly intervenes in his work as the rhetorical persuader, the maker of moral plots. On occasion he is extravagant in his judgment on the world. Elsewhere his notion of character, his way of structuring his tales according to the moral growth of a single life, his sense of the rational and conscious powers of the human mind to overcome instinct, free him from the shackles of Puritan dogma and moral intransigence. In spite of the "dramatics" (311) the silence of suffering alone is renounced.

Unwilling to turn his back on the "defeat of the cause I had served as a soldier" (323), Caputo retains his concern for a country that America in 1973 has appeared to renege on. In the epilogue he returns to Saigon in 1975 in spite of the jeopardy that the visit entails. The need to observe events at first hand, to renew his acquaintance with the world he knew, is overwhelming. "I cannot explain this feeling. It just seemed I had a personal responsibility to be there at the end" (323). Caputo's argument remains the same: not with the Vietnamese people but with a government that refused to commit itself to the pursuit of "truth" (312) in Vietnam. In retrospect, it is not the Vietnamese, he claims, who are the enemy; it is not they who are "threatening to rob me of my liberty" (315). Caputo's argument is that of the separatist who believes in free will; his has been a disobedient crusade for the truth "which the whole proceeding was designed to conceal" (313).

4

Soul Speech

= The Puritan Dilemma =

THE MANIPULATION OF AN AUDIENCE BY VERBAL MEANS AND "intense verbal" performance was common in the New England colonies in the seventeenth century. Sermons in the plain style were deemed the opposite of the "swelling words of humane wisedome," criticized by John Cotton in 1642, which "makes mens preaching seeme to Christ (as it were) a blubber-lipt Ministry." That was not the way of Christ, who, rather than give men "a kind of intimation, afar off" had actually spoken "their own in English as we say. . . . he lets fly poynt blanck."[1]

The duty of providing a plain-speaking testimony was not always easy to reconcile with the need to represent the sermon as an emotional experience and one in which the audience underwent an emotional reaction while listening to it. On the one hand, it was considered the duty of the saints and those who aspired to visible sainthood to talk about their conversions or their sense of grace in an open and public manner; on the other, as Patricia

Caldwell has pointed out, the idea of an intimate and public narrative, a story that "people tell about themselves . . . inevitably imposed an artistic standard of performance" (159).

Testimony was a matter of sincerity. A rhetorical performance in the pulpit or in print, one full of dramatic flourish and extravagant metaphors, would not draw a church member " 'out of his sinfull estate into fellowship with Christ' " (Caldwell, 159). Professions of experience, rather, should be "such as may be of special use unto the people of God" and should not degenerate into "soul speech." Faith, says Caldwell, was derived not from "an intricate arrangement of taffeta phrases" but from a "faltering account of what the believer simply and smartingly did feel" (96).

In determining who ought to be granted church fellowship, the New England Puritans listened attentively to the personal narratives of those who had journeyed across the Atlantic, rooting out the "subtle hypocrite" who professed his qualifications elaborately and extravagantly in order to "deceive the Church . . . by his golden words" (97). The Puritans were aware that proof of regeneration through words and signs was "particularly liable to abuse." If language was suspect, the words of conversion must be handled, as Caldwell says, "gingerly." In other words, "like live explosives, they are not for amateurs to meddle with and can go off in unexpected, dangerous ways" (102). Thus Thomas Shepard was genuinely distressed by what he considered the sinful distortion of language. Mistrustful of false eloquence and fevered exhibitionism, Shepard warned about hypocrisy concealed by the oratory of men who, through "a long story of conversion," were full of false prayers and "good works" (149), and who were guided by a desire for nothing other than "external applause and praise of men" (149).

= Golden Words =

In Vietnam writing, the Puritan dilemma of delivering an honest yet dramatically persuasive confession remains acute. There is a constant tension between those who narrate their experiences in a plain style and those who resort to the strategy of "soul speech." Both conditions are characteristic, though not exclusively so, of a confessional element in American writing, one that coincided with the mood of revivalism which came to the forefront of American life in the later years of the 1970s under the presidency of Jimmy Carter. The duty to testify to what one had seen and witnessed was a feature of the country's autobiographical impetus. In his commentary on the life stories of country musicians that appeared in the later years of the 1970s, Jac L. Tharpe uses the term "confessionals and testimonials" to describe the writing. Johnny Cash, Loretta Lynn, Tammy Wynette, and Jeannie C. Riley, are, says Tharpe, like "sinners in the hands of a merciful God, passive in their helplessness during their sinful years."[2] Popular autobiography during these years stressed not only the importance of religious awareness and belief but also the increasingly close relationship between religion as duty and religion as entertainment.

In the mid-1970s religion in America gave itself a more professional and public status and was increasingly designed to appeal to an audience through the medium of television. The electronic church, as it came to be known, emphasized the power of those who devoted their lives, as Claude-Jean Bertrand describes it, "to surfing for Christ on the airwaves of America." In the 1970s television was used as a highly sophisticated medium for those in pursuit of wealth and sainthood. The authoritarianism of the electronic church was rooted in a firm understanding of market potential and of the economic benefits that derived from baring one's soul in public for the benefit of others. The good looks and good fellowship of the celebrity church transformed the idea of the New England sermon into a corporate crusade, a public event in which Christianity became big business. In the 1970s and 1980s televised religion became a multimillion-dollar entertainment industry, targeting and manipulating an audience by means of an assertive and emotionally arresting message; and through bold advertising claims that promised success for those who followed a particular leader. By taking advantage of the revolution in satellite broadcasting and communications technology, superpreachers, like Jerry Falwell, Robert Schuller, Jimmy Swaggart, Oral Roberts, Pat Robertson, and Jim Bakker had a major impact on the standard and styles of performance testimony. With his oratory the visible saint of the electronic church was able to win friends and influence people by substituting "an intellectually simplistic entertainment" for the discipline and rigor of old-time worship.[3]

The partnership between broadcasting and the evangelical movement has been an undoubted influence on styles and strategies of narrative testimony in American popular culture. Recognition of the profit to be gained by televangelists has certainly influenced the language and testimony of those whose Christianity has long since lapsed. The literary response to Vietnam cannot be separated from what is going on in the surrounding environment, and the similarities in style that link the evangelists of contemporary America and those who discuss the problems of Vietnam should not be overlooked. Among those who profess a special or privileged knowledge of the truth, there is often a common assertiveness, an emphasis on credentialism and charismatic witness.

═══   The Old Trench Mind   ═══

The skills and subtleties of the man who bears false witness—Shepard's "subtle hypocrite"—is a major concern for the reader in the work of Michael Herr. In *Dispatches* the fulfillment of a Puritan legacy of testimony is subtly perverted by an entertainer who, with "his golden words," provides the reader with a "long story of conversion." In the writer's personal testimony—a mode of address promoted by Jimmy Carter and popularized by Jimmy Swaggart —southern evangelical excess is linked with Puritanical excess to create a work that is spiritually born-again in the sense that it deals with people in a state of awareness, men who have been where the action is and have thus been given, as Philip Caputo says, "a future" (*Rumor*, 304).

Dispatches is full of insights, cameo revelations about the nature of life, and the visionary capacity of those whose knowledge we are obliged to know. "Everywhere you went people said, 'Well, I hope you get a story,' and every-where you went you did" (31). The book comes across as a crusade for truth, but the opportunity to present that truth in as dramatic and colorful a way as possible proves too tempting. *Dispatches* plays host to a parasitical fiction, one that supersedes the professed intention of the reportage. As a fiction *Dispatches* exists to promote the self as a center of authority and to entertain the reader as a cultural consumer. Although, as Barret Mandel has argued, no worthwhile autobiography takes itself too seriously or removes from the text all trace of "pretense" and "illusion," the presence of that which is pretentious or illusory is so ably disguised in *Dispatches* that we are not always able to identify immediately what is "false and true."[4]

The appearance of covert fictionality in a work of apparent nonfiction leads Cedric Watts to describe this type of narrative as "Janus-faced" or "Janiform." The benefit that accrues to this narrative, says Watts, and its appeal are determined by a plot that provides "excitement" and promises "conclusiveness." In a covert narrative, autobiography is vulnerable to the exploitation of intimacy and the loss of good faith that ought to exist between the writer and his reader.[5]

Dispatches is an artful text which carefully disguises the legacy of what Robert Graves, in *Good-bye to All That*, caricatured as "the old trench mind,"[6] the idea of the war memoir as a solemn and truthful narrative. *Dispatches* strives to gain the reader's sympathy on the basis of the truths it purports to tell and the lies it purports to expose. What Herr appreciates is that the Achilles' heel of the personal narrative is verification, that the way in which we judge a performance, especially one that is keen to dramatize a morally authentic experience and an apparently bona fide condition of grace, is limited by what the author tells us. The reader's capacity for identifying a converting experience and the means by which it is ratified in literature has, says Herr, proved vulnerable to abuse. In the quasi-Puritanical conversion narrative, which the American writer has resurrected in Vietnam, too much emphasis can easily be placed on verbal performance, on "swelling words" rather than plain-speaking and truthful testimony. The reader can be duped by his own credulity. Such credulousness arises, in part, from the fact that autobiography has not been taken seriously enough. The problem is apparent in Nancy Anisfield's introduction to her *Vietnam Anthology*, in which she describes autobiography as one of the crudest and earliest forms of expression which American writers used to explore their experiences of Vietnam. She regards it sympathetically but not critically. "Autobiography," as she puts it, "is less complicated to write than fiction."[7]

The problem of locating moral authority in "golden words" is approached by Herr as a journey of investigation—both literal and literary. The narrator is a journeyman, a character who grapples with a problem he cannot solve, of how to identify the moral corruption of the Vietnam War in a world that remains—as does he—irresistibly fascinated by the language of violence. War writing is as much performance for the narrator as official propaganda is for those who support the war with their "overripe bullshit" (24). Herr's narrator, like Hemingway's Jake Barnes, projects onto others the very weaknesses that exist in himself. He cannot ratify the morality he asserts. His narrative is "self-dramatic" (16) and is based on the need to keep the reader entertained and amused in order to gain his intimate support.

Dispatches is an act of frenetic salesmanship. Scenes move with a desperate, episodic haste, the language is aphoristic and epigrammatic, the energy and pace all-consuming. The nervous instability of the "old trench mind," which comes from "close exposure to the dead," makes "for long reverberations" (16) in the life of the narrative. Herr has decided to maim the art of the man who elicits our greatest sympathy: the narrator of the text. He shares with Robert Graves the belief that "high-explosive barrages will make a temporary liar or visionary of anyone."[8]

= Games People Play =

Dispatches can best be understood in terms of a modernist strategy of unreliable narration where *histoire* and *discours* become discrepant. The book tells a different tale from the text it proclaims. As a polemic dressed up as war correspondence it begins disingenuously by identifying the danger of simplistic information, of being mistrustful, as Hemingway's Jake Barnes claims to be, of "frank and simple people, especially when their stories hold together."[9] This introductory strategy seeks to establish the moral and metafictional credentials of the narrator at the expense of someone whose "simple" story line appears foolish. The Robert Cohn of the text is an "information officer" from the MACV who, at the outset, explains the necessity for the destruction of Ho Bo Woods with "Rome ploughs and chemicals" (11). The officer is an apologist for "know-how" and "hardware" and, in the fight against primitive enemies, he speaks the language of the colonial "Mission." As an official propagandist he is a true believer in the exercise of institutional power and the magisterial influence of those who regard the woods as the natural territory of the Antichrist, a place to be conquered through cultivation and technological energies.

In seeking to create a symbolic distance between those who learn from personal experience and those who preach a doctrine of duty, the narrator of *Dispatches* presents himself as a moral individual and an opponent of the rule of military law. The information officer is a mouthpiece for those who wish to destroy Vietnam, but the narrator owes no allegiance to anyone. His values encourage us to dismiss the idea of a single, verifiable reality based on units of assembled fact—ground cleared, bombs dropped, numbers of enemy soldiers killed—and, instead, to accept a world composed of multiple realities and the multiple perspectives that inform those realities. Vietnam, we are told, is not a coherent experience, a place of logical or sequential actions and clearly defined forms and activities. It is a country that is inaccessible to the West, and it resists the language of the elect who wish to dominate it militarily. The tentative role Herr's narrator claims to adopt allows him to talk about his knowledge of the truth as being inadequate and provisional. What he claims to know is a war where "it was frequently difficult, if not impossible, to tell which side was winning or falling behind, losing ground or winning."[10]

What *Dispatches* appears to grapple with is the problem of how to contain modernist experience in structures that are largely irrelevant to it. Joan Didion addresses this problem in *Slouching towards Bethlehem* and *The White Album*. She describes her life as a writer in the later years of the 1960s as one of immense frustration. She speaks of the difficulties she encountered in trying to impose "a narrative line" upon "disparate images," images that appeared as part of an "improvised . . . script" but that "did not fit into any narrative I knew." This loss of faith in familiar styles of life and art—especially the idea that "an ending" is available "for every social scenario"—is part of the randomness of American life that seeps out of California and into Vietnam.[11] For the narrator of *Dispatches* the two cultures are interdependent: each is an extreme of "the same theatre" (14), each is transformed by the same cultural and subcultural energies. Both locations are surfeited with such a variety of styles and incidents (which happen in no apparent sequence and for no apparent reason) that the writer runs the risk, like Joan Didion, of becoming "paralyzed by the conviction that writing" is "an irrelevant act [and] that the world" as he or she understands it "no longer" exists. Joan Didion provides the context in *Slouching towards Bethlehem*: "If I was to work again at all, it would be necessary for me to come to terms with disorder."[12]

In *The White Album* and *Dispatches* the work of the writer, so it is said, is undertaken at a cost: loss of confidence in a recognizable reality, the constant blurring of fact and fiction, the ability of the culture to throw up "figures almost daily that are the envy of the novelist."[13] Writing causes disorientation: feelings of vertigo and nausea and severe visual disturbances. Although the writing is clearly necessary, it "has not yet helped me," says Didion, "to see" the purpose behind the act of composition.[14] What Didion refers us to is the problem of reading history in an incoherent age, an age preoccupied with the meaning of style yet unconcerned with the meaning of narrative, an age that lacks both linear form and narrative structure.

In *Dispatches* Vietnam appears but one step removed from Didion's California. The narrator, we are told, enters a world of fragmented forms; like Vonnegut's Billy Pilgrim, he becomes, so it seems, "unstuck in time." The journalist sets out to "represent" the world but realizes fairly soon that the world, as such, cannot be represented; instead, he finds that it is possible to "represent" only the discourses of the world. What the writer appears to discover, therefore, is a living metafiction, a state of mind and a place of action, a war and a landscape that constantly question their own identity, a country where the search for meaning constantly extends beyond the meager resources of conventional journalism. In turning away from the notion of a verifiable reality toward a reexamination of the way in which our versions of reality are constructed—how we conspire to agree on what reality is—Herr's narrator claims to have avoided the fate of the redundant journalist: he who wanders aimlessly in an obscure world.

Dispatches exploits a hybrid method of dealing with problems: "the factual authority of journalism and the atmospheric license of fiction."[15] As a journalist of the new, the narrator desires to unmask the lies of establishment reporting. He wishes to "tell the truth that shall make the people free"—a clear reference to the tradition of muckraking—and to place greater emphasis on subjective vision.[16] His viewpoint is grounded, so it seems, in the principle that each subject is the center of his world, viewing it uniquely, seeking to order it and confer value on it. All the old landmarks are gone. All one is left with is the self alone in a vast and seemingly anarchistic world. This relativistic viewpoint attempts to correct for our not being God and urges us to open ourselves to as wide a range of views as our limitations will permit, to avoid imprisoning ourselves any more than we already are. By boldly and candidly applying the principle of indeterminacy to autobiography, the writer appears to deliver a heavy blow to the traditional image of journalism as a medium able to separate fact from fiction. Instead, the writer overtly aims to stimulate the reader's attention and his emotions. The concrete detail becomes a device to foster verisimilitude, narrative is consciously organized through a scenic method, point of view is deliberately used for indirect commentary, and the people in the stories become characters. Truth is no longer something that can be simply pointed to by a statement; rather it becomes something to be revealed by the way the text is constructed. By claiming to adopt these modes of provisional inquiry, Herr's narrator is able to claim a radical distinction between what he does in Vietnam and what other journalists do, which is to "take the most profound event of the American decade and turn it into a communications pudding" (175).

Those who have sinned in their reporting are the older, more complacent journalists, the ones "you'd run into . . . once in a while at the bar of the Da

Nang press centre." They are the ones "who accept, without question, the propaganda of irrelevant fact built into the press releases of the MACV, the tourist-journalists, hacks who write down every word that the generals and officials told them to write" (175). By claiming to avoid the MACV, by seeking out the truth in the front line of action, Herr's narrator seeks to present us with "authentic" information in a language unaffected by the euphemism of command. Conventional journalism neutralizes the war's meaning; it disinforms those who listen, and it disables those who promote it. In a world where conventional journalism is irrelevant those who do not investigate the war's true purpose cannot be relied upon. Although the narrator may come across stories that are told "with the hair still growing" on them (31), stories that are sometimes "deceitful and counter-articulate" (32), each will convey a sense of the war's meaning and will indicate a range of reference in which information is "flexible" (19). By keeping an open mind on these stories the narrator will demonstrate, or so it appears, a generous spirit of inquiry. On releasing the folkloristic and tale-telling energies of the American abroad, in gathering various opinions, and by attributing to each opinion a provisional validity, he will be able to invest events with a huge symbolic complexity. The effect will be similar to that sought for by the early American romance writer. In piling up a bewildering variety of points of view, by employing the technique of the multiple eyewitness, the narrator will give us a literature of alternate possibilities, a broad canvas on which are painted many of the different faces of war.

What Herr's narrator wishes to insist upon, therefore, is a causal connection between the artifice of the narrative and the problematic "real world" of Vietnam itself, a world whose identity is highly provisional and insecure. The narrator presents the book and its mode of construction—episodic in form, pluralistic in opinion, self-questioning, plotless, playful, polemically diverse—as a dramatic metaphor for the American experience in Vietnam and the multiple realities that experience throws up. Naturally the reader must immerse himself in the role of the journalist and listen to the stories it has taken the journalist a year to understand. If the experience is disorienting, it will, at least, encourage the reader to ignore the forgeries of the hacks in the press bar.

The claims made for *Dispatches* over the years have been quite extraordinary. Few critics have not been daunted by the book and most have been overawed by it. *Dispatches*, it is said, demonstrates the inadequacy of conventional journalistic inquiry and forces us to reevaluate the established standards of war reporting. For some critics it even negates the achievement of writers like Ernest Hemingway, whose war dispatches seem, in comparison, "strangely anachronistic."[17]

But despite the claims that have been made, *Dispatches* is not the grand postmodernist text. The narrator may seek to deflect our attention when he says, of the hated MACV, "all that the Mission talked about was control: arms control, information control, resources control, psychopolitical control, population control, control of the almost supernatural inflation, control of terrain through the Strategy of the Periphery" (45), but the "control" he seeks to exert as a writer is no less emphatic. In *Dispatches* the uncertainty that is at the root of all metafictional landscapes is destroyed by the covert activity of the narrator. He is the controller of the text, an authoritarian who dispenses a wish-fulfillment fantasy of power and conviction. Like the old, omniscient author he changes things in the act of observing them, fabricating through an ultimately monologic discourse those structures of order that in the seventies reawaken the nostalgia of an earlier day. In *Dispatches* the narrator does not wish to call into question the means by which he conveys his information nor does he wish to provide fully or effectively a critique of the book's method of construction. As an autocratic influence in the text, he heeds the advice of Fenimore Cooper in *The Last of the Mohicans*: "It is a very unsafe experiment either for a writer or a projector to trust to the inventive powers of anyone but himself. Therefore, nothing which can be well explained should be left a mystery. Such an expedient would only impart a peculiar pleasure to readers of that description, who find a strange gratification in spending more of their time in making books, than of their money in buying them."[18] *Dispatches* is a text of instruction, not inquiry. For the narrator, experience is a function of the war's mystique and authority is determined by the quality of his credentials. To make sense of Vietnam is not a task the reader is equipped to fulfill, and his ignorance is a burden that can never be fully escaped. In confronting the war's mystery the reader must accept the didactic guidance offered by the narrative, and the wisdom of the man who has lived in the places where the reader is unable to go. Since the narrator has accepted a lengthy assignment the reader is obliged to accept the quality of his investigation. It has taken the narrator "a year to understand Vietnam" and by the time he is ready to leave, he claims to know "where all the stories came from and where they were going" (13, 32).

═══ Fabulation ═══

If *Dispatches* wishes to be considered a journalistic metafiction—elusive, uncertain of itself, unverifiable—then the narrator fails to realize his intention in the making of the text. In *Dispatches* Vietnam is presented as a sensible war in which those who exercise or administer power are seen as idiots and those who suffer the abuses of power are invariably heroic. In spite of the promise of difficulty, of elusive barriers to true understanding, the narrator creates a strict allegorical framework which employs the resources of fabulation for the purpose of providing the reader with easy, reductive equations. As Robert Scholes has defined it, fabulation represents an attempt to define and promote "a comic, grotesque," and "irreverent" landscape. The most relevant features of this kind of literature are a strong return to narrative as an organizing principle, "a rediscovered interest in the interface between oral and written forms," and an attempt to go back to the origins of creative writing, to what Jolles has called *"formes simples."*[19]

The narrator of *Dispatches* looks for stories that provide him with a means of communicating to as wide an audience as possible his faith in demotic and colloquial expression. In turning his back on the language and morality of established power, the narrator creates a value system in which freedom of thought and freedom of expression are associated with the fluent and "disengaged." Toward this end the narrator creates, like E. E. Cummings in *The Enormous Room*, a hierarchy of articulateness in which the most literate are the most villainous and the least precisely verbal command the most affection. Where the official symbolic structures of power are seen to dehumanize the elect, those who reject the values of an inherited language system are the ones most worthy of our attention and support. Herr's deputy offers us a world of definitive values by postulating pairs of extremes: conformists and outlaws, assassins and victims, spooks and civilians, "adventurers" and "drudges," "normals" as opposed to "beautiful lunatics," night and day, ground and air, grunts and lifers, writers and hacks. Vietnam is not a place of indeterminate action in which the reader loses control of his belief; it is a polarized landscape in which people gravitate to one form of action or another, where demarcated moral boundaries clearly exist and forces arise that thrust the characters into archetypal roles and elemental gestures. The man who is damaged in the making of history is the hero of the book. The man who escapes such damage—the rear-echelon officer, pogue, bureaucrat, propagandist—lives to exercise power over others.

Dispatches is a book of fairy tales in which roles are invented to celebrate friends and parody enemies. Just as there are good journalists and bad journalists—superheroes like Sean Flynn and "syndicated eminences" (177) or faded hacks in "their jungle-hell leisure suits" (37)—so similar distinctions exist between soldiers. Those who make a profession of war, and commit their lives to it, are invariably grotesque. The "lifers," unable to leave Vietnam alone, "tour" the country in the belief that "if we can't shoot these people, what the fuck are we doing here?" (31). All over Vietnam, says the narrator, are the "Green-Beret bushmasters, redundant mutilators, heavy rapers, eye-shooters, widow-makers" (35). In Vietnam if you look ugly you are ugly: physical distortion is a spiritual malaise. The writer sees it on the face of a marine: "He was walking by us now, and I saw that he had a deep, running blister that seemed to have opened and eaten away much of his lower lip. . . . He stopped for a second and looked at us, and he smiled some terrifying, evil smile, his look turned now to the purest evil" (166). On the comic edge of this nightmare is the commander who believes in the inevitability of victory, since America is "a nation of high-protein, meat-eating hunters, while the other guy just ate rice and a few grungy fish heads" (54). (The narrator intrudes, "He was talking fish but his dreamy eyes were full of mega-death" [55].) Officers in Vietnam are prepared to have their men "killed" to give their unit a little publicity. Some are obsessed by cleanliness (29), and others describe the quality of life at Khe Sanh as "clean" (123). In *Dispatches* fabulation transforms cartoon into lampoon, archetype into stereotype.

The most archetypal character and therefore the most heroic—because he undertakes his work as a "volunteer" (163) and not as a lifer—is the narrator himself. Vietnam, we are told, is the narrator's frontier, a place where he shares the untutored individualism of the soldier as cowboy, the man who lives outside the settlements where conformity to rules is the price for security. The narrator, like Raymond Chandler's Philip Marlowe, finds his destiny on the road. He attempts to change things through a vanishing code of voluntary individualism, justice, and, perhaps, celibacy. He likes to see himself move with integrity and toughness through a lonely world, rarely deviating from the code of a frontier knight in a society that makes stringent demands on his manners. He offers himself as the crusading journalist, a man whose courage is such that even the marines think he's "crazy" (168). Here is a man who seeks the approval of those for whom he writes, an insecure writer who goes in fear of being neglected. As the interpreter of a neglected war and the neglected veteran of a subculture that has its place within that war, the journalist requires public recognition. By "moving" (15) through the backwoods regions of South Vietnam he resists the imprisonment of static forms and appears to demonstrate the looseness of those whose expressions avoid the euphemism of command.

Dispatches is an advertisement for the war correspondent as eclectic hobo, a man who must travel the country in pursuit of stories in order to discredit the manners and opinions of those in the press bar. ("Some journalists talked about no-story operations, but I never went on one" [31].) The narrator says that he wants his letters to smell of the woods, for the heart of darkness, he claims, is not the forest but the briefing room. In *Dispatches* the loss of an available colloquial energy at the heart of American literature is made good—or so it appears—by those who inhabit the woods of Vietnam. In the campfire tales and camaraderie of the young marines like Mayhew and Day Tripper we seem to renew our acquaintance with the narrative skills of backwoods life: the art of braggadocio, swaggering self-assertion, parody, and bombast—forms of narrative that ridicule the wilderness, that convert terror into joie de vivre and helplessness into an exhilarating sense of power. When a black paratrooper glides past the narrator and says "I been scaled man, I'm smooth now," it leaves him wondering "not what he meant (that was easy), but where he'd been to get his language" (30).

The way in which the language of the West animates itself in the wilderness of the East is testimony to the power of American creativity. Graffiti says "everything": " 'Born to kill' placed in all innocence next to the peace symbol, or 'A sucking chest wound is Nature's way of telling you that you've

been in a firefight' was too good to share with anyone but a real collector"
(182). The slang of America becomes once more a means of renewing those
vital traditions through which the country creates a demotic sense of self. At
a difficult moment the language and fable of the common man, that living
speech which, as Whitman puts it, "is the lawless germinal element, below
all words and sentences, and behind all poetry, and proves a certain perennial
rankness and protestantism in speech" makes for creative sustenance.[20]

The underlying force of the entertainment in *Dispatches* is ethnocentric.
For all the narrator laments the loss of the wilderness at the outset, he shows
little interest in the lives of those who must bear that loss. To understand
Vietnam is to talk about "the war," not with the people whose country it is
but with the correspondents who visit it. "Because who but another correspondent could talk the kind of mythical war that you wanted to hear described. . . . Where else could you go for a real sense of the war's past? There
were all kinds of people who knew the background, the facts, the most minute
details, but only a correspondent could give you the exact mood" (181). The
war's true meaning can be discovered only in the language of like-minded
people. For this reason, "if you wanted some war news in Saigon you had to
hear it in stories brought from the field by friends" (41). Since *Dispatches*
is limited to the personal experience of its narrator, coverage of the war is
governed by the places the narrator has chosen to visit and the company he
has kept. His experience is the war's experience: the range of its discourse
is entirely contingent on what he has seen and heard on his travels. The
range of inquiry, therefore, is limited by the range of the author's quest, the
miles he logs, the people he meets. The war has no meaning in the places
the narrator has chosen not to visit; Vietnam as a country has no identity
beyond "men hunting men" and "death" itself, which "of course was really
what it was all about" (173). By going only to those places he finds exciting
the narrator provides us with a fast-moving narrative in which he is witness
to the central events of his time. The history of the war is a history of the
self and its social entertainments. What the reader is given is not war reporting
but highly desirable autobiography, not war dispatches but diary entries in
which a stranger (the narrator) becomes a friend.

Dispatches incorporates a vision of art that the narrator's observation of
war has encouraged. Pace and improvisation are vital elements in the book,
the sense of a world not wholly in control of its own energies but spinning
headlong and inexorably toward collapse. *Dispatches* profits from the violence
of Vietnam by concentrating almost exclusively on it. The narrator is a voyeur,
a tourist in search of horror and adventure. When the narrator says, "I was
there to watch" (24), we are reminded of what Hemingway said in *Green
Hills of Africa*: that for a writer to be exposed to war too long would damage
his sensibility. Thus, when the narrator reads of the news of a friend's death
in New York he is unable to go to sleep. He tries to remember what his friend
looked like, but all he is able "to imagine" is the horror of Vietnam, a world

of blood and bone fragment, much more compelling than the death of a friend from an overdose of pills. His mind is in the grip of its own fevered imagination, able to show no evidence of a sensibility qualified or controlled by personal reflection.

The emphasis on suffering as a way of promoting authenticity affirms the narrator's right to speak and our need to listen. In a world in which violence is idiomatic the narrator gains the double satisfaction of keeping the reader entertained and of presenting himself as a martyr in the quest for spiritual truth. He introduces us to the Tet offensive by describing the "huge collective nervous breakdown" (67) that "every American in Vietnam got a taste of" (62). The fear of being overrun by the Viet Cong, "our worst dread of yellow peril," is "realized" when the Vietnamese are seen "dying by the thousands all over the country" in their all-out push for victory. He describes the "total panic" that characterized the American response and the debilitating effect the Tet offensive had on the journalists, pushing them "closer to the wall than they'd ever wanted to go," until "actual youth had been pressed out of them in just the three days that it took one to cross the sixty miles between Can Tho and Saigon" (63). In his search for the nuances of violent energy the narrator is constantly on the move. Only a man who thinks quickly can stay ahead of the game. Culture as place is culture as space—the space made available by American machinery. The narrator substitutes one for the other (space for place), giving us a sense not of the country or of its language but of those whose stories talk about the country but have little to do with it.

Rootlessness is a way of monitoring the war: the endless shuttling within the country in search of violence is also a means of energizing the text. If the war world is a death world, the narrator's joy ride aboard the helicopter expresses an indiscriminate yearning for sensation. *Dispatches* is cluttered with death scenes, grotesque incidents, a snapshot catalog of theatrical life. Since violence is endemic, the language emphasizes the generality of suffering, the pervasiveness of death. Emphatic adverbs like "always" (19) and "everyone" (20), "totally true" (30), "unremitting" (34), "all" (40) refer the reader to the high level of occurrence of injury and pain.

This emotion is re-enforced by a style of writing that extrapolates the general from the particular in order to make elaborate claims about Vietnam—claims that are not borne out by the history of the war or the history of the war in relation to other wars. The paragraphs are stitched together in a seamless weave, but the reader is never asked to unpick the text. The writer shifts effortlessly from one yarn to another, going with the flow of his own "fluency," taking the reader from possibility to probability. In this wish-fulfillment world of violence "everyone around me was carrying a gun" and "any one of them could go off at any time, putting [you] where it wouldn't matter" (20). If soldiers "threw people out of helicopters, tied people up and put the dogs on them" (59), we need to know more about the frequency of the act and how such an act ought to be measured against other, less violent expressions of mission. There is no attempt to discriminate in *Dispatches* between what happened occasionally, what happened all the time, and what happened to everyone irrespective of who or where they were. John Converse's remark in Robert Stone's *Dog Soldiers* that " 'for most people in the line it was firing at leaves or points of light. There [wasn't] a lot of personal combat' "[21] would be looked on as an irrelevance in *Dispatches*. Because violence is ubiquitous it cannot be escaped. "It was like telling someone going out in a storm not to get any on him, it was the same as saying 'Gee, I hope you don't get killed or wounded or see anything that drives you insane' " (51). In *Dispatches*, to get wounded or to go insane is as natural as getting wet. That it didn't always rain in Vietnam or that you didn't necessarily go out when it did seems unworthy of mention. In a war where "going crazy was built into the tour" the "saturating strangeness of the place" (53) cannot be escaped. It thrusts itself before us, in places that "held such hostile vibes that you felt you were being dry-sniped every time someone looked at you. . . . After a while I couldn't get on without thinking that I must be out of my fucking mind" (20).

As a romantic pilgrim the narrator of *Dispatches* uses his observations of Vietnam to render the look of things through color, expression, surface, and spectacle. There is sometimes a shallowness of perception in the pictures we are given, a lack of depth, a striving to create a pictorial effect that is merely illustrational. Peter Rollins makes substantially the same point about the visual language of television news at the time of the Tet offensive in 1968. The confusion that surrounded Tet, says Rollins, originated in a set of "misleading visual dramas." These dramas, he says, supplied a series of compelling icons to which information would later cling and were so ingrained in the public mind that they could not be modified by subsequent reports. The putative "penetration" of the U.S. embassy in Saigon, General Loan's "gratuitous" execution of a Viet Cong suspect, and the "hopeless" battle at Khe Sanh seemed to confirm—because of the way they were presented— that the American embassy in Saigon had been violated; that individual rights were not respected in South Vietnam; and that, at Khe Sanh, America's toughest troops had collapsed in panic. What Rollins complains about in his analysis of much of the television news coverage—the camera angles, the types and lengths of shots, the editing, the way particular stories were used as microcosms to convey broader meanings—is germane to a study of the narrator's methods in *Dispatches*.[22]

History is stage managed in *Dispatches*. In his coverage of Khe Sanh the narrator repeats the mistakes the news networks made ten years earlier. Just as ABC's David Douglas Duncan focused his coverage on the burning wreckage of a C-130 in spite of the fact that at Khe Sanh, a relatively safe airport, only four major aircraft were shot down during the battle,[23] so Herr's narrator continually dwells on the tenuousness of supply lines to Khe Sanh in order to support the misguided analogy with Dien Bien Phu that he, like many of the network observers, believes is "irresistible" (85). "Khe Sanh was a very bad place then, but the airstrip there was the worst place in the world. . . . There was always the debris of one kind of aircraft or another piled up or near the strip. . . . It was so bad, so predictably bad, that the Air Force stopped flying in their star transport, the C-130" (76).

Since Don Oberdorfer's *Tet*, published in 1971, and Peter Braestrup's *Big Story* in 1977, it has been public record that the Lunar New Year offensive was not a major victory for the Communist troops and that few of the military objectives of the Tet attacks were achieved. In the version of Tet that we have in *Dispatches*, however, the American mission totally collapses. For example: "At Khe Sanh most bunkers were nothing more than hovels with inadequate overhead cover, and you could not believe that Americans were living this way, even in the middle of a war. The defenses were a scandal, and everywhere you could smell that sour reek of obsolescence that followed the Marines all over Vietnam" (89). Khe Sanh is a visually devastated landscape. It is pictured as a heap of smoldering wreckage, cluttered with "passion" (90) and the misspent worship of military dreams. "Heaps of equipment are on fire, terrifying in their jagged black massiveness, burning prehistoric shapes like the tail of a C-130 sticking straight-up in the air, dead metal showing through the grey-black smoke" (92). What is true of machines is true of the soldiers. "People would just get ripped up in the worst ways there, and things were always on fire" (93). What we have are pictures from a movie that flash across a wide-angle screen. What we see is a fascination with chaos, the horror of Mayhew as he watches the marine with an M-79 put an end to a screaming Vietnamese on the wire. "Mayhew looked out at the wire again, but the silence of the ground in front of us was really talking to him now. His fingers were limp, touching his face, and he looked like a kid at a scary movie" (117). What Mayhew responds to is the theater of war at its most entertaining. He, like us, becomes engrossed in the visual texture of an action-packed adventure story, a "movie" that relies for its effect—the way most conventional war films do—on the observer's fascination with violent incident. As a man who has been left "a little saner" (170) by the war, the moment of learning seems all but lost.

Those "special effects" that have made the war film a popular commodity now invigorate the writing of the journalist. His concern is not with the appalling civilian casualties of the war, or its persistent effect on the Vietnamese people, but his own self-conscious, cinematic energies. If Vietnam was prepared for in the video culture of the 1950s,[24] so the needs of that culture and its sense of style are effectively realized in the making of *Dispatches*. The narrator reminds us of those naive kids "who got wiped out by seventeen years of war movies" and who perform "little guts-and-glory Leatherneck tap dances under fire" (169) whenever television crews are in the vicinity. The cinema is now fully ingrained upon the sensibility of those who

fight and those who write. As the writer admits, "we have all been compelled
to make our own movies . . . and this one is mine" (153).

What *Dispatches* lacks is a sense of social inquiry. Observations and
indictments are glamorous and casual. There is no examination of the long-
term damage done by marines to the Vietnamese women whom they lay
before getting stoned, like heroes, on China Beach during R & R; or of the
damage sustained by the wives of journalists, patronizingly described as
"bored, distracted, frightened, unhappy" (187). Worst of all there are no
Vietnamese. If they do exist they are stylized and featureless. In the city they
appear to be defiled, in the forest diseased. If they support the Republic, they
exist under the corrupt influence of Western imperialism; if they support the
communist cause, they act like devils, ancient enemies in the ancient woods
whose natural home is the territory of the Antichrist.

For Westerners there is "glamor" in "danger" and "glamor" in corruption
(40). To live in Saigon is to sit "inside the folded petals of a poisonous flower."
The city has a poisoned "history"; it is "fucked in its root no matter how far
back you wanted to run your trace." In Saigon the past is "expelled . . . like
a toxin, Shit, Piss and Corruption." Saigon is an amalgam of rottenness; its
weather, its smells, its atmosphere are all polluted. "Paved swamps, hot
mushy winds that never cleared anything away, heavy thermal seal over
diesel field, mildew, garbage, excrement, atmosphere" (41). So absolute is
the corruption of the city that the people are barely recognized as human
beings, so dwarfed are they by the overpowering hostility of the environment
into which they are compressed. They scrabble through the streets like corrupt "puppets," "thousands" of them "in the service of a pyramid that wouldn't
stand for five years" (38), alleviating their "despair" and "impacted rage" by
"screaming obscure arguments at each other, cadging off Americans, stealing
tips from their tables" (39). Communication is not possible with the Vietnamese; their misunderstanding of life appears both "obsessive" and fundamental. A history that has been stolen from them by others reaps its own
perverted reward on the streets: "In the late afternoon the Cowboys would
leave the Cafes and the milk bars and ride down hard on Lam Son Square
to pick the Allies. They could snap a Rolex off your wrist like a hawk hitting
a field mouse" (39). The company of Americans is an obvious relief. As one
soldier who has lost his camera says, "I'm goin' back to the war, man, this
fucking Saigon is too much for me" (39). The Vietnamese survive not only
because they are corrupt but because they are able to withstand atrocity and
to commit atrocity. "All through the middle," says the narrator, were "the
Vietnamese, not always innocent bystanders, probably no accident that we'd
found each other" (42).

Comments like this require an explanation that is not forthcoming in
the text. Instead, what we are given is a view of a people who are doomed
by the fatality of history, a catalog of racial judgments offered on the basis
of what appears to be true, not what is known from personal contact. The

Vietnamese are guilty because they are different, because, unlike the Americans, they observe their surroundings but do not admit their reaction to them. Like the ARVN soldiers who congregate around the "stacked" bodies of marines, they stare silently and appear "death-enthralled like all Vietnamese" (71). "Death" may be the narrator's specialty, but Vietnam isn't.

If the South is suspect, the North is ghoulish. The NVA are the freaks from the horror show, creatures from the black lagoon, spooks and gooks whose world is night and the obscurity of the woods which are dark with something other than night. In their presence Herr's persona embodies a contradiction at the heart of the American soul. If the woods are capable of inspiration, they are also the place of our moral undoing. Nature can liberate colloquial and ceremonial energies, but it also shelters the Puritan blackman. When the narrator refers to those "proto-Gringos who found the New England woods too raw and empty for their peace and filled them up with their own imported devils" (46), he refers to his own historical experience.

Dispatches conforms to Leslie Fiedler's belief that at times American literature "seems a chamber of horrors disguised as an amusement park 'fun house,' where we pay to play at terror." Here is all "the cheapjack machinery of the gothic novel . . . called on to represent the hidden blackness of the human soul and human society."[25] In *Dispatches* the burden of "blackness" is shouldered by an invisible enemy—one that sees but cannot be seen—an enemy whose vagueness at the time of battle and whose "haunted" values are spine-chilling. In the Saigon-Cholon area there are four Viet Cong battalions that nobody can pin down, "dread sappers, guerrilla superstars" who "didn't have to do anything to put the fear out" (40). At Khe Sanh, the North Vietnamese "suddenly" materialize after midnight and take the camp at Langvei with a "style" that sends the Marines "insane" (94). Not only have the Vietnamese used tanks to overrun the camp but they have done so with an eerie silence that terrifies the marines who survive. As the terror builds to a frantic pitch, the narrator imagines wave after wave of Communist troops overwhelming the American positions. The delirious, irresistible attack on the defenses of Khe Sanh becomes a dramatic expression of "ghostly" (95) theater, imagined but not actually witnessed. The reader is thrilled, barely able to withstand the assault, as the prose achieves a breathless intensity.

The feeling of terror at Khe Sanh is emphasized by the uncivilized wilderness. Khe Sanh is Montagnard country, a historically unattractive place for those who seek to subdue the woods. The Montagnards might be allies but the Highlands where they live is a "sinister" and baffling place smothered in triple canopy jungle. The narrator finds it frightening and offensive; it inclines him toward a Puritan mind-set that his backwoods style ostensibly renounces: "The Puritan belief that Satan dwelt in Nature could have been born here, where even on the coldest, freshest mountaintops you could smell jungle and that tension between rot and genesis that all jungles give off."

The Highlands are "spooky beyond belief" (79), and the Montagnards who live there are "a kind of up-graded, demi-enlightened Annamese aborigine." Anthropological inquiry is passed over and the narrator prefers to describe in detail the physical effect of their appearance on Western observers. The Montagnards, he says, have a "sheer, awesome ugliness" that makes the Americans who are "forced to associate with them a little uncomfortable" (80). Their home is a "ghost-story country" full of vile "surprises" and the occasional "horror" of the hidden enemy of the North.

As a cultural text *Dispatches* is agoraphobic. The only spaces that excite the narrator are the ones inhabited by Westerners and, in particular, by the "radical, wigged-out crazies" of Vietnam, the grunts and correspondents that the narrator describes as "an authentic subculture" (189).

What that "subculture" endorses is a vision that repudiates seriousness, since to be serious, in Sartre's terms, is an act of *mauvais foi*—"bad faith." Seriousness has taken America into Vietnam; the earnest pursuit of imperialist goals has created the insanity of a genocidal war. In contrast to the idea that there is one right way—the American way—in which things ought to be done, the counterculture offers an idea of play, a stylish philosophy that is able to deny, as Johan Huizinga puts it, "the absolute determinism of the cosmos."[26] In the presence of extravagant authority, play becomes a necessary act, a means of preserving our sense of freedom through a creative demonstration of our sense of self. By being what he is—a creature in the pursuit of unity in the face of chaos—the player enters the human community, the true camaraderie of life in Vietnam. By preserving his awareness of the absurd, he affirms his own condition, he becomes a creature of rules and values. As Paul Fussell tells us, "seeing warfare as theatre provides a psychic escape for the participant: with a sufficient sense of theatre, he can perform his duties without implicating his real self."[27]

= Transcending Vietnam =

It is the ability to perform under stress, to protect one's self through farce and parody that is perceived as being the real achievement of the counterculture in Vietnam. The narrator's friends, Dana Stone, Tim Page, and Sean Flynn, are pantomime artists who play-act their way through the Vietnam War. They are, we are told, great adventurers, the "gamecocks of the wilderness" who wander endlessly in search of truth.[28] If Sean Flynn is "glamorous" (158), then Tim Page is "extravagant" (189), the self-made hero as world entertainer. Page is also the narrator's alter ego, a man whose language and life-style are a living demonstration of the need for show and self-publicity. Page is the archetypal "sixties kid, a stone-cold freak in a country where the madness raced up the hills and into the jungles, where everything essential to learning Asia, war, drugs, the whole adventure, was close at hand" (189). The reputation Page has, and the "great affection" (189) in which he is held, proves to the writer the value of "goofing" (197). It also explains the essential irrelevance of understanding Asia. Page is not of Vietnam but above it. He describes the Vietnamese with all the vanity and narcissism of the arch poseur. "Minh phung, auk bguayang gluke poo phuc fuck fart, I mean you should have heard those beastly people" (190). Vietnam, to him, is best understood through the styles of the sixties, by examining the war on the basis of a wisdom received from elsewhere: "history, rock, Eastern religion . . . travels, literature" (191). For Page the war exists to prove an ideal that is previous to it. The exclusivity of his world means that he sees Vietnam not through the icons of those who live there but through those who go there to work, play and fight. The montage Page makes of the war from his hospital bed in New York and the emphasis on "us" and what made "us happy" undercuts the conviction "that Vietnam was what we had instead of happy childhoods" (195). Vietnam is no more deprivation than it is opportunity. The war does not inhibit the sixties. What it gives the narrator is an opportunity to demonstrate its style and playfulness.

In *Dispatches* the war is confronted through gestures and ideals that are not germane to it. If this is true—as I think it is—and if the book concludes—as I feel it does—with nostalgic memories of American friends, then why the claim that it took the narrator "a year to understand" (13) what happened in Vietnam? What is it, we ask, that we need to understand so badly after all? And why the need for the pretense of difficulty? What, in truth, is the mystery of the message that the LURP cannot give us in the opening section?

The importance placed on the culture of the West (as a reference point for understanding the East) appears to undermine the value of the war as an influence on personal learning. If the material that we need to make sense of Vietnam is located in Western sources, then what is the mystery that removes Vietnam from Western understanding? If Vietnam is seen as a magnetizing force for our energy and our style, then, by definition, where there is no style there is no Vietnam. For this reason Vietnam as a country does not exist in *Dispatches*: its language isn't spoken, its customs do not thrive, its traditions have no bearing on the outcome of the war. The casualties of war are the casualties of energy: "Out on the street I couldn't tell the Vietnam veterans from the rock and roll veterans. The Sixties had made so many casualties, its war and its music had run power off the same circuit for so long they didn't even have to fuse" (206). The high emotional cost of the sixties is paid for in the same way by the same people in different locations, each performing an identical role. If this is the case, then the lesson of Vietnam is reduced to a minimum. If "Credentials" can mean listening to the music of Jimi Hendrix, we may as well listen. It is as good a way as any of learning about life.

Dispatches is a concoction that has little to do with Vietnam, a lot to do with the man who calls himself Michael Herr, and everything to do with what America is and the expectations of its reading public. The writer's desire to remain of interest to the culture he comes from and the one he now finds himself in results in a work that is all things to all people. Not only does the writer base his claim as a spokesman for the war on personal experience and moral necessity, but he produces a narrative that retrieves the wisdoms of the sixties. What the book lacks is a sense of its own self-contradiction. Although the writer appears to have straddled both decades, to have effectively satisfied the needs of his readers, he does not acknowledge that his desire for drama, the impulse of the sixties, and his need for investigation, the requirement of the seventies, prove incompatible. Just as Sean Flynn, the "great actor" who is last seen biking to Cambodia, got "swallowed . . . up" (203), so did the movement of which he was a member.

5

Odd, Unsovereign Flags

THE AMERICAN NOVELIST AND THE AMERICAN PUBLIC HAVE found Vietnam, as a country, difficult to square up to. Western versions of Vietnam remain predominantly self-enclosed and ethnocentric. Peter Marin perceives a "fundamental failure" in the American consciousness, an inability "to extend our own sense of human reciprocity or responsibility past the ordinary limits of family or nation to include those unlike ourselves."[1] Given the enormity of the human and ecological tragedy in Vietnam—3 million dead, 5 million wounded, 800,000 to 900,000 children orphaned, millions forced off the land, over 14 million tons of high explosives dropped, 19 million gallons of poison dumped on cropland and forest in U.S. chemical warfare operations—it is striking, as Noam Chomsky has written, that the "devastation that the United States left as its legacy has been quickly removed" from the national consciousness.[2] The payment of cultural reparations has not been forthcoming. In one of his lectures on human rights Jimmy Carter explained that America had no responsibility to give Vietnam any assistance because "the destruction was mutual." In other words, "we went to Vietnam without any desire to impose American will. . . . I don't feel that we ought to apologize or to castigate ourselves. . . . I don't feel that we owe a debt." As Noam Chomsky has said: "If words have meaning, this must stand among the most astonishing statements in diplomatic history."[3] But, as Chomsky goes on to point out, what was also interesting was the indifferent reaction to this remark among the liberal press and intelligentsia. The absence of any comment, almost as much as the statement itself, posted a warning to American writers that the Vietnamese people were not deserving of any recognition.

Many writers, says Ross McGregor, have shied away from recognizing the continuing problems of Vietnam. They show only a passing concern for the Vietnamese people whose "appalling suffering" they prefer to "background." "Lacking sufficient knowledge" of the people "to feel comfortable in characterising them," many of the novelists, as McGregor says, "merely sketch them" while concentrating on the American tragedy. "Although the war was fought externally amidst another people," he writes, "the American literature which emerges from it is self-absorbed and introspective."[4]

The charge of self-interest is difficult to refute, and there are good reasons why it has persisted. Certainly the Vietnam veterans—as a large percentage of those who have written about Vietnam are—have felt the need to come to terms with their own experience before they dealt with anyone else's. In most cases that experience was extremely narrow and did not allow for social intercourse with civilians. In the war the American soldier found himself culturally isolated from the Vietnamese people. The point is vividly illustrated in any number of novels in which, as Anne Malone tells us, "the fragments of the Vietnamese language at the soldier's command summon up only the most superficial features of Vietnamese life but convey succinctly the Americans' alien and intrusive presence in the land."[5] For a writer to enter Vietnam in his fiction, particularly if he wasn't an accomplished novelist, and to deal with a people even his own government had failed to understand, was a daunting challenge. In the aftermath of war there was little reason, if any, why the Vietnam veteran should accept that challenge. The immediate priority was to write about himself, not about a people with whom he had found it difficult to establish relations.

Those who did show an interest in the Vietnamese or in Vietnamese problems were often taken to task by the American press. Robert Muller, who led the first delegation of veterans back to Vietnam in the early 1980s, was shocked to find, on his return, that he was "criticized . . . for having the audacity to go and talk to the Communist leaders of a country with whom we do not have formal relations." Muller "came to understand" that it was the United States, not Vietnam, that was "suffering" from its "failure to end the war. To encounter the amount of hatred and bitterness from so many Americans toward the Vietnamese after having seen them look upon us as friends and allies and having witnessed them place the war in perspective, a part of their history, said an awful lot."[6]

For much of the 1970s and 1980s the conduct of the American government provided a stern warning to those who wished to help the Vietnamese. The U.S. government pursued policies that attempted to destabilize the Communist experiment in Indochina. In 1977 when India tried to send a hundred buffalo to Vietnam to replenish the herds destroyed by the war, the United States threatened to cancel "food for peace" aid to India. The Carter administration even denied rice to Laos where the agricultural system was destroyed by American bombing. In 1983 Oxfam America was not permitted to send ten solar pumps to Cambodia for irrigation, and in 1981 the U.S. government sought to block a shipment of school supplies and educational kits to Cambodia by the Mennonite church. Even though the American public in a *New York Times* poll of July 1977 showed that two-thirds of Americans supported sending food and medicine to Vietnam and a majority favored economic assistance that would have helped the country rebuild, the U.S. government consistently refused the Vietnamese people any help, thereby ensuring that postwar Vietnam remained on the brink of economic ruin.[7]

The American public has never been sufficiently well informed about the plight of the Vietnamese people or sufficiently motivated to voice its objections to what John McAulif has termed a "failure" of "political leadership."[8] As the experiences of Robert Muller (an active supporter of the establishing of economic links between the United States and Vietnam) have confirmed, Vietnam veterans have not been encouraged to develop an understanding of the Vietnamese. Even allowing for the vast numbers of boat people who have been permitted to live in the United States, one of the continuing tragedies of the war is that too many people "seem willing to consign" the people of Vietnam "to the periphery of a self-absorbed American consciousness." *Time* has described this attitude as one of "manic narcissism," and Peter McInerney sees the response as "a prolonged action of self-dramatisation by the nation."[9]

= A Cinema of Self-Interest =

With the exception of a cluster of alternative documentary films such as Felix Green's *Inside North Vietnam* (1968) and Emile de Antonio's *Year of the Pig* (1969), or the low-budget feature *The Iron Triangle* (1989), American cinema has appeared deeply suspicious of Asian culture and has portrayed the Vietnam War as an American, not a Vietnamese, tragedy. This is particularly true, says James C. Wilson, of "pseudo-Vietnam movies" such as *Taxi Driver* (1976), *Rolling Thunder* (1977), and *Heroes* (1977). Films like *Coming Home* (1978) "create the impression" that the war was an exclusively American tragedy, and *First Blood II* (more commonly known as *Rambo*), at the time of its release in 1985, was blamed by Peter Kiang of the Boston-based Asians for Justice for a severe rash of violence against Asian people in the United States. These films provide an impression "of the physical and psychological trauma suffered by Vietnam veterans," but few suggest that the Vietnamese might have suffered, also. To watch these films, says James Wilson, "one might assume that the Americans fought each other in the jungles of Vietnam."[10]

Most of the Vietnam war films pay homage to the myth that history is made by Americans and that Asian culture is largely unworthy of dramatic treatment. The film *Platoon* (1987), the first major Hollywood film to deal with the war in almost ten years, was feted by the critics as marking a watershed in the development of a liberal spirit of analysis and inquiry. "*Platoon*," said David Halberstam, "is the first real Vietnam film, and one of the great war movies of all time. The other Hollywood films have been a rape of history. But *Platoon* is historically and politically accurate."[11] Martin Scorsese said of Oliver Stone, the film's director, "No one else is doing the things he's doing. He's out there by himself."[12] *Platoon* demands our respect, we are told, because it signifies that the cultural and psychological remoteness of the American people from their Vietnamese enemies is now at an end. Here is a film made by a veteran that reflects a nation's willingness to come to terms with its own mistakes, to bare its soul and its grief in public, to recognize the crimes it committed, and to declare unambiguously its revulsion for what it did in the muted gloom and darkness of the jungle. Here is the reawakening of the liberal conscience for all to see. Here is an America that has turned the corner and said good-bye to revisionist history and Rambo myths.

Yet *Platoon* is little different from the films that preceded it. It is another example of an ethnocentric American film that satisfies a liberal conscience by appearing to come clean on the question of American atrocities in Vietnam. The purpose of much of the film is to make Vietnam synonymous with America, to blot out the culture of the host country with the paraphernalia of American machinery, with the words and rituals of American soldiers and the massive evidence of American dead. What *Platoon* opens up is familiar territory, the dope and dementia, rock-and-roll war. This is America's version of Vietnam—not Vietnam, but Nam, where the war is jungle and the jungle is hell and nothing else matters. At best the Vietnamese people are patronized with token, pitifully inadequate roles and a dutiful but shallow acknowledgment of the atrocities committed against them. The difficult truth that the film ought to have brought to our attention is completely ignored. As Max Hastings says, "It was not the isolated cases of American murders of civilians, or even the commoner incidents of careless or reckless bombing and shelling, that cost their cause so dear. It was the subtler impact of years of casual, careless American discourtesy toward the Vietnamese people, cultural condescension for a nation without a dozen television channels, open contempt for them in a thousand ways."[13]

Perhaps the film *Good Morning, Vietnam* goes some of the way toward acknowledging the existence of such "contempt." But again it places its primary emphasis on the character and culture of the United States—especially its music and the restorative vision of the 1960s—rather than on the Vietnamese people, most of whom support or assist the central character in his discovery of Vietnam. Asians are at their most lovable, the film seems to be saying, whenever they perform their party tricks: play baseball, learn American slang, engage our emotional sympathies in the love scenes. As long as the Vietnamese are recognizable and familiar, and yet willing to modernize themselves, they are acceptable. Once they become Viet Cong guerrillas, the show's over.

= *The Quiet American* =

The tendency to ignore the social fabric of Vietnamese life in the popular and political culture of the United States is a recurrent rather than a recent phenomenon. The stereotyped role of the Vietnamese in American comic books such as *Marvel, DC*, and *Power* during the war and, more recently, in the 1980s, gives some indication of the extent to which we are prepared to use popular culture as a way of perpetrating racism.[14] The tendency to push the enemy out of sight in the popular comics has been continued in fiction. According to Asa Baber, the American novelist has reneged on the chance to provide his reader with an image of Asia and has failed to convey the sense of place on which all Vietnam literature must depend. Such is the public indifference and so endemic are the feelings of racism in American life that the novelist has been scared away from the subject. Baber's *The Land of a Million Elephants*, a novel that attempted to deal with the Vietnamese in 1970, was never reviewed. The only explanation Baber can provide is that the novel's hero was an Asian wise man, Buon Kong, not a white man, and that the American people "couldn't relate to that."[15]

The problem of cultural isolationism was first observed by Graham Greene in the 1950s. Greene's novel, *The Quiet American* (1955), perceives the American involvement in Vietnam as a tragedy of manners, and it identifies a continuing problem for the American people in their social and cultural relationships with the Vietnamese. In *The Quiet American* Vietnam has become a slough of despond. The pilgrim, in the person of Alden Pyle, has a duty "to do good" (18), to save the country from political ruin and the sin of communism. As the member of an economic legation, Pyle is "innocent" (31); with his simpleminded intellect he wishes "to improve" things (18), to spread the message of Christian democracy, and to halt the menace of red atheism. But Pyle does not learn from the place in which he lives. His eyes are closed to a devotional world that reveals itself in moments of idleness. For the older "colonists" (157) like Fowler, Pyle's "innocence is a kind of insanity" (162), a sublime condition of guiltlessness that American dreamers, with their obsessive belief in the role of the West, "their private stores of Coca-Cola and their portable hospitals and their too wide cars" (31), impose on the world. Relationships with an enemy are prohibited, as is acquainting oneself with the enemy's landscape.

Pyle is the antithesis of Fowler, the English narrator. In Fowler's Vietnam, relationships are possible at all moments and meanings cannot be contained within roles.

> [Pyle] would have to learn for himself the real background that held
> you as a smell does: the gold of the rice-fields under a flat late sun:
> the fisher's fragile cranes hovering over the fields like mosquitoes:
> the cups of tea on an old abbot's platform, with his bed and his
> commercial calendars, his buckets and broken cups and the junk of
> a life-time washed up around the chair: the mollusc hats of the girls
> repairing the road where a mine had burst: the gold and the young
> green and the bright dresses of the south, and in the north the deep
> browns and black clothes and the circle of enemy mountains and the
> drone of planes. (25)

Vietnam is Fowler's "home," not his mission. He gains access to it through meditation and opium smoking, actions that lack any clearly defined social purpose. Pyle is engagé; he has no capacity for imaginative inquiry, no ability to observe the epiphanies that come to those who spend their time "living in the open" (144). Pyle's Vietnam is contained in his perception of its criminality and negligence. Where Fowler lives in awe of his surroundings, Pyle is impatient with them. Where Fowler is fascinated when Phuong does "her hair differently, allowing it to fall back and straight over her shoulders," Pyle is irritated, critical of "the elaborate" (12) and decorous approach. Pyle can understand Vietnam only as a representation of remembered debate and previously inculcated opinions. "He never saw anything he hadn't heard in a lecture-hall," Fowler tells Vigot. "When he saw a dead body he couldn't even see the wounds" (32).

Fowler is jealous of the new colonialism that Pyle represents. Pyle is seen as a political tourist whose "mission" of improvement is at odds with a world that reveals itself in its idleness, in the chatter of its streets and alleys, in the mannered triviality of those who sit around "doing nothing," like the women in Fowler's house who gossip on the landing outside the urinoir. Vietnam, as Fowler discovers, can be known only in its throwaway moments. Thus the key to the mysterious explosions in Saigon is revealed when Fowler roots through the clutter on the Quai Mytho, the crowded theater of its warehouses, and the "pantomime set" of Cholon. "I could see the strange Picasso shapes of the junk-pile by the light of an old lamp: bedsteads, bathtubs, ashcans, the bonnets of cars, stripes of old colour where the light hit"

(125). Fowler is able to see, "with difficulty," not only the junk and the clutter but what lies beyond: "the narrow track" that leads to the house of Mr. Chou, and the discovery of molds that are used for the plastic explosives that Pyle imports. Patience is required in the company of those who "pay no attention" (125) to intruders, like Chou's family. They identify themselves by the noise they make at Mah-Jongg, a game that is likened to the sound of "shingle turning on a beach after a wave withdraws" (125). In this closely observed landscape, gestures are profoundly important, the "occupations" of the elderly, the brewing of strong tea, the rinsing of cups, the act of spitting. Like the Englishman John Head and the Dutchman Van Braam in Pham Van Ky's *Les Contemporains* (1959) Fowler tries to encounter the East through observation in order to appreciate the naturist mysticism of the country and the communal identity of the Vietnamese.

The manners of an established culture have little meaning for a vigorous evangelist like Alden Pyle. In his attitude he reminds us of an earlier Bostonian, the Puritan Mr. Wentworth in Henry James's *The Europeans*. Like Wentworth, Pyle has acquired the formality of vision that makes him intolerant of the customs of other countries. As a "quiet" but dedicated missionary, Pyle is governed by a righteous philosophy of anticommunism in which life is discipline, not opportunity, and ideas are gleaned from reality instructors like York Harding. Harding's work, *The Advance of Red China*, is regarded by Pyle as "a very profound book," a perception that clearly anticipates the approaching tragedy of American involvement in Vietnam. In *The Quiet American* that tragedy is defined as the result of deficient imagination and cultural ignorance. Pyle's Vietnam is a dogma of the elect, and his views represent the antifictional prejudices of his Puritan forebears. Predictably, Pyle has "an enormous respect for what he called serious writers. That term excluded novelists, poets and dramatists unless they had what he called a contemporary theme, and even then it was better to read the straight stuff as you got it from York" (24).

= The Secret Reality of the War =

The critic Gordon Taylor sees *The Quiet American* as "an established point of reference for those interested in problems of literary response to the war"[16] (note the assumption that Greene is responding to the war rather than to the Vietnamese or to the conflict of values that might exist between those who live in Vietnam and those who merely visit it). He also believes that the novel is no longer of concern for those of us who wish to understand the war's " 'secret' reality" (301). The abolition of formal geography, the replacing of a country by the events of a war, the fluidity of political and moral belief —these issues, says Taylor, have swallowed up the idea of a fixed place and created "a black hole" in "space"—one whose "concentrations of chaos" are "too pure and powerful to be resisted" by conventional estimates of character, location, and plot. In this environment language must be commensurate with experience and "the images of timeless color and line" in Greene's novel (303) can no longer contain aesthetic form, which has become too jagged. American writers have superseded the achievement of an old colonial like Graham Greene and have created "meanings" that "fix" the war firmly within the American "national consciousness."

Since what we are dealing with, says Taylor, "is a subject resisting definition by literary precedent" (295) the Vietnam experience in recent literature benefits from the "revised angles of literary approach" and the "literary experimentation already under way in the 1960s." American writers, as Taylor defines them, "find their own ways of differentiating themselves from Greene's example" (296), and Taylor sees this as a vital and legitimate separation if our experience of the war and, by implication, the literary consciousness of the United States are to develop. Vietnam writing, says Taylor, must be seen not in the context of the country (Vietnam) but in the context of an American aesthetic. *Dispatches* is important because it extrudes pure American energy. "The nervous jags and adrenaline bursts of combat situations come through in whipcord loops of words whose cadences are threaded with the rhythms of rock and jazz, laced also with the terminology of electronics, and stitched to human facts by the authentically rendered speech of the grunts" (300). Herr has no obligation, says Taylor, to incorporate the "cadences" of Vietnamese speech since the war in Vietnam—and therefore the American presence—has overrun the country. "Words come from the other side of a line, or from deep within a warp," and the writer is compelled to enter that "warp," to enter the "black hole" of moral and linear space (307). The task is one of "finding forms commensurate with the extremity of the experience," of "transcribing" the energies of an atonal war. At the "extremity" of experience Herr risks the abolition of his own existence in order to identify the lack of outline, the absence of moral or physical boundary in Vietnam (301). The pursuit of new spatial energies generates new literary material and a new Vietnam, one that replaces the politics and purpose of an ancient country and an ancient war. Herr's work, says Taylor, is the realization of the spirit of the age, a symbol of abstract form in a country in which the loss of recognizable territory is a consequence of Western interference. In *Dispatches* the narrator's initial admission, says Taylor, supports this view: "It was '67 now, even the most detailed maps didn't reveal much anymore; reading them was like trying to read the faces of the Vietnamese, and that was like trying to read the wind. We knew that the uses of most information were flexible, different pieces of ground told different stories to different people. We also knew that for years now there had been no country here but the war" (11). What is required, says Taylor, is a new cartography, a definition of modern geographic possibilities, of states of citizenship and nationality in which the spokesmen on events are not the Vietnamese but the newly conscious or "born again."

Confronted by the awesome energy of the United States, Graham Greene cannot be updated, says Taylor, but he can be effaced. "American writers have now begun to make of the war what they must, in order to tell us what Graham Greene could not." *Dispatches* puts the old colonial voyeur in his place, which is "the background" (308). Says Taylor, Greene's "age, nationality, main concerns as a novelist, and early 1950s vantage on French and American influence in Southeast Asia, to say nothing of twenty years in literary-historical as well as geo-political time between his book and Herr's would obviously and unsurprisingly make for fundamental differences in approach and literary execution" (306–7). Since the Vietnam that Graham Greene knew does not exist any more, says Taylor, any discussion of its social fabric no longer makes sense. The "quest for alternative form" and the presence of "alternative literary strategies" reduce the need to observe a world through its civilians. Herr writes a "very different" novel "from a center Greene seems at once still to occupy and no longer usefully to provide" (296). The decision that Herr has taken, says Taylor, under the imprint of postmodernism, to fuse and combine "the resources of several genres rather than settle into established prose patterns" allows us to "reflect internally on problems of literary procedure presented by new social and psychic 'information' " generated by the war (297). In a war "where traditional rules no longer apply" the postmodernist text is an act of liberation, an expression of cultural democracy which frees the reader from the limitations of history and the procedural constraints of those who equate Vietnam with recognizable territory. As Philip Beidler confirms, the task of the Vietnam writer is "to create a landscape that never was, one might say—a landscape of consciousness where it might be possible to accommodate experience remembered within a new kind of imaginative cartography."

To critics like Beidler the metaphors of navigation and cartography give a firm indication of the writer's disagreement with tradition and his need to imagine the Vietnam War as "a place with no real points of reference."[17] The writer, says Thomas Myers in his book *Walking Point: American Narratives of Vietnam*, undertakes a hazardous but necessary duty. He is a "key figure" in a war in which the conventional grids of historical and military reference are absent or deficient. As personal narrator he is the man at the "forward" end of experience, he is "the eyes, ears, and brain" for those whose progress depends "on his intuition, his powers of observation, and his creative decisions." The point man sees what no one else does. He probes "the new terrain" of Vietnam, able to "use his finely tuned senses to record and to assess changing situations, unexpected problems." He translates his suspicions and visions of the country into practical pursuits in the narrative; as "guide and protector" he sees the heart of darkness in Vietnam, "the thick undergrowth of mythic space" where "the enemy is clearly positioned and well equipped."[18] The point man is a privileged witness who observes a world that is always menacing and an enemy that is always adversarial. Because of the difficulty of making sense of the enemy's movements, "the imaginative products of the newest point men are necessarily incomplete, inherently unstable, and deeply challenging" (32).

While Myers clearly emphasizes the importance of personal history in the construction of literary narrative, his analysis defines the war in Vietnam as an exclusively American affair. As a person who treads "on new mythic ground" (8) the point man acts as a "custodian" of Western values, a scout or detective who seeks out a hidden "foe of prodigious power" (33). The duties of the point man, says Myers, as well as his loyalties and obligations, are those of a Westerner, a man willing and able to identify the enemy to a disadvantaged reader and to warn that reader of his presence in the text. The job of the point man is not to intercede on behalf of Vietnam but to see the war as an extension of "new American terrain" (33). Since Vietnam is no more than a war zone and the Vietnamese people are never any more than physically sensed, the writer notes their position in the text, but does not consider their culture or society aesthetically noteworthy. The point man is committed to an American adventure, says Myers, an excursion in which the Vietnamese people—since they cannot be understood—assume a subordinate role in the novel. By implication, a novelist who writes from a Vietnamese point of view, or who downgrades the American presence in the text, is liable to be accused of abandoning his primary duty, which is to distance the reader from the Vietnamese.

= Exploring Vietnam =

Those writers who resist the tendency to see Vietnam as a place of military activity in which the American experience is preeminent have received scant attention in literary criticism. In 1988 W. D. Ehrhart voiced his "despair with the neglect of Vietnam war poetry by the academic community," a neglect that is damaging precisely because of the interest the war poets have shown in the Vietnamese people. Even though the range of poetic writing on Vietnam has been considerable—especially since the publication of a "seminal anthology," *Winning Hearts and Minds*, in 1972—what disturbs Ehrhart is that his article on Vietnam war poetry, published in *Virginia Quarterly Review* in 1986, "remains, to my knowledge, the only comprehensive survey of Vietnam war poetry in the public domain."[19]

Some relief for Ehrhart has been provided by the English critic Jeff Walsh. In his recent studies of Vietnam war poetry, Walsh directs our attention to those soldier-poets who address the problem of their own cultural separation from Vietnam. Of all writers, says Walsh, only poets have been willing "to demonstrate a profound awareness of the structure and feeling of Vietnamese culture." Writers like Jan Barry, Walter Macdonald, Basil Paquet, John Balaban, and Bruce Weigl are, in a sense, an embarrassing presence in the literature of the war. Their work illustrates the extent to which most Americans in Vietnam were "unable to transcend their own ethnocentrism" and "were separated from the country they were ostensibly liberating by the gulf of language, religion, family institutions and politics." American poets, says Walsh, have found the Vietnamese people much less threatening than have other groups of writers and have shown themselves more susceptible to the influence of custom and culture. This "underlying attachment to the tradition and order of Vietnamese life" is particularly apparent in the work of John Balaban, a writer whose understanding of Vietnam derives from his work with injured children during the war years, his particular interest in Vietnamese oral poetry, and his collection of songs published in translated form in *Ca Dao Vietnam* (1980).[20] Balaban's work and the impetus for it— rooted as they are in the life and rhythms of a rural and traditional world— run counter to that "American experiential axis" which has proven such a commercial success in recent years. Balaban's poetry shows an awareness of "Vietnamese culture and custom" and "is predicated on a Vietnamese register and structure of feeling." Since Balaban "has no burden of personal guilt to escape," his work permits "a freedom of viewpoint and subject matter" that takes him away from traditional preoccupations.[21]

In our discussions of the Vietnam War, those who write about the Viet- namese people are often relegated to the periphery. In criticism we continue to regard the Vietnamese as second-class citizens, culturally impoverished, socially unimportant, and aesthetically dull. Their presence has yet to fire the imagination of those of us who bring to Vietnam much of the cultural baggage—and the cultural prejudices—of a vast colonial undertaking. The tragedy of indifference is the continuing tragedy of the war itself: the failure to recognize that the war in Vietnam belongs to the country, not the country to the war. For Graham Greene this was the problem that lay at the heart of the American dilemma in Indochina.

=== The Forgotten South ===

At a conference on *Vietnam and the West* held at the University of Wales, Swansea, in 1988, the English novelist Mark Frankland spoke eloquently on the problem of "The Forgotten South" and of the difficulty he felt existed in re-creating a world that "had disappeared without being properly recorded" —a world that not only had "vanished" but also that too many people easily "despised." Frankland knows Vietnam not as a soldier but as a correspondent based in Saigon from 1967 to 1975. After his departure he recalls seeing *The Deer Hunter*. "It seduced me with its marvellously accurate American

scenes," he writes, but "it repelled me by its ludicrous depiction of the Vietnamese." The film, says Frankland, "set a pattern for many later American
movies and novels about Vietnam" in which "the South Vietnamese and the
French who dragged America into the first Indochina War against the Viet
Minh came to be presented as the worthless causes of the degradation, mutilation and death of young Americans." For Frankland "the process had
reached its almost logical end in Stanley Kubrick's *Full Metal Jacket*. My
memory may deceive, but I think that the only South Vietnamese in Kubrick's
movie with speaking parts—and they are tiny ones—are two pimps and two
prostitutes. There is also a Vietcong girl sniper whose role is similar to that
of the brave but lethal Indian in Westerns. The American Vietnam War
movie—I mean those centered on action in Vietnam—will have achieved
perfection when there are no native characters to be heard or seen at all."[22]

In Frankland's novel *The Mother-of-Pearl Men* (1985) the "native" world
of Vietnam and, in particular, the city of Saigon, reveal their identity in
layers.[23] Frankland offers us the chance to consider a country that is visibly
beautiful but culturally obscure. Obstructions to clear-sightedness are placed
in our path. Vietnam requires patience as well as stamina. Saigon is hazy,
sometimes smogbound; in the morning it is wreathed in the smoke of charcoal
fires. As a political and business capital the city is overcrowded and suffocating; we feel the tensions of a densely packed, thinly partitioned city, with
its émigrés and infiltrators. We enter a place of subversive and seething
energy overridden with the paranoia of imminent collapse, an underground
of labyrinthine tunnels, shacks, and back alleys, of buildings with corridors
that wander in a maze through secret, airless, and obscure rooms, of windows
and doors that open up to an atmosphere of "bad temper" in the streets and
offices, an aggressiveness made worse by the realization that in the stifling,
midsummer, oriental heat, one cannot go anywhere "without being spied on"
(15). But for all the burden of tension the novel carries on its journey through
the alleys and boulevards of Saigon, there is an openness of spirit in Frankland's work, a willingness to ignore the risks and encumbrances and wander
through obscure passageways. It is in these places and in these rooms, airless
and smelling of incense, that Vietnam finally reveals itself, amid the obscure,
unattended furniture and the forgotten contents "thick with dust" that sometimes glow with "the faint luminescence of mother-of-pearl" (109). Frankland's Vietnam reveals itself to those who observe it as an imaginative exercise
and to those who pursue it with courage and tenacity. Little is conclusively
proved by that pursuit and, as a dramatic experience, little of substance is
achieved or resolved. The complexity of Vietnam's transaction with history
has created a surface of complex appearances and textures, and the social
and cultural identity of the country is exposed and peeled away only in layers.
Frankland is aware, as Lucy Nguyen tells us, that "Vietnamese culture is
strikingly syncretic" and that to know the country is to understand the overlay

of "Confucianism, Buddhism, Taoism and Roman Catholicism" that "co-existed harmoniously there until the advent of Communism."[24]

In *The Mother-of-Pearl Men* the legacy of colonial influence—the presence of Chinese, Japanese, Portuguese, French—has resulted in an eclectic range of belief, one that predates the arrival of Western capitalism and the Marxism-Leninism of North Vietnam. The willingness of Vietnam to assimilate—though not always successfully—a variety of dissimilar cultural and ideological influences, all of which have played a part in the making of the country, manifests itself in a peculiar openness and a genuine spirit of inquiry as well as a feeling of restlessness. It is the spirit of the past—the conflicting influences of Eastern and Western imperialism—that has given the country its dense, subliminal graining, the "mysterious glowing colours" (136) of mother-of-pearl and ivory inlay.

The nature of syncretic faith and feeling is expressed in the Cao Dai religion. Caodaism combines Eastern and Western faiths—Buddhist, Confucianist, and Christian imagery—in an extravagant "show" of color that befits, as Graham Greene puts it, "the invention of a Cochin civil servant." In *The Quiet American* the Cao Dai festival at the Holy See in Tanyin is a fantasia of color in which "all truths are reconciled" (85). Partnership is the key word. "A Pope and female cardinal. Prophecy by planchette. Saint Victor Hugo. Christ and Buddha looking down from the roof of the cathedral on a Walt Disney fantasia of the East, dragons and snakes in technicolour" (83).

The Mother-of-Pearl Men extends the range of Greene's suggestions. Frankland gives us a novel that is both a celebration and a lament for a country that cannot resolve its generous yearnings for the outside world or provide for itself an affirmative definition of its own self-image. As the repository of trends and traditions Vietnam is to Frankland what it is to the filmmaker Emile de Antonio in *Year of the Pig* (1969), "the site of competing discourses rather than . . . a single unified text, a fact."[25] In an age of American cultural imperialism the country's achievements are easily overlooked. When confronted by the vast displacing power of the American military establishment, the syncretic quality of Vietnamese history is something "no one cares much to think about any more" (8).

Frankland's Vietnam is an oblique place. Like E. M. Forster, Frankland approaches the Orient as a land of mystery, and he interprets its effect on those who live in it and those who come to it. Both writers explore the relationship between the ancient and complex patterns of Asian civilization and the more "advanced" beliefs and activities of the West. Both writers question which worldview more effectively satisfies humanity's quest for certainty, although the answers both these writers provide are neither confident nor entirely spiritual. In *A Passage to India* and *The Mother-of-Pearl Men* the clash of cultures is between a subject people and a colonial regime. In both cases the host environment is found to be equivocal, intricate, and strange; for the Western visitor nothing is immediately identifiable, nothing quite fits, and reason and form are easily frustrated. In India the natural world is implacable and malign; in Vietnam it is debilitating and deceitful. Vietnam abolishes barriers between animate and inanimate forms, confuses the essential distinction between objects, and encourages feelings of profound irritation. Like *A Passage to India, The Mother-of-Pearl Men* is able to temper those feelings of irritation with a promise of discovery. In both novels man's capacity for curiosity and the boundless possibilities of his imagination lead him to assume that there are always further realms to be penetrated.

In Frankland's novel that sense of possibility is beyond the reach of most American civilians who work and live in South Vietnam. The cultural complexity of the country is something the United States is ill-equipped to deal with, for it sees Vietnam as a place in which to seek confirmation of the truths of Puritanism and colonialism. Vietnam exists to be controlled and administered as a fortress. The elliptical manner of the Vietnamese people is seen as a plot to deceive the virtuous. Any real intercourse is avoided, and despite the cry of bringing "civilization" the American purpose is merely to patronize the culture of a subject people. Official relationships take the place of human ones, social intimacy is limited, and those who rely on colonial goodwill must ingratiate themselves in order to receive it. Divorced from the land and the people who live on it, the American Raj lack intellectual curiosity and act like cold fish in the excessive heat.

Frankland sees the American in Vietnam as an interloper, a stranger who lacks the cultural experience to unravel the delicate web of Vietnamese life. Culturally underresourced, its appreciation of Vietnam impoverished, the American mission does not distinguish between the various classes of life in Vietnam—peasant and merchant, bureaucrat and aristocrat, métis and bourgoisie. Instead, the Americans see the Vietnamese as an undifferentiated social mass, a melting pot of unpredictable "adolescents" (141). According to Phap Long, the eccentric devotionist monk in the Pagoda of True Enlightenment, the Americans do not begin to compare with those who have come before them: the French, Japanese, or Chinese. "Strangely, one hardly notices the Americans," says Phap Long. "They are noisy but very obsessed with themselves. They do not know how to sting us like the French" (106). To identify with the spirit of Vietnam is to rid oneself of cultural conceit, "to understand," as Michael Bishop tries to do, "how seductive" Vietnam "must have been" for the first French settlers who were given the "chance to combine Europe with the tropics in a kind of beauty the earth had never seen before" (10).

Bishop is our guide and Frankland's choice of a lucid reflector, an innocent abroad who is capable of perceiving the seductive linkages that exist between Europe and the Orient. Bishop is a diffident character whose gentle manner is considered most likely to win the confidence of the mysterious Thai, an English-educated Vietnamese half-caste who, as the novel opens, is wanted by the West and has defected to the Viet Cong. Bishop, who works for a commercial bank in Saigon, is given the job of persuading Thai to leave the Viet Cong and then delivering him safely to British control. Bishop is selected for the job by Gruson, a British diplomat who works in Saigon, because he has that "aura of reliability that someone like Thai finds very reassuring" (119). Bishop is also curious. He is willing to peer into the depths of the Vietnamese underworld, to ignore the presence of Puritan ghosts, until the Vietnamese people reveal themselves—like the frog that comes at night into his garden—without fear of betrayal.

Bishop's Vietnam is an uncertain world of eclectic belief, a country that chooses not to offer the reader the "clean adventure" or the sort of story that is "only appealing" to the "ignorant" (131). Bishop's work takes in extremes of etiquette and aesthetic manner; his inquiries show a keenness to observe those acts of "casual American discourtesy," a willingness to record the small, flickering gestures that might provide some essential clue to the climate and culture of Indochina. The quest is generous yet doomed to failure. Bishop's Vietnam is constantly attempting to escape itself, to obscure the torment of its own divided personality, to resolve the dilemma of a disparate mind. The country puts up contradictory signs. It is symbolized by the Saigon barman with "a cast in one eye that protected him from enquiring stares," yet still allowed him "to enjoy the impression he made" (178). Bishop's talent is an ability to discern the styles of assimilation and discord, the coupling together of dissimilar energies and modes of expression. Yet little if anything of what Bishop discovers is shared by those ensconced in the Western enclosures: the hotel bar on Tu Do Street, for example, to which most of the Americans in the novel gravitate and from which they observe a hostile and unreceptive world.

Bishop avoids a life of static encounter; he moves through the city and "the countryside" (165) in search of practical and aesthetic experience. As he says, "the chance to do something, now that it had been presented to me, seemed more attractive than an evening with the whisky bottle" (137). His opportunism gets him involved, as Maurice Tan says, in "a very complicated business" (41), a world rich in artifacts and memorabilia, a country layered over with inscriptions and colors and the fragments of a barely observable history.

In the house of Thai's cousin we come across something of the essential range of that historical experience, the extent to which the affairs of life are governed by the pursuit of exotic manners:

> I walked round the big room. There were three large cupboards against the back wall, each inlaid with fine mother-of-pearl flowers, far grander than the ones in the old woman's house: I found the mother-of-pearl's acid, underwater colours oddly threatening. Incense sticks and a bouquet of plastic flowers, their colour almost vanished

beneath the dust, stood on the top of each cupboard. Photographs hung on the walls, showing people in both Vietnamese and Western clothes. In one of them some young men in flannels and shirts stood round a low, long-bonneted car. . . . Perhaps they were Thai's father and his brothers, so alike then but now scattered by the years of war and transformed into fighters and non-combatants, sceptics and believers. (62)

Bishop observes the clothes, the costumes, the decor of Vietnam, the clutter piled up beneath the hard and simple surface of violence. By rummaging through a discarded past Bishop is able to discover the comings and goings of a culture that is caught up in the business of protecting itself, a country that is "sensitive," as Do himself is, to the faintest "unwelcoming look" (123). Bishop's Vietnam is a country of impressions where identities merge one with another and the reference points of social exchange appear to dissolve in the shifting light.

For those who lack empathy the natural world is a source of irritation. As the seasonal rains fall and bring relief to Saigon, Bishop's journey to rescue Thai nears its completion. For Harry Wynant, a young American banker, the ceremonial quality of the rain has no meaning. "What a country" he says, "what a goddamned country. Nothing here happens by halves. It's either dry or it's pissing down" (148). For a man with a "petulant" manner Wynant could hardly be further from the truth. The soul of Vietnam, as Thai once says, is in "no-man's land" (95), perpetually engaged in a dialogue with history, torn between the promise of an eclectic inheritance and the ideal of realizing an imagined self. For Wynant, Vietnam is unfamiliar territory. Since it is unfamiliar it can only be resisted, cleaned up, detoxified. Heat requires not rain but good air-conditioning; tension is alleviated not by natural process but by switching "parties" or one's choice of hotel. "I'm just off to the Continental to have a drink with some friends," says Wynant to Bishop. "That Caravelle slays me. The air-conditioning's only fit for a morgue. It beats me why they don't build places like the Continental any more: solid walls, plenty of air and ceiling fans" (149).

The need for a "solid," protective, Puritanical environment is indicated on a number of occasions. The American embassy is described as a "prison-like mass" with "high white protective walls" (128), and the military base Bishop drives past on the road to Bien Ho is ridiculed by Bishop's companion Ba. "Americans had only a ghost-like existence for him [Ba]. They were a flock of exotic birds who by some chance of nature had broken their flight in Vietnam but would not stay for long. He often commented on them but never suggested that they would ever change anything that was important in his life and thinking" (29). Ba rejects the American presence as a historically valid or valuable experience for Vietnam.

American social attitudes inhibit the development of a genuine rapport.

The lack of conspiracy or intimacy in America's relationship with Vietnam is exposed by the Francophile sympathies of the Vietnamese. The importance of French as a conversational language and the prevalence of Catholic religious activity in the "villages" (29), gives some indication of the extent to which colonial affiliations remain a possibility in the contemporary world. Bishop comes to understand what the French have achieved, in spite of the heat and "the noise and harsh sunlight." He has an artist's eye for landscape and the willingness of the traveler to enter that landscape before the sun is up. Bishop wanders through the streets of Nguyen Du in appreciation of its picturesque forms. "It was very pleasant there, with handsome brown-tiled villas built by the French and tall, smooth-trunked trees along the streets. It was beautiful in the early morning when the light was gentle and the air was grainy and smelt of charcoal fires." In a reflective mood Bishop believes he is walking back into history, so strong is the presence of "the dream of the Frenchmen who had built the city and planted its trees" (10). The foundations of the city streets offer an exemplary statement on those charismatic acts of partnership in history. As the narrator of *Into a Black Sun* puts it; "Vietnamese streets are a mixture of France and Asia, an octopus sitting on a chessboard, some intersecting in a grille pattern and others radiating from an open hub" (130).

In Saigon the Vietnamese have retained the styles of architecture that testify to the achievements of the past and to European standards of civility and cooperation. The Cercle Sportif club has "not changed since the time of French rule, with no air-conditioning but fans in the ceiling, old copies of French newspapers and huge armchairs designed for European bodies." Gruson, whose attitude toward the Vietnamese is similar to that of the American Raj, regards the mongrel culture of Vietnam as a debasement of true ideals. The food of the club "French in concept and Vietnamese in execution" (22) is, for him, a measure of the way the Vietnamese "have attacked" (rather than experimented with) "the decent old colonial standards of this club" (21)—whatever they were. Bishop, in order to uncover his quarry, must disregard such beliefs. He must look to an understanding of the meaning of partnership and overcome a tendency to regard the Vietnamese as mere "children" (22).

Acts of partnership, when properly undertaken, bear rich fruit. For Bishop the seed is sown when Ba—whom Gruson regards as a "hopeless character who hangs around doing odd jobs for journalists" (23)—calls at his house two evenings a week. "He had apparently decided to take me under his wing and to help me 'understand the situation' as he put it. This meant telling me the latest Saigon political gossip, a jumble of names, rumours and intricate theories of plots and intrigues. The lessons began the moment I pulled back the grille" (39). What Bishop begins to learn is that if Ba is not always reliable as a "guide" (40) to Saigon, he is a perfect exemplar of Vietnamese culture, that "world of half-Eastern, half-Western sounds" that one hears in the nightclubs of the city and in the "yearning" expressions of life in the village (124). Through Ba, Bishop gains access to a society that is colorful and "restless" (7). He learns a language of life that compels his attention because of its "energy" (8) and unworldliness. At times that energy is diffuse and abstracted and the mind gets tangled in the shifting loyalties of the moment. With Ba, and to a much greater extent Thai, the mother-of-pearl quality of Vietnam is flawed by an absence of self-discipline, by too much "confusion" and "contradictory" (40) opinions.

Occasionally the energy is more focused and persuasive. Thai's uncle, Maurice Tan, is a skilled performer and informer whose style is rooted in the confidence of his class. Tan's "costume and manner" remind Bishop "of photography I had seen of fashionable Vietnamese taken in the 1930s" (47). With his glossy hair and black-market Gitanes, Tan drinks scotch and ice in a club called the Pink Night. He also drives a "black Citroen, the kind you see in old French gangster movies," the body "beautifully polished and the walls of the tyres . . . painted white" (41). Who Tan works for and what he is after we are never sure except that his main concern is to collaborate with Bishop in getting Thai, his nephew, out of the country and away from the clutches of the North Vietnamese who threaten to undermine the values of his "home" (42). Tan's aspirations are those of a man who sees himself as a connoisseur of the values of the old South, the artful collaborator who has borrowed his manners from the West in order to convey his affinity with Western culture. Tan speaks fluent French, was baptized a Catholic, and lived in Paris as a student.[26] France was "marvellous" (44), but Tan has also fought with the maquis against the French in Vietnam. Tan steers a difficult course, therefore, between acting as an acquaintance and as an accomplice. For Gruson, "he's too close to the communists and he's too close to the French" (51), yet from what we can see he remains his own man. If he disapproves of the overwhelming infusion of colonial artifacts, he willingly appropriates what he wants.

In his quest "to combine Europe with the tropics" Tan is intolerant of Vietnam's failure to do likewise, its lapse into the syncretic at its most vulgar. He sees it as a duty to instruct the Vietnamese on their occasional crassness, to show how life ought to be conducted, how one ought to behave artfully in public. In the Pink Night Club a Vietnamese woman in white trousers sings a song to the music of the "Blue Danube Waltz" while "the audience listened with astonished admiration." Tan is horrified at the lack of decorum. For him it is "astonishing" that "after one hundred years of Western civilization" the Vietnamese people are capable of acting in such a "ridiculous" way (44). To prove the artful capacity of his race Tan takes Gruson and Bishop to a restaurant in a "dusty little town" outside the city. There he delights in "teasing" (55) his guests with an order of eggs that contain fertilized yolks and the embryos of chickens. Having unnerved Gruson, he then sets about the job of restoring his confidence. He does this "in a theatrically conspiratorial manner" (58) with a plan to get Thai out of the countryside and into Saigon. As a master of provocation Tan is successful because of his willingness to explain himself through illusion and disguise, his ability to sharpen his wits in public, which is one of "the specialities" of the Vietnamese (54).

Yet Tan is politically weak in that his propositions have little to sustain them other than the whimsical energies of partnership and the Vietnamese love of a "change of skin" (43). Vietnam is littered with layers of skin, the cast-off faiths of fathers long dead. The Vietnamese, compelled to express their sense of self in social relationship, are committed to pursuing new forms of experience with those who visit them. As relationships shift and displace one another, the metamorphosis of Vietnam, the sloughing-off of skin, involves a transformation of manner but not of identity. In the world of cultural tourism, entertainments might change but most of the activities remain the same. As the girl says in Hemingway's story "Hills Like White Elephants," "That's all we do, isn't it—look at things and try new drinks?"[27]

New drinks, like new faiths, may imply lack of strength or long-term stability. As Father Quan says, "We Vietnamese have a talent for martyrdom. Do you know that there are many martyrs in the Vietnamese Church but not one saint. I often think about that. The communists—they have plenty of martyrs, too. Poor Vietnam. So many martyrs when what she needs is just one or two saints" (137).

The waywardness of Vietnam is self-evident to a pragmatist like Gruson. For him the Vietnamese are "a melodramatic people" who like to feel sorry "for themselves" (43), even though, says Gruson, "feeling sorry for yourself . . . can become a habit." Better the stability of an enduring faith than the talent for enduring martyrdom. "Let me tell you a good rule," says Gruson to Bishop. "When things get tough, pick a side and stick to it. . . . If you want to get anything done you have to pick a side" (180). Thai cannot pick such a side; he wanders from one intellectual view to another. The affiliations may change—French colonialism, Marxist-Leninism—but for Gruson they remain an expression of Thai's—and Vietnam's—fecklessness and "arrogance" (180).

Other potential problems remain. Partnerships cannot always be supervised and recent events have ruined the people's trust. South Vietnam is not always committed to aesthetic partnership or cultural assimilation; the etiquette of the country has become hard-edged and much of its idealism has been overturned by the presence of unwelcome strangers with their harsh accents and uncompromising manners. These exiles, northern refugees who came to Saigon after the Communist victory over the French in 1954, have a different understanding of cultural exchange. Tan regards them as unprincipled opportunists who do not fulfill the promise of generosity in their social affairs. They are possessed of a selfish and entrepreneurial cunning, says Tan, and their understanding of culture is limited to the principle of

selling one's soul to the highest bidder. For Tan, the spirit of northern affiliation is not expressed through a love of European culture and civilization
earlier embraced by the South, but through a hard, grasping materialism that
finds its fulfillment in the narrow, acquisitive values of America.

Tan sees the relationship between the northern emigrant and the American colonizer as an affront to civilized partnership, a business deal that
offends against the spirit of mutual tolerance in Vietnam and that, therefore,
breeds suspicion. Thus "when the Americans came it was the Northerners
here who learnt fastest how to get on with them. One of our cousins who
was a general until he annoyed the president told me that most of the American agents here are Northerners and I believe it. They are selfish and cunning" (43). For Tan the dominant ideas of partnership in the South are now
determined by the marketplace. The quest for new opportunity by the exiled
northerner, and the American desire to protect a valuable commercial market
in Southeast Asia from falling into Communist hands, mean that Vietnamese
society has become much less concerned to register its sense of a relationship
by upholding a belief in graceful or commemorative objects. Relationships
now exist for reasons of personal and political gain; transactions flourish that
provide no benefit to the social community.

In the new Saigon the need to maintain one's privacy, to protect one's
world from unwelcome intrusion, breeds paranoia. Altruistic life has been
ruined: the city is now full of "foreigners" (91). Those who work in the service
of foreigners are easily threatened by the prospect of unverified alliances.
Colonel Dinh, for example, forces an innocent métisse like Jeanette to spy
on Bishop by becoming a whore. Dinh, who is head of the secret police, is
deeply neurotic and appears in public dressed in a "tight-fitting camouflage
combat uniform" (45). In a world of fluid and shifting relationships Dinh's
ruse de guerre is also an expression of insecurity. As Tan says, Dinh "isn't
really sure what's going to happen here," and so he acts "like a man on a
raft in the middle of the sea. . . . he does very nasty things to anyone who
he thinks might overturn it." In the city where violence is indiscriminate
Dinh is "nervous and . . . very dangerous" (46); for this reason he will ruin
anyone who seeks to threaten him or is capable of "playing a trick on him"
(111). Dinh is in the business of denying Vietnam the art of its own illusion,
symbolized by the mysterious texture of mother-of-pearl. Dinh has brutalized
himself and his culture; he moves in a world of Western energies and false
collaboration and revives those memories of expatriate life in the postwar
American novel of the twenties. In Frankland's Saigon we enter once again
a war-hangover environment where the contours of reality are vague and
distinctions between civilian and soldier are no longer possible. Here are the
hard, impersonal transactions where the innocent are ruined by the ruthless,
"where one day's friend might be another day's enemy" (*Into a Black Sun*,
60). In the whimsical banality of those who threaten aggression—in the
grenade-tossing antics of Tam Heo—we confront the cruelty of the war-torn

mind and the boredom of those who wander the city in search of casual destruction.

There is, however, the promise of redemption, the promise of an act of good collaboration between Thai and Bishop that reminds us of the partnership between Jake and Montoya in *The Sun Also Rises*. Thai is the opposite of Colonel Dinh; for him partnership is not a protection racket but an act of self-exposure or risk. If Dinh is the spiritual northerner, Thai is the master of the art of illusion, and his remoteness is spiritual and self-referential. To investigate Thai is to enter the polychromatic world of history, to lose one's bearings, to allow oneself to get blinded by a light that shines at different states of intensity and reveals a landscape in a state of continuous change: "Soft colours were coming back to the overgrown garden and the palm trees beyond it. The air was fresh. It was a different country from that of the midday sun: gentle and hopeful where the other was harsh and despairing. But which was the real country? The search for Thai seemed to be taking me more and more deeply into the midday with its exhausted colour and pressing heat" (70). In attempting to enter that country Bishop suffers from obstructed vision and refracted experience. Given the element of surprise and self-transformation in the Vietnamese landscape, it is not always easy for him to identify those who seek legitimate partnerships. In pursuing Thai, Bishop must enter "no-man's land" (95) where appearances change and identities merge with little explanation.

Thai's Vietnam is a battle-charged landscape of warring knowledge and indeterminate belief; he is its symbol, riven by the complex divisions that exist between religion and ritual, between the politics of violence and the comatose life of the opium den. Thai's restlessness is Vietnam's; its shape is his: its protean form, its history and idealism that shift back and forth between affiliation and rejection, between various aesthetic experiences and the histories that shape those experiences. Thai travels in the spiritual landscape of the métis, the halfway world of the half-caste, the pigmy warrior wracked with the anguish of his peculiar intelligence, and the peculiar appearance of his body: "half child, half old man" (8). Thai's Vietnam is the dissolving crystal of its own history, a world that breaks under the strain of containing the anguish and ambiguities of the self. As Bishop and Jeanette make love he cannot help "thinking of the contrast between Jeanette's body, smooth and firm like a new fruit, and her face which when ill-tempered had looked as old as rage itself" (86).

Self-contradiction is a feature of the country's social life; it is confirmed by the secretaries that Bishop works with who wear the ao dai with cardigans over them, as if "putting them on gave them a different, more substantial and European air." This sense of barely endured cultural schizophrenia is a constant concern for Bishop in his attempt to understand the Vietnamese obsession with opposites. The problem is outlined early in the novel when Bishop spends "an uncomfortable evening" with one of the senior bank officials. This character is a man of outward calm at his work, but in the presence of his wife, he is someone who appears "on the point of drowning." The conflict within the official is intense. "He seemed to look upon his prosperity—a little villa, a Peugeot, large diamonds in his wife's ears—as fairy gold that might vanish at any moment." The worry does not last. At work the following day, Bishop watches him, "his calm restored and seemingly a different man" (15).

Such changeability gives the impression of incompleteness. Insofar as this is manifested in an evolving political will, the problem, as Gruson puts it, is "that most people in this awful country are fed up with both sides." If this "adds up to a sort of freedom" (118), the tension created can be unbearable. As Thai enters the pagoda to achieve an "exorcism" (73), so Vietnam rids itself of divided belief through the purgatorial experience of Marxism. Just as the country strives for "tranquility" with a "plan" (122), so Thai accepts the "extraordinary calm" of the monks in the pagoda. As one of them tells Bishop: "You are right to help Thai. I have talked to him in the past. He is restless but good. He is worth saving for he can help others" (74).

Whether Thai, who is overloaded with idealism, can help himself is never conclusively shown; Thai "has seen both sides and he knows that neither is whole" (139). Thai sees himself, therefore, as the bearer of Vietnam's history and destiny, a man who carries the yearnings of those who, unfulfilled, died an early death, the "wandering souls" who have "nowhere to go" and enter the bodies of "living people" in order to "possess them" (75). Thai's confusions are those of his country and, through him, Frankland reminds us of the lapses of political and religious will that are endemic to Vietnam. If the guerrillas celebrate the arrival of Tet on a Sony radio, Thai does it with a "Vietnamese swiss roll." What Frankland gives us is that comic dependency of a "serious" (34) world on the things that are also sentimental and transitory. Nothing is funnier than Thai's fixation on Cornel Wilde as a curly-haired Chopin in *A Song to Remember*, or the Toyota calendar that decorates the wall of the Pagoda of True Enlightenment where the monks are nourished on processed cheese, French bread, and cocoa.

Thai cannot be saved by the political rescue that Gruson proposes; nor can Vietnam be rescued through the archaic political mission that the United States proposes. As Bishop realizes, "How did you rescue anyone in this country? How did you rescue Thai from the battles that were going on in him as much as around him?" (140). If Bishop must lose his naïveté he must also retain his humanity and trust. "Suspicion was part of the curse. It could paralyse you as effectively as any fear of Tam the pig" (54). Without the friendship or loyalty of a man like Ba nothing is remotely intelligible. On its own Vietnam is merely "a theatre of fools in which I had become a bit part player" (172). For this reason Bishop is angered by the injury to Ba's son and the killing of Do, and he feels affection toward Father Quan and the métisse Jeanette, both of whom "had been hurt in some way" (179).

Bishop's ability to find out who has caused that hurt is never conclusively demonstrated. Thai disappears into Cambodia, perhaps "because he wanted to" (186). Or he may have been killed—by whom and for what reason remain unclear. Nor do we understand the motives of the Cambodians or why Thai's mother should wish to have a relationship with them without the approval of Gruson (who then loses interest in the whole affair). Bishop's achievement is the effort he takes to arrive at a point where all possible lines of inquiry have been pursued, and his refusal to indulge in those tantalizing strategies of deception that occasionally take his fancy. Bishop learns to deal respectfully with a world that trusts him only fitfully, a world without rules or guaranteed outcomes, a world of tension in which the heat is unavoidable and the rains are slow in coming. "And though I longed for a resolution of the tension I must have known that it would not come. I had left the world of games played according to rules, of family propriety and honourable business without realising what was happening and there was no easy escape back to it" (132).

The honesty of the inquiry shows up in the quality of the writing and the quality of feeling that lies behind it. Bishop's strength is that he avoids complacency and the easy moralizing of the disenchanted like Wynant. "I'll tell you one thing," says Wynant. "This country has a curse on it. It is bewitched'—he stretched out the two syllables—'and anyone who's silly enough to get muddled up with it has only himself to blame if he gets hurt" (148–49). The idea of Asia as a muddle takes us back to E. M. Forster. The contempt both writers have for the arrogance and closure of the colonial mind is overt if not absolute.

In Frankland's choice of Michael Bishop we see a way of accepting the necessity of Asia as a mystery in language that avoids the need for a muddle. Bishop's language conveys a sense of a prose not bound by its own thesis, a prose that can stretch itself, that can enter a landscape that lies beyond American graffiti and American myth. In his observation of the middle class, Bishop takes us into a society that for most writers does not exist. We encounter a society that ignores "the bars that made money from the Americans" (134) and that spends its time in the evening observing the "latest material in the tailors' shops" or "the craftsmen's boutiques that sold ivory and lacquer ware and objects glinting with mother-of-pearl inlay" (134). Yet beneath the illusion of contentment in Bishop's landscape lies the menace of something threatening and the obscure, but nonetheless powerful force of self-disagreement or self-disgust. The language of the novel has a tension and an edge to it; it indicates tranquility but seeks to incorporate a disorder that will ruin it. The changes in the writing are sometimes imperceptible. In the journey to Ba's house we move without fuss from contentment to contained menace:

> There were market gardens on both sides of the road and the fresh morning air carried the smell of young vegetables, the smell of any English garden on a summer day. The village was at first just as

> reassuring. It was only two miles off the main road and looked sub-
> urbanly prosperous. Small tiled houses stood between neat clumps
> of palm trees, well-tended flowers and bushes. But towards the end
> of the village the palm trees grew thicker and here we turned off
> down a track till we reached a clearing across which stood a house
> far larger than those we had just passed. . . . A pig was penned into
> a space near the veranda and there were some unhealthy-looking
> chickens around the steps.
>
> Ba got out and shouted something in Vietnamese. There was no
> answer except from the hens who raised a feeble cry of alarm. Ba
> hurried in front of me and disappeared inside the house. The veranda
> floor was covered in chicken droppings and feathers. (61)

Bishop's landscapes are always liable to change in appearance, to shift from
the poetic to the grotesque and, if necessary, to look both ways at precisely
the same time. Here is Do's death: "He was lying on his side with blood
coming from beneath his head. There was only a touch of it on his mouth. . . .
There were already flies on it when I got back. I drove them off and they
settled on a piece of rotting fruit close by in the gutter. Their backs glittered
in the sunlight like chips of mother-of-pearl" (170).

Bishop's perception of Vietnam is that he can neither make sense of it
in terms that retain their shape and texture nor exert substantial control over
it. There is some recognition that what he may have looped into is a world
of "wily energy" (162) and "intrigue" (147), where feats of deception—as
Thai's mother so artfully demonstrates to Gruson at the Caravelle—are etched
like mother-of-pearl within the culture. Bishop's mission, like Thai's life, may
achieve very little, like a small particle of cosmic matter played on by a force
field whose energy source is undetectable. Yet our complicity with Bishop is
considerable. His limitations set the standards and the level of vision obtain-
able. We never know more than Bishop; and, since there are places he cannot
go and bases he cannot touch, we are unable to see beyond his attachments.

There is no resolution to the problems of Asia, and this is the point at
which *The Mother-of-Pearl Men* and *A Passage to India* part company. There
is certainly no Godbole, the wise fool, the man of harmonious contradiction
whose appearance suggests a reconciliation of East and West, if only in the
Hindu acceptance of disaster and invasion. In Frankland the foolish are not
always wise and the wise are not always foolish. They simply coexist. Contentment is available in drugs or in the ascetic utopian religion of Phap Long.
If Godbole exists, he is a priest without a God, a quack and a conjuror, like
the founder of the Pagoda of True Enlightenment, the Superior An Minh
Phuong, whose incantations have gone unanswered since 1941. If Vietnam
is a place of tragedy, it is also a place of foolishness where the spirit world
can sometimes combine with the whimsical for the sake of entertainment.
An absurdity perhaps, but one that is worthy of investigation.

PART
II

*Errand
in a
Wilderness*

6

*Contemporary
Critical Theory
and Debate*

VIETNAM WRITERS HAVE SHOWN A WILLINGNESS TO MOVE IN accordance with the changing circumstances of American life and their own particular needs. No longer do they live in the shadow of war writers like Joseph Heller or Kurt Vonnegut, nor do they appear as willing, as has been suggested, to develop a range of postmodern characteristics. Vietnam literature rarely disputes its own identity nor does it challenge the credentials of the author, except where the author is patently fraudulent. The reader may be uncertain about the nature of reality, but he is usually given enough components to construct a context from the various discourses within the novel in order to stabilize its meaning.

As a reference point for American writing in the 1980s, the idea of Vietnam's "abiding unreality" has worn itself out.[1] Tim O'Brien, as if to counterbalance much of the critical discussion that surrounds his novel *Going after Cacciato*, has stressed that "for me Vietnam wasn't an unreal experience; it wasn't absurd. It was a cold-blooded, calculated war."[2] It is little wonder that readers feel confused when comparing O'Brien's remark with the arguments commonly made by the critics. A good example is Philip Beidler, who has written a major survey of Vietnam writing, and who says that the war was the product of "some insane genius for making reality and unreality—and thus, by implication, sense and nonsense—as indistinguishable as possible." The idea that America's involvement in Vietnam was an aberration, the extended reaching out of some insanely resourceful mind, serves no useful purpose anymore—and the better writers, in many cases, have discarded it. Contemporary history confirms the need to look at Vietnam as more than a self-enclosed event. If we accept, as Philip Beidler does, that Vietnam was "a place with no real points of reference, then or now,"[3] then present-day questions like the impact of Vietnam on American foreign policy in Central America, or the role of the Vietnam veteran in the "Olliegate" scandal, can be easily pushed to one side.

Critics persist with arguments to the contrary. The war, it is said, has no origins in "traditional" history but reflects a midcentury obsession with science and technology that in turn supports the assertion that war should be fought "as proof of its own possibility."[4] According to Thomas Myers, Michael Herr's *Dispatches* remains the definitive text, not because it analyzes the role of colonialism in Vietnam, but because it enlarges our sense of the conflict as an aesthetic experience. *Dispatches*, says Myers, assumes "not only the primacy of the imagination but also the necessity for inventing new aesthetic strategies for the rendering of new history" (146).

As a symbol of "new history" the war in Vietnam, says Myers, cannot be understood through the use of traditional narrative. Vietnam is a fiction that explores its own making, a "supreme work of the American imagination" (144), and as such it requires from the writer an act of imaginative transcription and "textual alchemy" in which the war "is pressurised, tested, and finally, transmuted within the laboratory of personal sensibility." For Myers, the novel demands that the writer abandon the "traditional modes" of narration and that the reader accept a central contradiction: that in order "to remember the war, one must (first) reinvent it" (146). In refusing to accept Vietnam as "old" history, Myers insists that the "message" or meaning of the war "resides" in the workings of the "personal imagination." The Vietnam War is so confused, says Myers, it cannot be seen as an event that offers the reader a sensible view of the past. If the war signifies a lack of tradition, then the text must signify a break with tradition. "The Vietnam war is not a finished event," says Myers, but an invitation to revision; it is "not a destination but a point of departure, the catalyst of individual consciousness that enfolds it and shapes it" (148).

For Myers, the Vietnam War is an event of aesthetic possibility rather than an example of discrete history; it offers the writer the chance to accommodate himself to postmodernist life: "Fragmented, surreal, episodic, ungiving to singular readings, and resistant to convenient closure, the war seemed not the extension of an established tradition but something more akin to a collective nervous breakdown, an overload of the mythic circuitry that the managers sought to thread through the paddies and villages of an unreceptive culture" (143–44). For Myers, therefore, the received traditions of history are far less important than the inventions of the moment, the urge to make history what it ought to be—worthy of the age in which we live—an innovative text in which the writer discovers "within the materials of individual consciousness a historical lexicon and syntax with enough originality and power to do battle with those of the master narrative." The Vietnam writer is a "self-reflexive agent" of the new, and the "exploration" of history is an activity the reader encounters not in a world of "pre-existing truths" but in the "partnership between event and the creating imagination" (147–48).

= Paco's Story =

This quarrel with received history is not always easy to support, and the argument that Vietnam is an exceptional event is not always realized in the literature. In fact, Vietnam veterans are particularly concerned to establish continuity between the trauma of Vietnam and related problems in American life. Many of them are keen to set their experience in a wider historical context, establishing connections between what they have suffered in the war and other casualties in American history. In *Paco's Story* Larry Heinemann compares the Vietnam veteran of the 1980s with the homeless victims of the Great Depression. *Paco's Story* is haunted by the memory of the past, the traumatic history of the dispossessed who are deprived of love and the comforts of community. As a "vag" aboard a Greyhound bus Paco reminds us of the migrants of the 1930s who took to the road in a desperate journey of escape from social victimization. His search for work in the town of Boone recalls the problems of the hobos in John Dos Passos's *U.S.A.*, the yearnings of those who live on the road with their tawdry dreams of glamor and ambition in Nelson Algren's *Somebody in Boots*, the thwarted attempts of the Okies and Arkies to recover from eviction in John Steinbeck's *The Grapes of Wrath*.

What fascinated Sartre in American fiction of the 1930s fascinates Heinemann in the 1980s. In *Paco's Story* we reencounter the picaresque solitary on "the long American road"; we are witness once more to the "constant flow of men across a whole continent . . . the hopeless wanderings of the hero in *Light in August*, and the uprooted people who drifted along at the mercy of the story in *The 42nd Parallel*, the dark murderous fury which sometimes swept through an entire city, the blind and criminal love in the novels of

James Cain."⁵ The carelessness and indifference of the American community toward those who have suffered at the hands of others, through birth or history, is reintroduced as a central theme in American life, and it does much to undercut the idea that the alienation of the veteran in the 1980s is without parallel. In a world of words and empty promises Paco hits the road at the end of Heinemann's novel "thinking, Man you ain't just a brick in the fucking wall, you're just a piece of meat on the slab." As he leaves the Texas Lunch in Boone he retains a forlorn belief in the American frontier. As he says, " 'There's less bullshit the farther west you go.' "⁶

Heinemann takes issue with the idea that contemporary life demands from the writer a postmodern narrative, and he rejects, in particular, the need to invent "new aesthetic strategies for the new history" of Vietnam (144). Nor is he in the business of measuring the war on a sliding scale of tragedy. The narrative of *Paco's Story* connects with the history of other wars and other wanderers; it works on the principle that a story is told best—as Melville's Ishmael says—in a language of "careful disorderliness." *Paco's Story* is a loose-leafed ramble through Paco's history, from the moment he survives the devastation at Fire Base Harriette and the wasting of Alpha Company to the loss of his emotional company and the injury Cathy inflicts on him in her letters in the rooming house in Boone. *Paco's Story* is a jaunty theatrical excursion, a work of colloquial history written and spoken by the members of Alpha Company who were blown away at Fire Base Harriette. The colloquial expressions of the dead provide the reader with a collective rendering of proletarian speech, a clustering of narrative voices and oral histories at the grass-roots level of American life.

In *Paco's Story* the cultural voice of American democracy is observed in the telling of stories and in the fragments of history attached to those stories. Colloquial speech, by its very nature, demystifies the memory of war and absorbs the extravagance of the devastation that occurs at Fire Base Harriette into a lively vernacular experience. The personal narrative of the soldiers brings intimacy to the war, an intimacy that reduces (through the heightened realism of everyday speech) the exceptional status of those who were killed. Heinemann exploits the oral traditions of American folklore. A certain joki-ness infiltrates the text and the worm's-eye narrative roots out the buried feelings of Paco in a meandering, knockabout manner. The spoken form determines the feelings of the reader and establishes a complicity with the past. The traditions of storytelling are animated by Vietnam as Vietnam itself is animated by history. The war, therefore, acts as a spur to the narrative potential in American life; it establishes continuity between the dead of Fire Base Harriette and the legendary mentors of American folklore.

If Thomas Myers is correct, the war in Vietnam serves only to discredit history, not to animate it, and stories that are told about the conflict can have no bearing on events that precede it. What Vietnam gives us, says Myers, is a radical and unusual literary experience, one that transforms the writer's view of history and his understanding of literary form. According to Myers, the literary "protagonist is not merely affected or altered by the history he helps to write; he is spiritually and emotionally annihilated by it, reshaped internally so that his new state becomes a dark joke that only the initiated can share" (31).

The idea that the veteran is a member of a secret fraternity, "spiritually" divorced from a colloquially literate, proletarian past, is one that Heinemann firmly resists, as do the unnamed narrators who commit their colloquial selves to the telling of Paco's story. Vietnam, says Heinemann, teases out the inherent theatricality of the American adventurer living an experimental life. The dramatic mannerisms of the characters and the joie de vivre of the narrative remind us of the nineteenth-century Yankee peddlers, the gypsy crews, strolling actors, minstrels and evangelists—that plethora of performing Americans who roamed through the frontier settlements of the West. In the provincial culture of Boone or in the woods of Fire Base Francesca, we are also reminded of New England's history, the "chimney-corner" tendencies of the Puritans and the tale-telling ways that accompanied the growth of settlement life in the villages and towns of the eastern seaboard. Heinemann brings into sharp collision, in other words, a variety of historical narratives and grammars. From Ernest's recollections of World War II to Gallagher's memories of his father in Chicago, from the bombast and braggadocio of a confidence man like Jesse in Boone to the yells and blather of the backwoods narrators, the vernacular tradition retains its appeal in American life and confirms the importance of colloquial speech.

Heinemann's wish to make Vietnam—in spite of its secrets or inner realities—a social experience for the reader is not supported by a criticism that remains preoccupied with the aesthetic possibilities of "new narrative" or "new history." The argument, for example, is frequently put forward that the writer can no longer communicate to the reader, through realistic language, what the war was like, since the war by definition was not realistic. Jerome Klinkowitz describes Vietnam as "that most incredible of places,"[7] and John Hellmann argues against the usefulness of social realism since it identifies a "plausible" and probable course for events and is "too restricted . . . to convey the hallucinatory ambience" of Vietnam. Writers who use realism, it is said, are forced to labor "over the construction of a credible fictional representation of an inherently incredible actuality."[8] Realism, it is argued, with its requirements of plot, verisimilitude, and characterization is wholly inadequate as a filter for experience and as a way of coping with what Alfred Kazin has described as "the manic plenitude of American destructiveness." Since the war was unreal, says Kazin, then any "serious novelist" who tries to describe Vietnam will find "himself outdone."[9]

Kazin's argument is vigorously supported by Donald Ringnalda. Realists, he writes, do not discover the "shapeless contingencies" of Vietnam nor do they "probe dark recesses"; instead, they "trace surfaces" in the war and imply "a sense of controlled continuity and rational ordering." Vietnam lacks such "continuity" and historical reference. The war, says Ringnalda, "was qualitatively different from anything [most Americans] had experienced in their history." It posed exceptional problems: an "impenetrable jungle" and "an *indigenous* enemy" for whom "the formidable landscape was home," a lack of loyalty in the civilian population, and the inability of the American forces to "distinguish friend from foe." In confronting these new and exceptional circumstances the American writer, says Ringnalda, challenges "the illusion that absurdity can be defeated" and argues strongly the position that "you didn't *learn* anything from the Vietnam experience." The most successful books, he says, "most certainly are not novels that try to make sense of the war." In fact, "they're all quite mad." Insanity is inevitable where writers combine "postmodern" speculation with "blue-collar experience."[10]

Ringnalda returns us to the argument put forward by Thomas Myers that Vietnam has "defied conventional attempts to record it" and has resisted "conventional" methods of interpretation (5). Imaginative literature, says Myers, ought to be seen not as the creation of history but as its arbiter: a "self-conscious aesthetic expression" that makes sense of the war on the basis of personal rather than public experience (9). The "historical novel" finds itself in a combative role, says Myers, and is obliged to reply to the "forced harmony of popular culture and official revision" (8). For this reason the most authentic and imaginative records of war literature are those that provide the reader with information on the "interior" or "buried" histories the war contains. Ethnocentrism has its virtues. The Vietnam memoir, like the Vietnam novel, is "hermetically personal" (72). "Many of the books speak powerfully and convincingly on the level of immediate experience, but as they assemble the daily horrors and boredoms of the tour of duty in Vietnam, they often seem to abdicate the tasks of larger historical vision and cultural connection" (39).

Myers relates the lack of historical vision to a lack of political vision. The root of the problem, he says, is the ragged response of the American government to the appeal for support by the Democratic Republic of Vietnam in September 1945. The refusal of the United States to support Ho Chi Minh, says Myers, allowed the French "to resume colonial status" (24) in Hanoi after the defeat of Japan. The subsequent "phases" of American involvement, which "are discernable after the French defeat in 1954" (25), disprove any notion of the Vietnam War "as a unity." The lack of coherent purpose behind the subsequent embroilment resulted in the war evolving not as "a single narrative but [as] a number of successive and simultaneous wars within a war, a loose collection of political, ideological and military vignettes that would not conform easily to the form of the collective mythic novel in which previous American wars resided" (24).

= The Postmodernist View =

For Thomas Myers the absence of a "master narrative" in Vietnam derives from the lack of attention given by politicians to the war's "historical and cultural roots" (27). The absence of narrative is regarded not as a deficiency but as an opportunity for the writer in assessing the new reality of the 1960s and the openness of its plots and structures. In the desire to pursue "new history" the American military provide the writer with an opportunity to create "new literature" (31).

A characteristic of the literature, which "came of age during the 60s," says Michiko Kakutani, is its disagreement with traditional narrative structures. "A fragmented approach to storytelling, a reluctance on the author's part to interpret events or speculate about characters' motivations, a tendency to see everything in the present tense, as though the past or future were impossible to connect—these techniques which recur with startling frequency in Vietnam novels," say Kakutani, "are the same that have begun to filter down from the postmodernist masters of the nouveau roman to mainstream American fiction."[11] A favored postmodernist activity is determining the quality and relevance of a text by examining the nature of its disability, the extent to which it has suffered deliberate injury and breakdown—"brain damage"—in the act of composition. Thus, in Vietnam literature, the failure of the brain to convey messages that make sense of the world may be observed in the schizophrenia—or as W. L. Webb puts it, the "split consciousness"—of those who possess an "amiably psychotic view of the world."[12]

In the neurosurgical ward of fiction, the death of the novel is playfully announced. The brokenness of the Vietnam experience is embodied in the form of its finest literary casualties—in their lack of sequence and structure and in the spoiling tactics of those opposed to causal progression. Vietnam is a muddle, a thing of uncertain definition, a war that for the United States was not declared a war at all but a conflict that degenerated into a self-disputing, self-questioning text. No one knew the plot in Vietnam—not even the author—because the author changed his approach so often and had no idea of the kind of structure he was seeking to create. Much of what America did militarily in Vietnam was based on a strategy of exhaustion, a doctrine of attrition that itself was exhausted, an ideology that reflected the "used-upness" of those who deployed conventional force in an unconventional and indeterminate age.[13]

Kakutani applauds the efforts of postmodern writers like Michael Herr or Stephen Wright but is critical of the fiction of James Webb (*Fields of Fire*), Winston Groom (*No Bugles, No Drums*), and John M. Del Vecchio (*The 13th Valley*), novelists who are excessively naturalistic and "clean," "more typical of World War II than Vietnam," and unable, according to Kakutani, to convey the dislocation of the war. In an implausible war plausible narratives have no place. A fiction that prefers to explore its own making and that incorporates a formal principle of uncertainty and untidiness in the writing is the one best equipped to acknowledge the experiences of contradiction and the deranged features of contemporary life. The "finest" novels, those that read history correctly, see Vietnam as a symbol of disorientation and futility. Novels that resist interpretation, that "try to leave it up to the reader to decide," that come apart at the seams in the act of reading, are able to conjure up the "heightened weirdness" of an insurgent world. "For the most part," says Kakutani, "Vietnam was not a war of conventional battles and historic campaigns. From the soldier's point of view, it had a strangely episodic quality: ambushes and fire-fights, interspersed with long periods of monotonous waiting, melted into a kind of existential haze; it was frequently difficult, if not impossible, to tell which side was winning or falling behind, losing ground or winning."[14]

What Kakutani gives us is a version of Vietnam that is pure Americana, one that is more ideal than real, more imagined than actual, and one that is largely deferential toward those whose work can be easily assimilated into the canon of postmodernism. The observation, for example, that fewer than one soldier out of five in Vietnam ever saw combat, or that statistically the war was much less dangerous, less traumatic, than Britain's Burma campaign or America's campaign against the Japanese in the Pacific during World War II, is not considered relevant to what the critic believes to be important—so it is ignored. From the uniqueness of America's loss comes the uniqueness of America's experience and the difficulty of negotiating with an unpredictable and adversarial culture in which "values" are felt to be disintegrating. Vietnam offers an exceptional "incoherent experience"; it is a place with a "peculiar psychological atmosphere" which creates "a day-to-day surrealism that distinguished it from previous conflicts." In Vietnam, personal identity is in a state of profound "tenuousness," a feeling of "total ignorance" persists about "what the future" holds, and each moment is governed by "anxiety," "even those that [have] nothing to do with combat." In such a world the received traditions of war literature, naturalism and documentary realism, are inappropriate as "narrative strategies for dealing with the war" since, in a conflict that "so defies reason and the rules of causality," they appear unacceptably tidy and contrived. For the postmodernist critic nothing can mitigate "the hallucinatory mood" of the Vietnam War, the absoluteness of the chaos and the "progressive brutalization" of the characters it throws up. Vietnam is therefore an unprecedented nightmare born out of "the moral and political uncertainties of American involvement, the intense savagery of the jungle fighting, the heavy use of drugs and the extraordinary bureaucratic confusions of military life there."

In the quest for definitive evidence of a "formless" war, texts are discussed on the basis of their willingness to confirm certain established or approved experiences, not on their ability to open up areas of imaginative inquiry that lie outside those experiences. Vietnam is seen as a convenient asset to be stripped of all its corroborative evidence. The war is useful because it provides a fable of "bizarre complexities," and only those books that are able to capture the war's contradictions can hope to be "commensurate with the chaos."[15] In Vietnam the extreme experience is the definitive experience, and the value we gain from looking at the war is the extent to which it confirms our impression of history as chaos. Those who write about Vietnam therefore, have a central obligation to extrapolate from it a vision of history that the war, in its most extreme moments, willingly confirms and to discount the value and validity of those experiences that do not endorse the approved metaphors of breakdown. If, as Norman Mailer tells us, "the trouble with reality is that it isn't realistic any more," then the Vietnam War must be seen to extend itself into areas of experience where sense-making narratives do not permit themselves to go. Vietnam—which is to say, the American experience in Vietnam—confirms and accelerates the drift of twentieth-century history in which, as W. L. Webb puts it, "man-made apocalypses have exploded our culture and history, disrupting our deepest sense of what we are and making us doubt our sanity, even our creatureliness."

Vietnam offers the postmodernist critic an image of Western disfigurement; it provides him with a symbol of "the abounding contradictions of postwar American society."[16] Critics have become fascinated with Vietnam as a place redolent with the modes of modern experience—innovation, ingenuity, what Jerome Klinkowitz terms "military postmodernism"[17]—at the expense of its moral or social contexts. To observe America in Vietnam is to discover the crisis of contemporary history and the experimental consciousness of a country dynamically engaged in promoting its own standards of civilization and conduct. What the American experience in Vietnam reveals, says the postmodernist, is a level of sophistication and enterprise that is far more intriguing and relevant to the world in which we live than the primitive ideology of an aspiring third world country, or the social catastrophe that Vietnam has experienced in recent times. As Jean Baudrillard has acknowledged:

> It has to be said that New York and Los Angeles are at the centre of the world, even if we find the idea somehow both exciting and disenchanting. We [in Europe] are a desperately long way behind the stupidity and the mutational character, the naive extravagance and the social, racial, moral, morphological, and architectural eccentricity of their society. . . . It is a world completely rotten with wealth, power, senility, indifference, poverty and waste, technological futility and aimless violence, and yet I cannot help but feel it has about it something of the dawning of the universe. Perhaps because the entire world continues to dream of New York even as New York dominates and exploits it.[18]

Concern with the cultural preeminence of American values is evident in the work of the journalist William Broyles. After he made a trip to Vietnam in 1984, Broyles wrote an article for *Atlantic Monthly* in which he argued that the Vietnamese people—and especially the youth of Vietnam—had not retained a personal or cultural identity sufficiently strong to withstand, as W. L. Webb puts it, the "gobbling consumerism"[19] of America. The political and military failure of America to control Vietnam had, said Broyles, shown itself to be irrelevant. Where technological power and economic capital proved to be of little use in subduing the Vietnamese, cultural consumerism and the commercial triumph of Western values had become an irresistible attraction. Broyles records the impending defeat of native Vietnamese idealism and the loss of cultural self-belief. He sees the memory of proletarian struggle as a fiction that brings diminishing returns and the Vietnamese attachment to consumer capitalism as a process that will inevitably displace all other attachments, including the memory of political struggle.

Broyles is convinced that "though we lost the war our culture is clearly winning." In the bookstores Russian books remain unsold but English ones are bought straightaway. "Anything American is highly prized, particularly clothes. I gave a government worker in Hanoi a black LA Raider T-shirt," says Broyles, "and for two days he wore it to work." In the rush to embrace American products the purity of *dau tranh* (faith) has suddenly lost all relevance and meaning. In the war "everyone suffered together, and suffered for a goal that everyone could understand. When Ho Chi Minh said that nothing was more precious than independence and freedom, he clearly meant to include motorcycles, blue jeans, and tape recorders. But when one girl gets a pair of jeans and some makeup, then that idyllic world where one is for all and all for one and everyone suffers together is on its way to the dustbin." At the thirtieth anniversary of the liberation of Hanoi, Broyles witnesses performances of traditional music and a parade of celebration in Lenin Park. At the end of the concert there appears a group "with long hair and short outfits" with a lead singer who moves like Mick Jagger. The audience is spellbound. The Vietnamese, it appears, have already lost the cultural battle for the hearts and minds of the country's youth. The momentum of Vietnamese life, says Broyles, confirms the drift of Western history and the willing surrender of traditional culture to that history. Broyles makes the point, almost in triumph:

> And America is going to be much more difficult in this battle than we were in the others: our clothes, our language, our movies, and our music—our way of life—are far more powerful than our bombs. We represent something else now—we represent a future that many Vietnamese want, and that everyone, from the Communist Party Leader, Le Duan, to the simple peasant, knows the Russians cannot give them.[20]

= An Emergence of Sense =

This argument that the contemporary American experience takes precedence in the making of history lives on in much of our literary criticism of American writing and the Vietnam War. The endorsement of the United States as the dominant partner in its dealings with the world is reflected in our decision to use Vietnam in order to confirm a set of assumptions about the nature of contemporary experience. "If it sounds strange," writes Ralph Dahrendorf, elaborating his account of managerialist postcapitalism, "the strangeness is due to the strangeness of reality."[21] Reality is strange, yet strangely familiar, especially when it directs our attention to the all-consuming playfulness of the American literary experience. For this reason the critic encourages the reader to ignore those novels that cannot be integrated into the absurdist or postmodernist canons of experience and to endorse a fictional experience that confirms the Americanness of the world in which we live.

Stephen Wright's *Meditations in Green* has been highly acclaimed for its willingness to incorporate postmodern disorder as a formal principle in the making of the text. Wright's novel relates through a series of brief cinematic tapes the story of James Griffin, an intelligence adviser in Vietnam who becomes a drug addict in his effort to escape the memory of the devastation for which he has been responsible. The novel uses, says Michiko Kakutani, a dislocated form of composition more in keeping with the actual experience of the war than a work of naturalism or documentary realism. The abstractness of the country, the bizarre contradictions and complexity of the war, demands a response that is equally fragmented. *Meditations in Green* provides a fine example, says Kakutani, "of the American dream in disrepair, it offers a hyped-up and willfully subjective view of a society 'coming apart.' " Since Vietnam is possessed of "an incredible tenuousness of identity" it is dependent upon fiction to provide a metaphorical structure for the chaos of experience. *Meditations in Green* avoids the need for "a definite moral outlook," and "instead of holding up signs as to what is proper and what isn't" the book leaves it up "to the writer to decide." Wright's work, it is claimed, bears witness to the truth that "the finest Vietnam novels must be seen not so much in relation to other war fiction but in relation to other contemporary writing."[22]

The argument offered by Kakutani is further supported by Thomas Myers. Myers believes that the literary language of *Meditations in Green* gives the impression of a "jarring historical education," of a "memory" wrapped up "in a hallucinatory haze." He suggests that the stability of the text is threatened not only by "the residue" of what Griffin "became in Vietnam, a heroin-addicted, fragmented sensibility," but also by the present influences of America "that encourage dissolution, paranoia and alienation" (199).

The strong tendency in Stephen Wright toward dislocation, nevertheless, does nothing to bear out the idea that Vietnam is merely so much "debris down the drain of history" (51). The promise that conventional values will come loose in the novel is simply not fulfilled. However much Wright appears to move in pursuit of a self-referential narrative form, there is little internal evidence of those speculative plots, extraordinary suspensions, unresolved ambiguities, and self-contradictory structures that we associate with meta-fictional writing. In spite of the anarchic and fractured surface of the text, Wright is unwilling to play games with the reader that might destroy our sense of coherence, or to withhold the identity of the unethical and corrupt, or to obscure our awareness of the colonial errand as a continuing dynamic in American life. However much Griffin's personality is unsettled by his experiences with the 1069th, and whatever structural disturbances the text suffers as a consequence, its vision of history is coherently expressed through reference to Puritan vision and design.

For the American military in *Meditations in Green* Vietnam is a land-scape that reveals the mind and purpose of God; it is an open book that provides the reader with a detailed lesson in the management of temporal and spiritual affairs. In reading Vietnam the Puritan soldier is obliged to observe nature for signs and evidence of divine intent, for the information through which the wonders and providences of the natural world are dra-matically revealed. As the home of the Antichrist, nature is also a profligate wilderness which the Puritan magistrates of the 1069th are keen to subdue. As a place of potential cultivation the jungle must be cleansed before the seeds of righteousness are planted, stripped of its leaves and heathen roots before the earth can function as a "theocratic garden of God."

James Griffin, the central character in the novel, attempts to participate in this process. In Vietnam he is instrumental in rooting out the signs and providences of God's mission in the wilderness. In the United States he seeks to participate in a reformation of the land. The nature of Griffin's Puritanism changes as he moves from one continent to another. He becomes less of a magistrate and more of a redeemer, less concerned to rid the world of its covert growth and more preoccupied with the cultivation of a garden.

On his return to the United States Griffin tends plants and smokes grass as a necessary act of self-protection. Smoking grass is part of that process of meditating in green. It induces, through casual burning, a slow wholesome-ness, a state of mind that reverses the tendency to devastate the earth through burning and bleaching. Griffin, who was once "an impotent king locked in a tower," overcomes his elevated ministry and his dream of death—his ob-session to create "bright wastelands" (294)—with the role of healer. He recognizes "the single mystery" as he watches the growth of plants in his attic. "I read dozens of botany books but diagrams and nomenclature couldn't satisfactorily explain the direct wonder of one growing plant. You had to feel your way into understanding. I could see myself stripped to the skin, lying in a box of my own, swollen root burrowing into the ground. Blossoming all over" (311). The relationship between self-renewal and organic life is stated clearly and the therapy of nature achieves its triumph over the mechanical disorder of the scientific mind.

Griffin's emergence as a healer is suggested at the end of the novel when he leaves his room in the city in order to save the life of a person who looks like Anstin, a hated sergeant from the 1069th, whom Trips, a friend of Griffin, is bent on killing. Griffin "transcends tensions and moves . . . beyond the waste land," even though that action coincides with a moment of death and the "worldly defeat" of his friend Trips.[23] For the Puritan recluse who becomes an interventionist—like Faulkner's Gail Hightower—the difficulty of social adjustment in a hostile and unfamiliar world may always remain. Domestic arrangements may prove unsatisfactory ("This is not a settled life. A children's breakfast cereal. . . . The sunsets are no damn good here"). The stress of readjustment may prove a challenge that can only be dealt with through the "ghosts on my television screen" (8).

The extent to which Griffin undergoes a definitive historical change and sloughs off his Calvinistic heritage is limited. Thomas Myers suggests otherwise. He argues that Griffin emerges as "the new character within American folklore" (Myers 209), a post-Puritan westerner, "a reshaped Johnny Appleseed" (Myers 207) who commits himself to an Emersonian dependency and a transcendental ideal. But the transformation, although promised, is never completed; Griffin's urge to go on the road and replenish the depleted forests of the West is not fulfilled. Griffin remains a righteous grower, his dream built on braggadocio and bombast. "In the spring I'll wander national highways, leather breeches around my legs, pot on my head, sowing seeds from the burlap bag across my shoulder, resting in the afternoon shade of the laurel tree" (341).

In the unnamed city to which Griffin returns, the habit of living in a state of confinement is not easily relinquished. Motives might change, manners do not. Griffin meditates on the "Green Machine" (277), the once-despised natural wilderness, now re-created as a garden of vegetables and indoor plants on a floor-full of soil in a seedy attic. Yet he remains a spectator to his fate, allowing the certainties of nature—that closely monitored and uncomplicated world that thrives in his attic—to comfort him. His contrition for the damage he has done to the wilderness of Asia consists in growing plants at home. The salvation in his life, the steps he takes toward ecology, are rooted in the philosophy of what Charles Reich once termed "the Greening of America" in his book of that name. This is the bulwark Wright sets against an absurdist world: American pastoralism, the divinity of nature, the awe-inspiring persistence of the earth. But the word *America* remains important and ties us firmly to a Puritan past. As Griffin admits, his life is one of enclosure and stasis. "I rarely left the room anymore. The plants required attention, I required attention" (311). Griffin lives as a Puritan naturalist, a cultivator, a sympathetic gardener who ministers to the plants and watches for signs of actual growth. In the sheltered world of his attic Griffin experiences a softening of the heart. New growth and new life are idealized: "The seeds burst, and the soil broke and I used to lean against a box, eye to the ground, and monitor a miracle as tiny separate shoots, tender as a baby's fingers, poked curiously through a wall of earth" (311).

The burden of negotiating with a Calvinistic inheritance remains the tragic and disabling legacy of Vietnam. In Griffin's room the demons of the unreconstructed forest are obliterated. Roots and tendrils do not reach back to resurrect a vision of unsupervised forests. The attic is a protected environment. The miniature jungle that grows in boxes is shorn of its complicating foliage, its capacity to suffocate and tangle. What is lacking in the room is density of growth.

The need to retain control over nature provides an illustration of what Thomas Myers aptly calls "the war as unfinished business and ongoing obsession" (207). Land as a register of Vietnamese meaning is not a discovery that Griffin is able to make. Greenness as a feature of Vietnamese life is not acknowledged. The importance of the project is not the abstract presence of nature but the possession of nature. Since Griffin remembers "jungle decay" (314), the earth in his attic remains boxed in.

In *Meditations in Green* Puritanism survives. The vision that supported strategic hamlets lives on in America as a policy of protecting strategic earth.

7

Designing
Vietnam

IN HIS WORK ON DESIGN TECHNOLOGY REYNER BANHAM
suggests a correlation between the creation of an American culture and the
production of American skills and tools. The idea, says Banham, that a problem can be solved or resolved by the invention of a product has been one of
the formative beliefs of American history. Particular types of tools have been
created to accommodate particular types of experience, and product solution
has invariably been seen as a means of growth and territorial expansion.

In the early years of the American colonies, for example, geographic
expansion created a need for skills and tools that would limit the temptation
and trauma of the wilderness. As times changed so did the mechanics of
machinery and tooling. "Out of the dearth of specially skilled labour and the
enormous distances over which goods had to be transported," writes Banham,
"there clearly arose one very characteristic type of designed-in-America object; it is highly portable, usable by untrained hands, sophisticated in itself,
and capital-intensive."[1] The frontier experience led to the creation of tools
that could easily translate into different environments. According to Banham,

the object of choice is either a tool or a weapon: "It is the bowie-knife, the Winchester repeater, the Thompson submachine gun, the atom bomb. Or it is the die cast axe, the sewing machine, the McCormick reaper, the Fordson tractor, the Lunar Excursion Module."[2]

= Self-determination and Privacy =

If design has been a function of experience in America, experience has also been a function of design. The relationship between the invention of tools and the ideal of self-determination is a case in point, says Banham. It is of particular importance, as in Vietnam, when "physically and socially isolated men" try to "survive in untamed environments," and when traditional communities are destroyed and small, self-conscious, experimental communities are created artificially within "environments" that may be unfriendly or essentially pre-American. For Banham the features of these communities are shaped by the "asocial privatism" the versatility of the tool makes possible. The governing ideology of the community becomes introspective, and the community, because of the plurality of its skills and devices, becomes unwilling to incorporate the character of the larger public environment. Instead, the environment is tamed by virtue of the community's facility with tools and its range of physical equipment. The approach is invariably confrontational; conversations with the native people are discouraged and the preferred mode is analytic, self-enclosed and culturally reductive. As an American soldier succinctly puts it: "somebody had to show poor people better ways of livin', like sewer disposal and sanitation and things like that."[4]

= The Absence of Native Context =

Banham writes, "What American experience points up . . . is that the neatness of the engineering solution usually depends on phrasing the problem in such a way that most of its context is omitted, or at least enough of the contingent circumstances are set aside for a 'solution' to be proposed using available technology, albeit combined in a new and original form." When we discuss the omission of context in Vietnam what we often refer to is the problem of incorporating into the methodology of a neat "engineering solution" none of the established native features of a region. In the Vietnam War American designs appear as responses to perceptions of American needs, as things imposed from without rather than created from within. Notwithstanding the excellence of certain designs in Vietnam—sensors, nightscopes, medical equipment—Malcolm Browne compares the "essential difference" between the American and Vietnamese approach to war in terms of localized knowledge and localized response. "Viet Cong gadgetry begins and ends on the battlefield," says Browne, "while ours begins in America and is adapted for better or worse to the Vietnamese jungle. When the American gadget proves inadequate for the task it is sent back to the drawing boards, some of which are in Saigon but most of which are 10,000 miles away. Supply lines are attenuated, and the American military designer lives in a different world from Viet Nam."[5]

This absence of cultural nativism in the technology and language of the American colonial mission can be traced to the Puritans, who regarded the Indian as a heathen creature who could be rescued from his ungodly ways only through conversion and physical incorporation into the Puritan settlements. In the Puritan era the Indians were offered a Europeanized life where their physical and spiritual progress could be monitored. This belief in spiritual conversion and bourgeois assimilation reappears in the American mission to Vietnam.

In South Vietnam during the Diem regime, native people, such as the Montagnards, were forcibly removed from their villages and made to live in the prisonlike world of strategic hamlets. Many of those who were transferred practiced Confucianism or Buddhism or Cao Dai, religions in which attendance to the ancestors' shrine on the land was an important ritual. One of the mistaken premises of the strategic hamlet program, as the Communist Lao Dong realized, was that the Vietnamese were a socially mobile people and would enjoy the experience of moving from one region to another, as the Americans themselves had done in their own frontier past. As Jeffrey Race points out, the land question was of absolutely paramount importance in the Vietnam War. "No other factor looms so large in the consciousness of the peasant. Aside from the economic precariousness of owning no land a peasant feels a rootlessness particularly strong in Vietnamese culture, because the land has a special ritual significance for the Vietnamese. It is the focus of life and family activity. Closeness to ancestral graves and the fields the family has worked for generations provides the emotional security and strength which Westerners generally draw from prophetic religion."[6]

Through the strategic hamlet program we have an example of the danger involved in narrowing the context of a problem so that a "one-shot engineering" or architectonic solution can be neatly implemented.[7] The problem, once removed from any external reference, is put at the mercy of experiment and design. As a "tool" the strategic hamlets of South Vietnam proved insufficiently flexible and too tightly structured to cope with the problem they addressed. The nature of the problem—the identification and isolation of the Viet Cong and their sympathizers—could never be resolved by simple designs. The world of the strategic hamlet imprisoned the problem within a cultural cyst and left no room for intellectual discussion of the larger environment.

The obsession with customized landscape and the forced removal and separation of families were direct violations of Vietnam's rural and social traditions. In the opinion of William Gibson, the destruction of native villages and the forced removal of villagers comprised "the necessary first step" in the "reconstruction" of Vietnam from "a rural agricultural society" into "a modern urban society."[8] The provision of "yellow strategic hamlet pins, strategic hamlet stamps, strategic hamlet matchbooks, and strategic hamlet school note-books" reflected the desire to create a materialistic uniform environment topped with barbed wire, in which "the confidence and friendly co-operation" of the people was enhanced by taking their picture with "a Polaroid."[9]

The preferred way of encouraging sociable behavior in South Vietnam was to design environments that contained most of the facilities necessary for material well-being. The destruction of native habitat was a way of eradicating the unknown; if the landscape was ruined it was also reinvented and many of its features redesigned. Whether it was the bar, the hotel, the fire support base, the PX store, the hospital, the airport, the metalled road, the strategic hamlet, Cam Ranh Bay, or Saigon itself, South Vietnam came to be regarded by the United States as an insular or self-contained text best understood through familiar products: armed services radio, American television, popular magazines, transistor radios, IBM 1430 computers, M-48 Patton tanks, Coca-Cola bottles, Dial soap, shaving foam. Here we see the secular legacy of what Puritan poet Edward Taylor described as "beauty in the sanctuary" (Caldwell, 74). Here was a plantation of like-minded worshipers protected by "the Hedge," an assembly of the elect nourished by a feeling of righteousness in a heathen world. Insofar as the errand in the Vietnam wilderness was an inward-looking one of enclosure, it ignored the native environment and transformed the country into a place fit for Americans to live in.

The strategy is designed to induce agoraphobia, but sometimes the opposite occurs. For James Griffin in *Meditations in Green*, the wired enclosures in which the 1069th Military Intelligence Unit is forced to work have caused the return of "Childhood Claustrophobia." Amid a "hostile population" Griffin is kept "locked in." Outings, and the chance to breathe, are rare. "Except for a few KP's, a couple of latrine attendants and a handful of maids, everyone around was quite American, speaking American, eating American, driving American, reading American, rocking American, the sky itself crisscrossed dense on grandma's knitting with American aircraft and American telephone poles and American wire" (251).

America specialized in "quick fixes" in Vietnam. "What was missing was a little maturity—a recognition that the need for the house matters more than the tools required to build it."[10] The psychic inability of the tool to make an intelligible assessment of Vietnamese culture and society was deemed irrelevant. Soldiers were catered for on the basis that what they brought to Vietnam were the cultural assumptions of America's youth. Their needs were defined as those of a customer, an adolescent brought up in a highly charged consumer environment. A frenetic attempt was made to manufacture an environment that the soldier could understand; the emphasis was ethnocentric and highly customized. Even war zones were saturated with gadgets. It is not incidental that Mattel, one of the major toy manufacturers in the United States, was a principal weapons designer during the Vietnam War and that the early M-16 was called "a Mattel" because it looked like a toy with its lightweight plastic stock.

= The Deployment of Gadgets =

In Vietnam, American commodities were not only a dependable resource; they offered reassurance in an unfamiliar world. Physical equipment that denied the guerrilla the possibility of expansion, that cordoned off a protected environment from an insurgent one, was highly cherished. Rockets and machine guns, says Philip Caputo, "were merely technological equivalents of the gourds and rattles natives use to chase away evil spirits" (81), and the use of physical gadgets was associated with fencing off a political ideology. The idea of exorcising the devil, or at least of forcing him to stay on the outside of some insurmountable fence, may be observed in Robert McNamara's announcement on 7 September 1967 of the American plan to build a "barrier" between North and South Vietnam and to block the infiltration of North Vietnamese forces and supplies. The "barrier," announced McNamara, would consist of barbed wire, mines, and "sophisticated devices."[11] As an attempt to stop military incursions this idea of a *cordon sanitaire* was but one more example of an American designer's pipe dream, a quasi-Puritanical attempt by the government "to control physically people it did not understand."[12]

The deployment of gadgets for ideological and cultural purposes is a recurring theme in the Americanization of Vietnam. The war effort was an immediate beneficiary of the commitment to increased military capacity and technological growth in the space and defense industries by the Eisenhower administration, which was made in response to the Russian success with ICBMs and the launching of Sputnik in 1957. After Congress passed the National Defense Education Act in 1958, huge amounts of funds were pumped into the American educational plant. Of crucial importance in the design and development of military technology was the fact that scientists and engineers were able to move back and forth between the military, aerospace, and commercial sectors during the 1960s, since, as Jeffrey M. Schevitz tells us, the technology required to send a man to the moon, and to wage a war in Vietnam, was "virtually the same."[13] It has been estimated that in the mid-1960s between 60 and 70 percent of the nation's engineers were directly or indirectly related to the defense and space effort; in 1967, according to government statistics, almost 54 percent of all engineers in manufacturing industries were employed by ordinance, aircraft, electronics, and instruments, the four defense-aerospace industries. The escalation of the Vietnam War created numerous jobs for engineers and scientists in the military and aerospace industries. In the 1960s new organizations within the Department of Defense were established to coordinate the transformation of the weapons-makers' primary activities from the strategic systems necessary for an all-out war to the tactical systems necessary for fighting limited counterinsurgency wars.

In this way, the weapons-makers' work was integrated with the requirements of American foreign policy in the late 1960s. According to a Department of Defense report in 1966:

> In order to seek out systematically just what was needed by our forces in Southeast Asia, the military departments expanded their research and development efforts in Vietnam in conjunction with the Joint Research and Test Activity. JRATA had been created in 1964 with the specific responsibility of obtaining statements from field commanders on their most urgent needs and translating these into formal requests for the development of new technology, which were then given priority over all other "normal" requirements laid down by the military departments.[14]

By 1967 $2 billion of public and private money was being invested in the creation of think tanks for the purposes of developing scientific research and technology, much of which found its way into Vietnam. Think tanks also sprang up within the armed forces themselves to create weapons and counterweapons and to evolve new systems of warfare.

The emphasis on the specific creation of what Malcolm Browne calls "tangible gadgets" created a technological vocabulary and framework within which the Vietnam War was increasingly imprisoned. For military strategists, says Browne, "it was comforting to conceive of thought as something concrete, something that could be generated and stored in a tangible think tank. Not surprisingly, the vast bulk of thought that resulted had to do almost exclusively with tangible gadgets."[15]

= A Consumer's War =

To the American soldier this was not an altogether unwelcome response, given the consumer age into which he had been born and his belief in technology as a dependable resource. It is not surprising that *Stars and Stripes* constantly featured a buoyant and successful American technology on the cover of its news magazines in Vietnam during the 1960s and 1970s. Especially prominent were the stories about winning the space race. If the planets had succumbed to American technology, so must the peasantry of North Vietnam. Machine dreams such as these made sense to a generation, many of whose aspirations and expectations were governed by the appearance of new consumer products and attractive consumer designs.

(This applied to black soldiers as much as it did to whites in Vietnam. If the gadgets of Vietnam were the creations of a highly educated, urban-based, scientific elite, they did not discriminate on the basis of racial use. In fact they were offered as seductive instruments of expression and enjoyment. Although Vietnam is often referred to as a poor man's war, a black's war, a Hispanic's war, there is little evidence to suggest that blacks resisted the process of consumer socialization or that black levels of expectation did not adjust to those of white consumer-conscious adolescents. In fact, even though discrimination was rife in Vietnam, there is evidence to suggest that many blacks and Hispanics volunteered for the draft in order to experience the equal rights they were denied at home.[16])

In *Dispatches* the attraction of a Loach helicopter is sexual: "It was incredible those little ships were the most beautiful things flying in Vietnam (you had to stop once in a while and admire the machinery), they just hung there above those bunkers like wasps outside a nest. 'That's sex,' the captain said. 'That's pure sex' " (131). The effect the Loach has on the mind of the voyeur is compelling: "you had to stop . . . and admire." What the Loach offers to those who observe it from the ground is a stylish performance, a sleek sexual aesthetic. When the Loach plants its seed of destruction, it Westernizes the Viet Cong; it makes them historically and culturally sub-missive. Clean and elegant and beautiful, the Loach appears to absolve the pilot from all moral responsibility (sex is death and death is attractive), and, by virtue of its appearance, distances the observer from the consequences of the violence it inflicts.

In the streamlining of sexual weaponry and the customization of military equipment the range of "American gadgets brought to bear on the Vietnamese war [was] practically limitless."[17] Military industries geared their products to the expectations and sensibilities of the enlisted men. Remington, Colt, and Mattel realized that many of the soldiers who fought in Vietnam were men whose commitment to the army extended to no more than the 365 days they were required to spend in the country. Accordingly, the weapons industry balanced the soldier's obligation to fight and kill with his need to minimize the consequence of his actions. In Vietnam modern technology not only was able to demonstrate its range and firepower but also appeared able to cam-ouflage the physical evidence of damage. The bullet of an M-16 was designed to impact in such a way as to "tone down" the reality of damage in the mind of the person who inflicted it. The bullet, says Herman Rapaport, "tumbles when hitting the body, shearing off portions of flesh and bone. To be wounded by this bullet is to sustain extensive physical damage, but not so much that the body will never recover, not so much as to be 'inhuman.' "[18] The creating of an aesthetically acceptable wound distanced the soldier from the object of his attentions and obscured his knowledge of the consequence of his actions.

The existence of gadgets satisfied the expectations of a consumer market, and this applied as much to recreational commodities as it did to the various weapon systems. Vietnam was a production-line war which took place during a period of unprecedented domestic affluence. The gadgets of Vietnam, therefore, should not be regarded simply as products of laboratory experimentation, but as customized creations, items on the shelf which the soldier might take advantage of with his purchasing power and customer choice. The creation of surroundings that were well-supplied with goods and services, the presentation of war as the pursuit of commodity, reaffirmed the soldier's belief in the market. The need to know "how to do things the Vietnamese way" seemed unimportant to men who "knew they had" only 365 days to spend in the country.[19]

In *Meditations in Green* the PX store is "the largest building on the base," a place of almost Dreiserian mystery and luxury. It is entered with reverence:

> Soldiers of every rank crowded the narrow aisles, touching with dirty fingers the stacks of electric shavers, Japanese cameras, Olympic swimming trunks, the plastic packaging of hair driers no-one but an officer's mistress would ever use or want, not even having to buy, the touch alone sufficient, a moment's respite from the strife outside in the intimate contact of hand to synthetic as if these various goods and appliances were the last relics of a distant age of faith whose remaining magic, dim and uncertain, lingered about the few surviving objects of its ownership. (123–24)

It might be an extravagance to claim that "even the most remote outposts" received "top-drawer Hollywood movies, usually a new one every night"; nevertheless, a great "feat of logistics" was accomplished in providing the soldiers with book and musical-tape libraries, motorboats and water skis, and even a bowling alley. In Saigon swimming pools were also available, though "at the expense of the Vietnamese public from whom the pool was taken over."[20]

In 1968 the *Saigon Daily News* commented that providing troops "with as many facilities" as there were at home was "ludicrous." The energy required to satisfy consumer expectations, as if the drugstore and the shopping mall were just around the corner, was enormous. "War or no war, refrigerators, radio networks, newspapers, and *Playboy* magazines are a must all the same. You can by no stretch of the imagination figure out how many planes and helicopters and ships are needed to provide such amenities, and how many troops are used to doing the numerous non-combat chores."[21] The effect of consumerized warfare on the American soldier was never adequately understood, and styles of plenty and economic abundance were left unchecked on the presumption that the morale of the soldiers would benefit. But, as Malcolm Browne has indicated, the technological and material benefits of life in Vietnam consistently undermined the visceral urge of the soldier to compete: "War was all right as long as it could be carried out 30,000 feet over the battlefield on a nine to five basis with air-conditioned PX stores and swimming pools at the head-quarters compounds."[22] Moreover, a soldier's morale could easily be swallowed up by that product-driven structure. For this reason Robert Mason concludes his autobiography, *Chickenhawk*, with a warning that the helicopter pilot should not be regarded as an epiphenomenon of the manufacturing process, a commodity with a short life span, designed at Fort Rucker and offered for consumption in South Vietnam.

In American literature the nerve center of South Vietnam is a city of seething, expatriate energies and Western consumer values. For Robert Stone, Saigon is a colonial city transformed into a junkyard, a French estate redesigned as a back lot. In *Dog Soldiers* Saigon is a city of starers and loiterers, a dream dump of the Western imagination. It is a city of objects and objectlike people who are dwarfed and deadened by the material world. The scale of the chaos reminds us of Los Angeles in the American novel of the 1930s. As Alvin Kernan puts it, "As the fake encrusts itself on the fake, obeying no law except the need for the novel, the result can only be fantastic disorder, combinations of things unrelated, great jumbles, and the division of those things which properly belong together."[23]

The search for sensation not only perverts history; it fragments and rearranges the human character. In *Dog Soldiers* the American visitor is a crazed consumer, forced to survive in a landscape where the quest for the novel is monstrous and garish. Feelings of disaffection and impending riot lie beneath the surface. Saigon in the late 1960s, says Mary McCarthy, "is like a stewing Los Angeles, shading into Hollywood, Venice Beach, and Watts." The desire for profit is self-debasing and socially ingenious. McCarthy's Saigon, like Nathanael West's Los Angeles, "seems to exhibit both the promise of modern civilization and the symptoms of the decline of the West."[24] The immediate need is the purchase of commodity. On the streets "there is hardly anything native to buy, except flowers and edibles and firecrackers at Tet time and—oh yes—souvenir dolls. Street vendors and children are offering trays of American cigarettes and racks on racks of Johnnie Walker, Haig and Haig, Black and White (which are either black market, stolen from the PX, or spurious depending on the price); billboards outside car agencies advertise Triumphs, Thunderbirds, MKGs, Corvettes, For Delivery here or Stateside, payment on Easy Terms."[25]

For McCarthy, cultural opportunism is a deficiency in the South Vietnamese character, whereas for a writer like Mark Frankland it represents a feature of the country's syncretic tradition. McCarthy ignores the Viet Cong whose acts of cultural opportunism in the South were part of an effective guerrilla strategy. Communist insurgents in South Vietnam devoted themselves to imitating American needs and tools. They acquired and adapted a variety of items from the American military: U.S. Carbines, M-1s, M-16s. They also exploited the product dependencies of the American soldier to undermine his political will. The style of the Viet Cong was not high-minded, nor was it the product of a self-contained economic structure or a rigid system of belief. Insurgent strategy was parasitical, ingenious, and flexible. It was built on plagiarism, capture, and theft. It exploited the familiarity of American objects for subversive purposes and the soldier's need to reward himself by using the things he knew and trusted. When Viet Cong girls sold Coca-Cola, they used genuine Coke bottles and a cola substitute in order to camouflage the ground glass the bottles contained. Through his love for the product and his trust in American manufacture and design, the soldier literally bought his own death. He wasted himself through his purchasing power and his corporate loyalties.

═ Machine Dreams ═

Morris Dickstein's observation on the sixties takes an easy but misleading route: "Part of the decadent spirit of the sixties was surely Luddite. It saw machines, and was determined to break them or shut them down: the war was a machine, society was a machine, even the university was a machine producing cogs for society."[26] The liberation of one's race and sex through the smashing of a fog machine—as happens in Kesey's *One Flew over the Cuckoo's Nest*—may have been emotionally attractive to the counterculture, but it wasn't integral to the lives of those who went to Vietnam. The Vietnam generation was nothing if not product conscious and fashion conscious. In the fifties and sixties the language of style and material design cut across class lines, if not racial ones. Customization defined the scope of adolescent rebellion and provided a focus for creative expression. Cars and bikes, the inventions of a corporate, urban society, also became the means of expression for those who wished to distance themselves from the values cherished by that society. Cars may well have been the most conspicuous symbol of parental affluence in postwar America, but they were also, as Tom Wolfe has said, "the physical means of triumph over family and community restrictions." Cars were objects of performance: fictions of energy, thrust, experimentation, and style—a symbol of the willing acceptance by America's youth of the benefits of technology as a way of satisfying their "love of direct aggression."[27]

Technology was integral to the lives of those who went to Vietnam. Do-it-yourself technology and car customization was one of the most important and unifying features of American adolescent life during the years leading up to the Vietnam War. Philip Caputo's description of Lance Corporal Marshall is revealing: "a freelance knight of the quarter-mile strip, given to telling tales about back-road jousts won on his chrome-gilt steed, a chopped Chevy with a California rake, four-speed stick, four-eleven rear end, and a fuel-injected mill that idles with a throaty rumble and exploded like Vesuvius when he wound her out, red-lined the tac, and did zee-ro to sixty in five flat" (*Rumor*, 24–25). Some of the most popular music of the decade was devoted to machines, most of it was played on machines, and almost all of it was amplified and transmitted on machines. Many of the groups' names conveyed the importance of machines—the Hondas or Ronnie and the Daytonas—and Brian Wilson of the Beach Boys wrote many of his songs in appreciation of the automobile's lyric possibilities. The rebel, the musician, the engineer, the designer—each used the bike or the car to advertise his expertise. Machines demanded attention and were the principal means of attracting attention by those who performed with them.

Vietnam was a war that underwrote but did not necessarily discredit the belief in technology which the "massive infusions of money into every level of society"[28] had made possible in the 1950s and 1960s. The idea that personal security was determined by physical equipment and that the use of machinery was an essential means of self-expression is explored by Jayne Anne Phillips, a novelist in whose work "machine dreams make up much of what might ordinarily pass as the personal unconscious of the people she describes."[29] For Phillips the American soldier who went to Vietnam was obsessed by machines. He was not, as Nancy Anisfield suggests, "taken from the security of home and family" and "suddenly thrust into a world" where his everyday existence revolved around "sophisticated weaponry, military regimentation, and . . . an environment and climate totally alien to him."[30] Anisfield's anti-technological stance is a favorite of those who neglect the powerful reassurance technology provides. For working-class boys who went to Vietnam a belief in machinery was a way of maintaining a connection with home, a nostalgic reminder of the way things were. Machines reawakened the memories of the track. "I loved flying in helicopters because you went fast," says a soldier in *Nam*. "Its power, like having a Corvette. I got to do something I'd wanted to do since I was a kid, which was touch clouds."[31]

In reading Robert Mason's *Chickenhawk* we get a sense of the opportunities Vietnam offered to those who were proficient in engineering or who possessed navigational skills. Mason is a southerner who appreciates machine-made style. The same reflex abilities, hand and eye coordination, manual dexterity, timing and touch, that are necessary to drive a hot car at a speed approaching 200 m.p.h. are also needed to fly a fully loaded Huey into a hot landing zone under heavy fire. Similarly, in *365 Days* Ronald Glasser endorses the connection between the world of flight and the sensibility of the South: "There is not a Volkswagen in a parking lot at Fort Rucker, Alabama, or at Hunter in Georgia, nor a Scouter or Ford Fairlane running the roads. It's all Honda 500's and BSA Scramblers, Corvettes with the heads lowered and Dodges with 3.11 rear ends. The kids who choose to go there are of a type—lean and tough, mechanically oriented, obsessed with speed and daring, and incredibly brave" (195).

= The Southern Pilot =

Chickenhawk introduces us not only to the attraction of using customized machinery (many of the helicopters used in Vietnam were specifically designed or adapted for the purpose of combat) but also to the art and craft of the navigator and the knowledge that had to be assimilated as a condition of survival. During his training on an H-23 Hiller, Mason talks at length about his relationship with the instructor pilots—"mythical beings whom we held in the highest respect" (23)—and the skills those pilots transferred to only the best cubs. "All the parts wanted to go their own way, but somehow the instructor was controlling them, averaging their various motions into a position three feet above the grass. We floated above the ground, gently rising and falling on an invisible sea" (25).

We are reminded, not least in the use of water imagery, of the training of an earlier southern navigator—the apprenticeship of the cub pilot to the skilled riverboatman Horace Bixby—in Twain's *Life on the Mississippi*. In both cases the key consideration is the search for control and balance at moments of crisis, the use of cerebral and tactile power to feather and control delicate machinery. Like Mark Twain in *Life on the Mississippi*, Mason describes the creative tension that is a hallmark of the pilot's accomplishment, what Scott Fitzgerald refers to as "the ability to hold two opposed ideas in the mind at the same time, and still retain the ability to function."[32] The ambiguity at the heart of the American experience becomes a source of creative strength for both Horace Bixby and the instructor pilot, a way of establishing a line of control. Each writer refers us to the continual dialogue that takes place in the pilot's mind between the "language" of the elements—the need to achieve a personal understanding of the river or the air—and the random capacities of boat and chopper. Navigation is the art of coherent statement, the making of forms that retain their shape in spite of the horseplay of the natural world and the potential for anarchism within the machine. In the person of the pilot the dramatic amalgam is released into art. The pilot lives at the crossroads of American culture—the world of the machine and that of the garden—and he allows himself to be pulled in two directions. He is devoted to understanding nature as phenomenon at the same time that he is committed to the celebration of hard technological realities. He is the great coordinator of unfocused energies—wilderness energies, industrial energies. Through him, America is able to make sense of itself and to manage its own momentum.

Skill and science intermingle in the moment of competition—on the flight path or the race track or the Mississippi River. Twain describes the steamboat races in *Life on the Mississippi* as dramatic occasions. The noise, the smell, the massive crowds, and hard-working crews, the "consuming excitement"[33] of a great spectatorial occasion—these scenes are evoked in *Chickenhawk* whenever we observe the formation flying of helicopter pilots in the Ia Drang Valley. The pilot's skills remind us also of the stock car driver in the American South, of Junior Johnson, the legendary driver from Wilkesboro, North Carolina, with whom, says Tom Wolfe, a "whole . . . class of people identified." The lineage of the South lives on: transmitted through history from one machine to another, and from one charismatic performer to another. The daring of Bixby anticipates the exploits of Junior Johnson, and Junior Johnson has many of the qualities of the pilot who flies in Vietnam with the cavalry. Each is a version of what Wolfe calls "The Last American Hero," the last of a line whose style is passed on in the changing aspect of American machines.[34]

= The Helicopter as Icon =

If the helicopter allowed for the pursuit of stylized heroism, it also provided a display of corporate and governmental power. It represented what America had made of itself, technologically and militarily, and it represented, in an untamed environment, the elevated energies of corporate capitalism. The helicopter was an instrument of American belief, its job to outwit and subdue—outgun, outrun—an insurgent enemy. It also embodied a strong sense of its own Americanness, its own cultural iconography, its separateness from the world of the ground.

In deploying the helicopter, American design set forth a definition of military necessity and military possibility in spite of the nature of physical realities in Vietnam. Army officers argued that since it was extremely difficult to train large numbers of ordinary American soldiers in guerrilla warfare, "the Army does not need to adopt guerrilla measures. Rather, the helicopter can be used, once the enemy is found, to re-supply US forces so rapidly that 20 men can be landed every minute."[35] As Alisdair Spark has said, the helicopter seemed capable of doing "more than just solve the problems of countering insurgency, it appeared to transform the guerrilla equation" by "eradicating at a stroke previously intractable problems of ambush [and] manpower." The invention not only determined the response to the actual problem; it determined the response in spite of the problem and therefore obscured it. "Air mobility proved a seductive strategy for civilian and military policy-makers alike," and it gained in legitimacy for appearing to emulate "guerrilla mobility." The helicopter offered the symbolic possibility of fighting a range war with fast transportation, in this case the "cavalry." In fact, so strong was the army's preference for air mobility that by the end of the war the marines were experimenting with one-man lift packs in which each man, in effect, had his own helicopter.

The assumption that one could determine the outcome of a war by quickening the pace at which the war was being conducted—the idea that he who fights quickest always fights best—was summarized by Gen. William De Puy when he claimed that "the VC needs ten days to transfer three battalions. We manage five battalions in a day."[36] Senator Henry Jackson (from the state of Washington, whose prosperity depended upon airplane production) also enthused about the helicopter's versatility in similar terms: "The sky is a highway without roadblocks. The helicopter frees the government forces from dependence on the poor road system and canals which are the usual arteries of communication."[37] The idea of utilizing an implement of American design to solve a particular environmental problem reflected a historic belief in the ability of machines to operate effectively in wilderness conditions. The expectation was difficult to fulfill for the simple reason, as S. L. A. Marshall has pointed out, that if it is difficult to fight a jungle war with helicopters, it is even more difficult if this is done by denying oneself many of the advantages that traditional armor and land-based artillery units can provide. However much the helicopter "became the American touchstone, symbolizing a transcendent American power incarnate in metal," the fact remained that to rely on it was to make the "tacit admission," as one U.S. adviser put it, "that we didn't control the ground."[38]

In *Chickenhawk* Robert Mason's helicopter, the Huey, is a powerful cultural icon. As Mason says, the soldiers would gather around the Huey and talk to him " 'knowingly,' as people do around race car drivers" (245). The problem is that the Huey is not the exclusive property of the pilot, but reflects the differing aspirations of those who manufacture it, those who deploy it, and those, finally, to whom it is assigned. The expectations of manufacturers, strategists, and pilots may appear synonymous, but we cannot assume that they always are. The only consistency may be that all expect the helicopter to function in the interests of one side and not of the other. The extent to which the helicopter lends itself to a definition of what those interests are depends upon a variety of things. Here there is often a conflict of opinion, not only between the fliers themselves but also between what the military defines as duty and what the flier defines as personal style. Mason's gift is for an aggressive ingenuity; he accepts a calculated risk and extends the range and the territory of the machine in order to save lives. Feelings of "transcendent American power" and liberation are balanced by a constant admission that his source of energy is, at best, provisional and that "power" is at the mercy of those "on the ground." Mason has a strong sense of conviction in the importance of doing his job as a helicopter pilot to the best of his abilities; at the same time he has an equally strong awareness of the limitation of his status as the emissary of a culture whose mission seems increasingly suspect. Mason's attitude is an amalgam of idealism and duty tempered with survival instinct. What *Chickenhawk* offers is a demonstration of belief in the possibilities for action offset by an awareness of the imminence of death. The reason for the title soon becomes obvious. On the ground Mason is a chicken; in the sky he is a hawk.

Mason is an exhilarated learner. To survive for any length of time means carrying a "bag of survival tricks" (111), a collection of unorthodox skills that lie outside the military syllabus. While he may dream of getting out of the war, he cannot deny the thrill of being in it. He once says, after he has been grounded for ten days: "As I walked out to the flight line, I felt weightless with joy. My work had become my home, and I was glad to be back" (301). Mason describes his "work" as an act of supreme theater, what Kenneth Tynan has defined as "high-definition performance."

When Mason leaves Vietnam he goes home and takes up a job as a military helicopter instructor. Mason is aware that Wilkesboro, North Carolina, is not Vietnam. Working-class kids who go to Vietnam pay a heavy price for their recklessness and their dreams of glory. The risk of death for a helicopter pilot in the air cavalry is extremely high, and helicopter rescue missions, of the kind that Mason generally flies, are aborted only in the most extreme circumstances. Even though he has become mentally exhausted and reacts to the war as a cause that "enraged" him (395), he takes his work very seriously. In spite of his reservations about the war, Mason teaches the cub pilots what the "key experience" in Vietnam really is, what tricks and gifts are required for survival. He says: "I taught them stuff not covered in the school syllabus. The school was interested in getting numbers out of the door. I was interested in their survival" (390).

Mason does with helicopters what Junior Johnson did (for Tom Wolfe) with racing cars; he redefines the limits of performance and forces a machine to act out "the kind of play that challenged our skills" (278). Mason redesigns the structure of "work" to resemble that of "play" in order to make survival possible. Play can never be fully separated from the skills that are learned at the controls of the craft. For Mason, "just going out to resupply some patrols on a secure road was so bland that we played games to make it interesting. Resler and I took turns flying low level down the road, seeing who could hold the ship in the turns" (214). *Chickenhawk* is a celebration of skills and tools and the range of expression that tools permit. It lets us observe the Vietnam war as an offering to design, a centering point for a culture that is committed to personal expression through the use of material forms and structures.

In *Chickenhawk* space is ethnocentric (the air is American, the ground Vietnamese), and air mobility is an American skill. The language of Jesus nuts and rotor blades does not refer us to crucifixion but to elevated mission, a movement away from the Vietnam villages and the primitive hinterland. The rhythm of flight represents a simple experience of good and bad. Strength is retrieved by withdrawing from the ground. To stay grounded is to allow the demeaning energies of native society to undermine the purpose and vitality of American mission. To rise from the earth and to experience the pull of space is a morally and emotionally correct feeling; it is an action normally associated with the airlift of casualties to a safe American location. Rescue and healing thus become a movement into space and through space, a thrust toward the safer horizons of the imaginary city: "We flew east to Happy Valley at 3000 feet. I was always happy to be flying high. Even higher would have been fine with me. Very few pilots were killed by staying away from the ground. . . . The jungle was the enemy's ally, and as long as he forced us to fight in its strangling hold, we would lose" (102). Descent brings with it a confrontation with an obscure congregation, a face-off with the forest that tangles blades and hopes. Philip Caputo feels this acutely: "When the helicopters flew off, a feeling of abandonment came over us. Charley Company was now cut off from the outside world. We had crossed a line of departure all right, a line of departure between the known and the unknown. The helicopters made it seem familiar. Being American we were comfortable with machines, but with the aircraft gone we were struck by the utter strangeness of this rank and rotted wilderness" (79).

= Tooling: Home and Abroad =

In the "rotted wilderness" a soldier can either panic or act with the fervor of a Puritan saint. In Jack Fuller's *Fragments* Neumann devises "a goodwill mission," a plan to improve the "morale" of the troops and eliminate "habits" that "were becoming sloppy."[39] His troops, "the Blues," "tool on out there" (194) and "adopt a village." This is the home of an American scout, Apache, who lived in Xuan The but overcame the "apostasy" (143) of living with the Viet Minh. Neumann believes he can do something that the villagers cannot "do for themselves." He decides to renovate a dispensary that lies in ruins, overgrown with vines (145), and to protect the village from physical attack by the NVA with concrete block and mortar. In this "goodwill mission" the language of design and the designing of belief are "clear" and "righteous" (105). Fuller provides a definite answer to Crèvecoeur's question, "What is the American, this new man?" He is the contract worker, the landscape planner, the visible saint as entrepreneur who builds a "hedge" in which he enacts the colonial ideal of moral plantation. Neumann's structure is "strong and angular against the dark, formless threat of the jungle," its style is "alien" (157–58) to the natural environment which appears to contain a tropism for disorder. Neumann's expertise is self-centered; it derives from a desire to fill the space that belongs to others with American forms. Significantly, his first task in Xuan The is to take a mistress, to penetrate Tuyet's space, to develop within her "a big six-inch interest in pacification" (155).

Neumann's styles of life and art are those of a Protestant, and his "aura of authority" (31) is that of a contractor who works "in shifts" (147) with backward children. In contrast to the loose, "organizing principle" of "the seasons" (160) that permeates the life of the villagers, Neumann introduces a language of material design and conviction: "They understand when you give them things," he says. "Bricks and mortar. Plain and simple" (161). Xuan The is an experimental plantation for the Blues. As Neumann says "with one Rome plow I could have this bush busted in less than a day" (168). With its "solid bunkers" and "a moat" (169) the renovated Xuan The indicates the unwillingness of the American designer to incorporate the native features of the environment into his work.

The pretense of fortification is easily ridiculed by the Communists. When Xuan The is attacked and Neumann's hootch overrun, the authority of western architecture is undermined. The jungle cannot be controlled nor can the building of mission stations convert the people to Christianity. Policies of reconstruction are meaningless: "The bush kept trying to squeeze in on us, you see, to push us out" (114).

During the attack Neumann kills an intruder whom he finds in the hootch of his lover, Tuyet. The intruder is Tuyet's brother whom Neumann assumes, without proper knowledge, to be a Viet Cong. When Tuyet resists she, too, is killed, along with her younger brother and, finally, her mother. Neumann creates an appropriate set of targets on which to expend his frustration with those who appear to have betrayed his mission. What he sees as treachery is simply the action of a world he cannot capture, the closeness of a people whose culture escapes the moral enterprise and rubble-clearing activity of a "sweaty American" (149). When the NVA attack Xuan The, Neumann's "purpose" (149) counts for nothing. In the ensuing battle the Americans find it difficult to identify their opponents. "I imagined the enemy soldiers laughing," says Morgan, "as my shots tattered the trees high above their heads or harrassed the vegetation on their flanks" (200). In the jungle, as Morgan recognizes, "our problem was what we didn't know. . . . In Vietnam if something had any value, it was gone the moment you took your eyes off it" (205).

Only Neumann's return to the United States prevents the further loss of what is valuable. In rural America, where generations of farmers have devoted themselves to continuous clearing, one's view is no longer obstructed by the disorderly jungle or its inhabitants. Space, once cleared, does not intimidate. On the cultivated farms of Martindale, "the land stretched out flat all the way to the horizon, broken only by little groves of trees and the wire" (257). The relationship of family and "family farm" is emphasized as a defined ideal by the clear, unbroken view the family farm provides. The clarity of life is conveyed by "the calm, empty distance," the removal of wilderness, "the peaceful oblivion of the fields, the vacancy of the sky" (259). In this structured world of homes "nestling" between the trees "and the steeple of a church rising above the tallest limbs," nature has been subdued. Where the sound of gunfire from occasional hunters is "muffled by the open space" and is "barely heard" (254), there can be no menace.

In Martindale Neumann makes good the loss of Xuan The by "fixin'" things up for his wife and family. In "one of them good old farmhouses" (262) he protects himself with chicken wire, shingles, "brightly" (269) painted rooms and a tool shed, so that nothing can "threaten the home" (273). In a shack "rigged up with electricity" Neumann keeps "his tools all set out" (275) like "an animal enslaved by his weapons." As he recalls Xuan The, he massages a gun from "barrel to stock, rubbing his fingers on the oily blue steel" (280), as if to confirm the identity of his world in a statement of mechanical and sexual force. Neumann remembers the violation of his hootch by Tuyet's brother as an act of penetration, the threat of a rival. In the folklore of the American new-man, guns are the ultimate sexual referent. Tuyet's brother dies because he has no means of disproving the referent that imprisons him. "I didn't recognize the man. He wasn't from the village, but when I saw the rifle, I knew what he was" (277). To name a weapon is to define the person who owns the weapon. "The man was a VC. It was an AK-forty-seven. It lay there next to him in the dirt" (277). Neumann shoots because in a world of obscure truth and indeterminate action where the facts of life are "always slipping" (284), the use of guns can, momentarily, make the "facts" go away.

The Frustration of Capitalist Strategies

At $90 million a day the Vietnam War represented an immense and inflationary cost. The Communists realized, through a skillful reading of the logic of capitalism, the means by which they could effectively subvert the expenditure. The massive accumulation of plant machinery and capital equipment and the promise of physical release through action that the equipment implied, was countered by a guerrilla philosophy that did not accept the logic of attrition or the need for conventional military encounter. According to Philip Caputo, the experience of patrol was particularly frustrating since "there was no pattern to these patrols and operations. Without a front, flanks, or rear, we fought a formless war against a formless enemy who evaporated like the morning jungle mists, only to materialize in some unexpected place. It was a haphazard, episodic sort of combat. Most of the time, nothing happened; but when something did, it happened instantaneously and without warning" (89).

Since military engagements were often inconclusive or "anticlimactic"[40] the capitalist energies of the United States were in a state of constant suspension. The problem lay in determining how best to dispose of the accumulating reservoir of surplus. For their part the Communists were content to allow the reserves of energy to build up, to "let capitalism choke on its surplus values" and prolong the struggle by engaging with the military in ways that were random and inconclusive. "The Viet Cong knew," says Herman Rapaport, "that what Westerners want is a shoot-out at the 'Okay' Corral, that they see history in terms of a fascistic sacrificial machine where excess or surplus is ignited. . . . To sacrifice, to reconcile groups, to overcome conflict, to make peace, this the Viet Cong and the N.V.A. frustrated at every point." By using the arts of camouflage and ambush and by refusing to satisfy the expectation of a decisive battle, the Communist Vietnamese adopted a strategy that "did not enter into the capitalist mirror of production and consumption." Instead, they exploited many of those " 'repressed' layers of terror and suffering" which America brought with it to South Vietnam. Their behavior underscored, as Eric Wolfe says, the relationship between the possibilities of resistance, the development of a revolutionary ethos, and a certain constitutive distance from the social and economic logic of capital. The art of war for the Vietnamese rebel was an "anticlimactic" process, "just a movement," in which action was promised and gratification denied.[41]

In a world where the logic of production leads to the creation of unexpended energies and the accumulation of surplus power, those who fight are driven by the search for confrontation and climax. The absence of satisfactory resolutions, the frequency of inconclusive confrontations, the episodic nature of the firefights and ambushes—the random killing instead of the desired shoot-out—creates an atmosphere of increasing frustration.

In the literature and film of Vietnam, weapons not only resolve disputes, they create them. In the absence of known enemies it is necessary to simulate both targets and opponents since the performance of killing must always be commensurate with the tool that inflicts it. Where technology proliferates, it creates a market that inflames desire. When a soldier says that he kills "enthusiastically,"[42] he is invariably fulfilling the perceived potential of American machinery. In film and fiction the need to take technology to the limits, to act in a manner that is dramatically worthy of a mode of production—to match high-grade engineering with high-grade stunts—is common. (This is also true of a postwar world where, as Norman Mailer tells us, modern society is largely a continuation of the army by other means.)

In the America that the veteran Kowalski returns to in Michael Sarafian's film *Vanishing Point* (1971), surplus is endemic to American society. Kowalski, an ex-policeman with an honorable discharge, brings with him to America the stored-up energy of a veteran who seeks satisfaction. An ex-bike racer who now delivers cars faster than anyone, Kowalski exploits the benefits of a technology that can take him wherever he wishes to go and at whatever speed he wishes to travel. Kowalski cannot downgrade or domesticate his expectations of what technology can do for him, nor can he suppress the need to live dangerously in a world loaded up with more than he can handle.

Kowalski moves between a world of surplus and a world of boundaries, limits, and speed controls. His quest is to use up his energies in spite of controls, to drive his Dodge Challenger at maximum voltage from Denver to California toward a final, cataclysmic vanishing point, a point beyond existence. There is a sense of honor involved in this act, the spiritual fulfillment of a contract between man and machine which Sarafian intends us to empathize with. As Eric Mottram says, "Kowalski finally accepts defeat and crashes his car to explode in a police barricade of huge yellow clearage vehicles. He has used up his resources. There is no place for his courage, energy and driving skills."[43]

In the fictionalized or filmed versions of Vietnam, extravagant techno-logical violence, often carrying overtones of sexual release, is the American wish-fulfillment response to the frustration of guerrilla warfare. In *Apocalypse Now*, for example, Killgore survives but, like Kowalski, in a stylish way. Technology provides Killgore with a voice. He comes to his target on swelling Wagnerian strains with "Death from Above," a message imprinted on the sexual belly of his chopper. Killgore's sex is transmitted from a distance; it avoids the earthy contact and Vietnamization of Kurtz, a man with his bases broad and low who has no regard for the tools of civilization or for planting seed in cultivated land. Killgore's cavalry roam the skies at a distance from the land and subject it to assault with napalm, guns, rockets, and music. Killgore's exhibits the traits of the underground but his convictions are those of Westmoreland and the Pentagon. Killgore is the charismatic, corporate man: dangerous, adversarial, colloquial, and his beliefs are always those of the committed warrior.

With the aid of a customized sound system his chopper becomes his pulpit. In an audio-conscious, postliterate world, Killgore's message comes from on high, conveyed in a language that reverberates over the jungle floor. The message is clear. In a war where "you can't tell who's who" because the people "all look alike," then "the only way to take out your frustrations" is to "go out and shoot somebody."[44]

In Takeshi Kaiko's *Into a Black Sun* the American soldiers, under the direction of Captain Wain, discover a holy pond in the town of Huian. Wain attacks with grenades the pond around which the villagers are praying. Wain's explanation to the narrator is simple: "This fucking water contains a magic fish. We're in the middle of a strategic operation. We're trying to pacify this pond, with grenades and machine guns" (11). The town is full of rumor and the people attribute miraculous curative powers to the magic fish. The Min-istry of Culture and the Department of Psychological Warfare in Saigon "fearing an epidemic of superstition [have] ordered division headquarters to take some action. The fish was to be caught or killed, then displayed in the city square to put an end to the excitement" (12). Troops are dispatched. The pond is dynamited, dragged with a net, and then photographed by aerial reconnaissance. The "magic" fish, which has begun to appear in ponds in various parts of the province, is subjected to the full force of technological assault. As a source of mystical energy, real or imagined, the fish cannot be tolerated. Elimination is the logical response to a creature that is reputed to fly around (visiting different ponds in the province) without permission. As Wain says: "We'll sweep the pond with machine guns. If that doesn't do the trick, we'll call in a gunship tomorrow and loose off some rockets. That's all we can do" (12–13).

In James Park Sloan's *War Games* (1971) the problem of unsupervised energy and the anger of those who are unable to penetrate the mystery of the wilderness is resolved through fantasies of sexual conquest. Here, a young soldier, "impatient with unexciting duty," shoots a water buffalo and mortally wounds her. The men stand around to watch the beast die. "Then an idea began with an absurd boast, grew to a dare, and then to a bet. The men who had shot her were dispatched to her haunches to pull the buttocks apart. One by one the men approached and mounted her. The man who told the story believed—though no one could be sure—that he had been the one upon her when she died."[45]

The release of rage through catastrophe is also the subject of J. G. Ballard's postapocalyptic Vietnam western, *Hello America* (1981). Here, Killgore reappears as Charles Manson, a self-appointed president of the United States in a country now overrun with lush vegetation and exotic life forms. As Manson surveys the paradise of the West from a helicopter gunship he identifies as his enemies all the creatures of the wilderness, "massacring anything that moved."[46] In one particularly devastating sequence he murders deer, llamas, and a "bull-elephant trying to defend his small herd bathing in a Bel Air hotel pool." The bull is attacked and dies "in the bloody pool, still trumpeting in the boiling red water as the gunships circled around him like crazed sharks." The narrator senses that for Manson "life" is a "kind of disease." The contamination Manson fears is a virus bred in the wilderness. To control its spread Manson (aloof from the viral energies of the forest) administers death from the "glass partition" of a gunship. While Robert Mason rescues those whom the forest has sickened, Manson slaughters what he sees as the source of that sickness, the birds and animals—as if their physical attractiveness and fecundity threaten to spread pollution and disease.[47]

Fecundity and putrefaction merge in Vietnam. As the narrator remarks in *Into a Black Sun*, "the tropics are fecund and bountiful; but they're remorseless in their abundance, indifferent to the glut of honey, the ooze of putrefaction" (55). The natural world is as demeaning to Ballard's Manson as the vast and threatening sexuality of the whale is to Melville's Captain Ahab. It is a source of procreative menace, an energy center that flaunts its triumphant sexuality in the face of those it appears to have rendered sexless. Manson and Killgore are the self-appointed Puritan magistrates. Each employs the mechanical sex of the mad technologist as vigilante policeman in order to combat the sexual anarchy of a lawless world. Like the demented American Captain Wain, they act like "descendants of Captain Ahab, a strange, obsessive species, driven to fill the tormented soul with purpose and action" (165).

Where Melville's Ahab gets too close to the whale and is punished for it, Manson, like Killgore, retains his distance. In the Vietnam novel the abolition of distance brings with it the prospect of contamination. In Joe Haldeman's *The Forever War* (1974) William Mandella feels "unclean" when the Tauran aliens of Aleph Aurigae invade his space and bloody his suit.[48] Mandella speaks in the same "sick voice" that Alden Pyle uses in *The Quiet American* when the blood from the legless torso of a trishaw driver stains his shoes. In Haldeman's Stargate and Greene's Saigon, from science fiction through social fiction, the American way of war is the pursuit of purification. It is typically observed, says Philip Slater, "in the need to insulate carefully reared soldiers from the horror they cause."[49] In Vietnam, space is the condom for sexual technologists who fear infection, while "ethics," as Philip Caputo has said, seem "to be a matter of distance" (218).

8

Seeing
Vietnam

CIVILIAN AND MILITARY PERSPECTIVES ON MODERN WARFARE
are often revealed by the use of film narratives. The effect of these narratives
in American literature is commonly perceived as debilitating, as is the in-
sulation of the soldier that Philip Slater comments upon. The reference point
for criticism lies not in the analysis of Lawrence Ferlinghetti's Ladybird, who
assures President Johnson that "Vietnam was not a place but a state of mind,"[1]
but in John Aldridge's work on the American volunteers of World War I.
According to Aldridge the auxiliaries were possessed of a cinematic outlook.
"They were onlookers at a struggle in which, at the time, they had no personal
stake. . . . They were special observers, immunized by their nationality and
the good fortune of their service from all but the most picturesque aspects
of the war. As spectators, guests of the war by courtesy of the management,
they were infected with irresponsibility, thrilled at second hand by danger,
held to a pitch of excitement that made their old lives seem impossibly dull
and tiresome."[2]

＝　The Spectatorial Attitude　＝

The "spectatorial" attitude of the volunteers of World War I may have been shaped by the work of George Creel. Creel was head of the wartime Committee of Public Information and provided stimulating propaganda for the American people on the new motion picture screen prior to and during World War I. Creel was a man who "advertised" the war.[3] The distance many of his films created between the war environment of Europe and the expectations that civilians had of that environment is illustrated in Hemingway's short story "Soldier's Home." Krebs, who is probably not a volunteer, has remained with the marines on the Rhine until the summer of 1919 and returns home much later than the other American soldiers. The townspeople, "thrilled" by the language of the "atrocity stories" and the war reporting, have now become bored with "actualities." The filmic narratives Krebs brings with him do not conform to any of the approved filmic texts nor do they confirm the expectation of war as tourism. "There is a picture which shows him on the Rhine with two German girls and another corporal. Krebs and the corporal look too big for their uniforms. The German girls are not beautiful. The Rhine does not show in the picture." A "reaction" has set in among the people of the town. In order "to be listened to at all" Krebs has "to lie."[4] The transience of pictorial definitions reminds us of the "reaction" of Kismine in Scott Fitzgerald's "The Diamond as Big as the Ritz." She, too, developed an interest in the war but, having "seen a photograph of some wounded Serbian soldiers," had "lost interest in the whole proceedings."[5]

The photogenic quality of war is examined in Mary McCarthy's *Vietnam*. To its discoverers, Nha Trang beach is not a war zone but a garden in the wilderness awaiting cultivation, a visual delight that offers the possibility of exploitation though enclosure. Traveling in a C-130 McCarthy hears the pilot and the copilot discuss their "personal war aim . . . to make a killing, as soon as the war is over, in Vietnamese real estate." "From the air, while they kept an eye out for V.C., they had surveyed the possibilities and had decided on Nha Trang—'beautiful sand beaches'—better than Cam Ranh Bay—a 'desert.' They disagreed as to the kind of development that would make the most money: the pilot wanted to build a high-class hotel and villas, while the copilot thought that the future lay with low-cost housing."[6] Technology provides a panorama: it gives the pilot a chance to observe the world not as he knows it but as he hopes his clients might come to know it; and to imagine the metamorphosis of wartime killing into a peacetime "killing" in real estate. Below him, nature contains an observable design, a plan or pattern that may be interpreted on the basis of symbols: quality of sand, depth of shoreline, nature of rock and tidal flow. The important principle is the quest for a pictorial form that reveals itself in a sensible way and from which we derive dynamic inspiration.

The quest is both a commercial adventure and an allegory of Puritan duty. This notion of duty originates in the idea that the visible world has been granted spiritual status by God and is part of a divine plan in the unfolding of His elaborate—and profitable—mission in the wilderness.

Like McCarthy's pilots, the New England Puritan was an observer of landscape; his mission was that of the spiritual tourist who sought "to transform particular incidents into exemplary events, to transform individual experience into cultural fact."[7] The "exemplary events" were divine providences, revelations that provided clues to His divine plan and the spiritual correctness of the pilgrim's errand. "Exemplary" pursuits were rewarded with exemplary providences, manifestations in the physical world of divine purpose. All of God's creation was an open book which bore witness to His existence and purpose. Regarding this, Calvin had said, "God hath not only sown in the minds of men seeds of religion . . . but hath manifested himself in the formulation of every part of the world, and daily presents himself to public view, in such a manner, that they cannot open their eyes without being constrained to behold him."[8] The Puritans believed, therefore, that no part of nature was without a role to play in God's plan. Through the diligent and devout use of allegories men could discern a literal correspondence between a set of natural objects or phenomena and a separate and detachable set of spiritual truths. Arguing against the idea of an inner light, the Puritans believed that truth was to be observed in the external world. Only by the careful observation and analysis of the hardships imposed by nature would man discern the divine messages intended for him. The Book of Nature had been provided for man as a means of persuading his rational capacity that he had been chosen. In the pursuit of observation colonial life was intensely visual, intensely theatrical. Providences made the populace attentive to the manifestations of divine will. God was both performer and director, the supreme presence who tutored his congregation in New England in a master class. Since God was the artist and the world His stage, the colonists were both an audience who were to witness His work and actors who received instruction—through the wonders of the natural world—on the nature of spiritual performance in New England.

The "spectatorial attitude" has remained a characteristic of American mission, but in the literature of Vietnam the quality of vision—the extent to which the observer is involved in discovering the scope of God's plan in the wilderness—has been severely reduced. Visual experience is now confused with edited evidence; information and instruction now take place through a screening process in which one's direct contact with the world—and those who live in it—is limited. In Bobbie Ann Mason's *In Country* and Steven Wright's *Meditations in Green*, for example, the environment of Vietnam—remembered or actual—has become spiritually and physically inaccessible. The use of film as a means of exploring culture has created an outlook that is governed by myth and conjecture. In the photographic negatives of military intelligence and the cinematic text of the Hollywood film, the audience is instructed through the use of signs, each of which is a visual allegory and directs the observer to think about the world in a stereotyped way. Film is not simply a medium of information but a vast repository of ideology and bias.

In *Meditations in Green* American military intelligence assigns individuals to the task of gathering information on the movement of the enemy in the hinterland of Vietnam. The central character, James Griffin, is an "image interpreter," a man who translates the features of the "pictures" taken by cameras, strapped to "the belly of a Mohawk," of "suspected hostile activity" (43). Back in the world of Hopewell, Kentucky, Sam Hughes, in Bobbie Ann Mason's *In Country*, scans the diaries of her dead father and the television programs of an equally dead provincial culture in a world where direct testimony and historical discussion are not encouraged. In the military and provincial communities of America Vietnam is understood through "the interdiction of a lens" (*Meditations* 276). In the filmic landscapes that define Vietnam, what we encounter in both novels is an emotional blur, an image on a screen which has no authenticity. The colloquial expression of those who have lived and fought "in country" loses out to the lure of extravagant "interdiction"—the dreams of photographers. Although the Puritan vision is retained in Vietnam, the opportunity for individual awareness and witness is diminished. The expatriate soldier and the provincial civilian are equally devoted to receiving information through a mediated text. They share the belief that film can provide an unequivocal means of explaining "what it was like" (160) in the war zones of Vietnam.

If the camera eye has become God's eye, then film has reduced the act of witness to an act of tourism. Film creates surrogate patterns of language and experience that provide reassurance. In a post-Puritan landscape the spectatorial attitude is no longer a dynamic mode of activity; information technology has become antisocial, it encourages passivity and unquestioning obedience. The American observer still retains the allegorical associations of his heritage—pollution with wilderness, communist with Antichrist, plantation with protection—but he is prone to be a dreamer, imposing on the world meanings that are melodramatic. God is displaced by other forms of intelligence while the observer relies on optic nerves that are stimulated by the power of "preposterous phenomena." The devotional energy of a secular "congregation" of film addicts reminds us of the "dim, anaemic wonder" that possesses F. Scott Fitzgerald's Twelve Men of Fish.[9]

For those who believe in the availability of the Book of Nature, there is still hope, but it is only discovered after an enormous struggle. *Meditations in Green* and *In Country* are positive that hope resides in the living theatricality of nature and in the power of personal testimony and faith. The lesson is difficult but nature still teaches. As Emmett puts it in *In Country*, "if you can think about something like birds, you can get outside of yourself, and it doesn't hurt as much. That's the whole idea. That's the whole challenge for the human race. . . . I've watched 'em. There are things you can figure out, but most things you can't" (226). In the swamp of Hopewell, Kentucky, something of the power of godliness is revealed to Emmett as it is to James Griffin in *Meditations in Green*. The power and persistence of the natural world (which still retains its providential appeal) holds out the prospect of a spiritual future in spite of the attraction of popular culture and film ideals.

The lesson is a long time in coming. For most of *In Country* and *Meditations in Green* the wilderness is remote and the attraction of film is difficult to resist. John Lahr makes the criticism forcefully:

> In the land of moonshots and mass marches, the theatrical metaphor is increasingly apt. The President *stages* his public appearances; the Yippies *make scenes*, advertising *sets the mood* for consumption. In fact, as foreigners are quick to note, everything in the U.S.A. is one big production. America is a twenty-four-hour sensory assault, an electronic bombardment of diverse dreams. Image competes with image; and in this stalemate it becomes harder to see and feel.
>
> Television and film are distractions to most Americans. The scope of their audience and commercial investment is so large that "truth" becomes a commodity to be packaged for consumer needs. America—a society defined and deluded by its dreams—is obsessed by technology which sustains its amnesia.

In contrast, says Lahr, the living or "legitimate" theater "is a landscape industry" with the power to release individual hope and potential. "In a society whose historical memory is congenitally short," says Lahr, "we must have images which make us remember, not forget."[10]

The status of public theater in Hopewell, Kentucky, confirms Lahr's indictment of American life. Personal revelations of faith are discouraged, for the town has lost all public awareness of the past and the desire to redeem it. The power of electronic images has condemned the community to silence, and the sensory assault of popular culture has displaced historical inquiry. The living drama of testimony that, as Lahr puts it, "coaxes us out of our houses and into a new community" is not understood.[11] Surrogate forms of social theater—the professionalization of witness on film—have gained an unqualified status. Spiritual inquiry has been delayed by the advent of an intrusive urban theater in which "truth" and public revelation are forms of "commodity to be packaged for consumer needs." Since Hopewell is culturally absorbed and has lost the power of public speech, it denies the veteran the opportunity to address an "audience" through the "living theater" of public address. Hopewell has not yet participated in the autobiographical restoration of faith. No one remembers the war for fear of remembering themselves.

Those in the "audience" who desire conversion—like Sam Hughes— wait for a sermon that never comes. For Sam the subject is buried with her father. Public history (the war) and private history (the death of her father whom her mother is unwilling to recall) have been almost irretrievably lost as a topic of conversation. In a world where experience has been absorbed by cinematic images history has no public function. Problems that don't exist on film are not considered problems at all, and the infrequent appearance of Vietnam on television relegates the war to a subject of limited social concern. In a culture devoted to the sight of men who eat bicycles on television's "That's Incredible," the veterans' narrative is shunted aside. In Hopewell, Vietnam has become a second-rate crisis in a world of fabricated conflict, its meaning subsumed within the medieval folklore of sci-fi videos, HBO movies, evangelism, and the teacup tragedies of the soaps and serials. For Sam the whirling energies of the music videos provide release: "99 Luftballoons kept dancing in her head—all those h-bombs going off. Legs by ZZ Top. Panama by Van Halen. Flesh for Fantasy by Billy Idol. So many videos were full of disasters, with everything flying apart, shifting, changing in the blinking of an eye" (229–30). The charisma of the stars belittles the contribution of ordinary people. On the streets and screens of Hopewell the illusion of peaceful integration is preserved, and so the disability of the veteran becomes an embarrassment.

═ *In Country*: The Posthistorical ═
Southern Consciousness

In Hopewell, film papers over the cracks of embarrassment that surround Vietnam. For the most part the movies and videos continue to reiterate the familiar threadbare themes of the fifties: that the ills of society are mostly moral ills or inflicted by the presence of alien, atheistic threats; that a cure for those ills lies in the preservation of an unquenchable optimism and a sense of good neighborliness; and that laughter is the best medicine at a time of political or social tension. In the 1980s the movies of Hollywood remain more or less the same in spite of Vietnam. The popular film and the bestselling book receive their support from a persistent undercurrent of wish fulfillment and fabulism. Trivial pursuits distract one's attention from the language of tragedy, since trivial pursuits have become the tragedy.[12] In Hopewell, the evasion of political issues, personal needs, and social responsibilities is the key to the complicity that exists between the public and popular culture. Those who wish to remember the war must do so by traveling outside the community. History is tolerated only when cordoned off in a designated place, like the marble and granite monument erected in Washington to honor the dead of the Vietnam War.

What Hopewell offers its citizens is southern confinement, not southern culture. For Mason the southern provincial town has become the symbol of a particularly virulent brutalism; it stands as a place with no available tradition, with a tendency to flaccid thinking and mediocre intelligence, dominated by the media, which in turn are manipulated by money forces. Stripped of its traditional resources, Hopewell stumbles along with only surrogate

words and stale ideas to keep it going. The occasional glimpses Mason provides of an organic community characterized by permanence, faith, intimacy,
and binding tradition belong to a previous age—one represented by the veteran Dwayne who "died" with his secrets; the other by Dwayne's parents,
Pop and Mamaw, the last survivors of a narrative-conscious, vernacular
South.

During their trip to Washington, Mamaw sits on her bed in a motel,
"oblivious" to the material sensations of the world around her. While she
reflects on "her geraniums, near the sink in full bloom," Sam and Emmett,
her companions, are "propped against pillows and sip the bourbon Cokes and
watch T. V." (18). The show, like the traffic on the interstate, cannot be
interrupted or prevented. Those who watch it are overwhelmed by the force
of the narrative; like an "endless river" with unstoppable "energy" the life of
America whines like "a rock song." Sam "likes" it, but Mamaw is lost. She
struggles to compete with its momentary "show" of "strangeness" and energy.
Her questions indicate the isolation of her language from the narratives that
defeat her: "Why are y'all laughing so? Did I miss something?" she asks of
a television program. The question is not irrelevant but distracting. Sam tells
her not to "talk . . . this show's real good." When Mamaw phones home, her
reported conversation about the rain in Hopewell is unpersuasive. On a clear
night in Maryland and in a motel full of modern appliances, Mamaw's an-
ecdotalism is out of place. The sadness of the moment is not so much the
insularity of her speech but the extent to which it appears unimportant—
buried beneath "blues and greens" and "a luxurious shag rug" (19).

In the wasted and buried communities of the South, history is relinquished. The loss of narrative is the fault of "strangers" who, as John Dos
Passos puts it, have taken "the clean words our fathers spoke and made them
slimy and foul."[13] To recall the history of the immediate past is to recall defeat.
Vietnam is a reason for that defeat; it provides an explanation of why the
working-class South, which sent a disproportionately high number of soldiers
to Vietnam, requires distraction. Sam's mother, Irene, recollects her own
loss—the death of a husband at nineteen years of age. "I can't live in the
past. It was all such a stupid waste. There's nothing to remember" (168).
History, including the memory of a teenage pregnancy, is best forgotten. In
a world loaded up with consumer machinery—video recorders, space invad-
ers, stereo systems, compact discs—Irene becomes the mechanical bride.
With her life like "a soap opera," she goes to Lexington to live in "a brick
ranch house with a patio and wall-to-wall carpeting" (5) and a husband she
calls "Lorenzo Jones." Like the town she lives in, Irene has lost too much of
herself already to have anything left to give to the veteran. In a world where
mass communication has made each civilian an expert on the war, his stories
are irrelevant. The people have "got twisted around in their heads what it
was about, so they can live with it and not have to think about it" (79). Ten
years after the war concluded, the culture prefers the painless technicolor of

Jesse James Meets Frankenstein's Daughter to stories of maladjustment and posttraumatic stress.

The veteran is a threat to the community, a source of disobedience and potential embarrassment. He more than anyone is alive to the threat of disinformation since he more than anyone was persuaded by the media to believe in Vietnam. The veteran exposes the cultural capitulation, the willful exchange of a communal wisdom for the vacant idealism of "made for television." What he points to is the creation of a culture in which the narratives of the market provide the sole inspiration for the myths of the community and a major resource for its social conversation. By testifying to the importance of fellowship and camaraderie, the veteran may, if he wishes, directly confront the anomie of his culture and the peripheral survival of republican themes in the American town.

For most of the novel the veterans of Hopewell refuse to accept the social challenge their presence in the community implies. The emotional lives of the veterans remain buried and unthreatening. Sam's uncle, Emmett, assigns himself to the activities of adolescence—to popcorn and TV dinners, the sentimentality of Mary Tyler Moore and the sci-fi myths of the re-releases—in order to demonstrate his quiescence within the community. If film as a forum for understanding life is the fraud on which the mythological edifice of Vietnam was built, the veteran is prepared to accept the deceit. He submits himself to a process of false witness, to improper "seeing," to a life of deteriorating vision and a set of ideas "mediated by the film industry" that cannot "be empirically tested against direct experience." Given that the movies played a crucial role in fostering "the idea of a clearly identifiable evil" in Vietnam, one "which could only be subdued by superior force,"[14] their capacity to provide a frame of reference for structuring experience in the postwar era remains intact.

For much of the novel Emmett prefers surrogate history to personal history and blubbers with affected grief at the final episode of "M.A.S.H." By watching television Emmett can disappear beneath the opaque surface of life in Hopewell; he can acculturate himself and embrace triviality in order to avoid the agony of constant alertness. In refusing to talk about the past Emmett can gain the dubious privilege of belonging to a small-town American secret fraternity: a Masonic lodge that restricts its membership to those who have agreed to a vow of silence. Sam is warned away from the subject of Vietnam not because her questions are unhelpful but because they are indiscreet. Women ought not to ask questions since they "weren't over there" and "can't really understand" (107). For a veteran like Pete, Sam is a threat since she seeks to disrupt the mystery of the clique. "You don't know how it was, and you never will. There is no way you can ever understand. So just forget it. Unless you've been humping the boonies, you don't know" (136).

In a male-only world Sam has no way to acquire knowledge, except through film and television. She becomes preoccupied with her quest for evidence that will bear witness to the underground suffering of Hopewell's veterans. Sam is a restless adolescent with a strong sense of natural justice, but her concern for the welfare of the veteran has been shaped by the dramatic conventions of Hollywood. Joan Didion defines these conventions in her essay "Good Citizens" as a function of the styles of life and art that inform the notion of liberalism in Hollywood. In "the peculiar vacant fervor of Hollywood," says Didion, and in the morality and motion of its films, "political ideas are reduced to choices between the good (equality is good) and the bad (genocide is bad)." A "curious vanity and irrelevance" characterize so many of Hollywood's "best intentions," says Didion. These "intentions" of good citizenship are apparent in the way "social problems present themselves . . . in terms of a scenario, in which, once certain key scenes are licked . . . the plot will proceed inexorably to an upbeat fade." In the predetermined language of "a well-plotted motion picture," the prevailing ideology "is faith in dramatic convention. Things 'happen' in motion pictures. There is always a resolution, always a strong cause-effect dramatic line, and to perceive the world in those terms is to assume an ending for every social scenario. . . . There are no bit players in Hollywood politics: everyone makes things 'happen.' "[15]

= The Symbolism of Agent Orange =

In the early seventies the "ending" that the television industry supplied Vietnam was based on the premise that the veteran had become an unfortunate psychotic. As Gloria Emerson tells us, "On television the Vietnam veteran is always a psychopath who hallucinates and thinks he is in a firefight. The police and SWAT teams are gentle and patient. Not wanting to hurt the veteran who is armed and shouting again to his platoon they wait it out and capture him with great cleverness. The veteran is led off. He will receive the best medical treatment. There are wonderful psychiatrists waiting to help."[16] As Emerson says, "some lies are hilarious," but Sam Hughes falls for them. The "faith" she has in "dramatic" conventions and the structures that lead to the "resolution" of problems are inspired by her view of films and television. As a "good citizen" of Hopewell she makes "things 'happen.' " Her interpretation of war—deriving perhaps from her memory of Watergate as a television series—is based on the idea of a dramatically arresting line of inquiry, a narrative structure in which war means violence and violence means injuries that progressively worsen. For Sam the legacy of Vietnam is the covert suffering and illness caused by Agent Orange. Agent Orange provides Sam with a vividly arresting symbol of her uncle's suffering and a reason to explore his odd and solitary manner. For Sam, Emmett's brooding is caused by a progressively worsening skin condition, a toxic illness that masquerades as "delayed acne." Emmett's skin problems have become a visible "event," the means by which the mind and the body have made things "happen." By linking a diagnosis to an illness Sam is able to create "a strong cause-effect dramatic line," and by directing Emmett's attention to the veterans' hospital in Lexington, to "assume an ending" that the medical treatment will bring about.

Sam believes that if the social life of the veteran is a problem, it can "be solved by the good will of individuals." The term *Agent Orange* is satisfying to her on an aesthetic level. In a careless society Agent Orange is an illness contracted from careless use. The lack of provision for the illness among medical facilities and welfare agencies suggests not only a lack of awareness but also that the illness is grounded, like the war itself, in its own mystification. Sam is attracted to Agent Orange not simply because it provides her with a useful term to explain the problem of posttraumatic stress but because the condition it refers her to is exotic and colorful. Since the term *Agent Orange* conjures up a dynamic alliance between the visual and the secretive, it appeals to her sense of the gothic and the melodramatic: "The Army sprayed all kinds of chemicals over there," she says. "If they had waited to have me, I might have been born without a spine, or maybe I'd have flippers" (148).

In Sam's imagination Agent Orange has become a science fiction disease in which the body of the veteran appears to have hosted an alien form. The process of contamination is mystical but thrilling, as Emmett realizes. When Emmett visits Irene in Lexington he tells Sam that he arrives at "the climax" of the movie *The Invasion of the Body Snatchers*. He also suggests that his body has been taken over by an alien power, as in Sam's imagination it probably has. The event has forced him, so he claims, to act unnaturally. "I believe my body was entered by aliens and I was transported" (157). In Sam's scenario the veteran is victim and potential entertainer. For this reason she is fascinated by the man whose impotence is cured when his penis is inflated "with salt water" and pumped up "when you touch a button." Science creates disabilities and then fictionalizes the problem with a cure. "Sam imagined his [Tom's] penis expanding and growing, like Pinocchio's nose. Modern technology could do anything, she thought" (128).

Agent Orange is the gothic horror to which Sam is attuned by popular culture. She latches on to Agent Orange as one would a consumer product. What that product offers is self-assurance. As C. W. E. Bigsby tells us, "popular culture deals in certainties. From the hard rationality of the detective story to the hermetic moralism of the western, from the closely structured and self-justifying pop song to the necessarily self-defining contour of the cartoon popular culture presents a model not merely of balance and completion but also of confident assurance—an assurance contained in the product itself and therefore projected on to those exposed to it."[17] As a choice of illness

Agent Orange is totalitarian, a centering point for Sam's experience that denies her access to the ambiguities of feeling. Sam's idealism, therefore, is undermined by the culture that shapes her thinking. The danger is discussed by Marshall McLuhan:

> Once we have surrendered our senses and nervous systems to the private manipulation of those who would try to benefit by taking a lease on our eyes and ears and nerves, we don't really have any rights left. Leasing our eyes and ears and nerves to commercial interests is like handing over the common speech to a private corporation, or like giving the earth's atmosphere to a company as a monopoly. Something like this has already happened with outer space, for the same reasons that we have leased our central nervous systems to various corporations.[18]

Sam, like the good citizens of Didion's Hollywood, looks "for the sermon in the suicide," "the imposition of a narrative line on the disparate images" of posttraumatic stress in Hopewell.[19] In a community where Vietnam is rarely discussed openly and her father's death is obscure, Sam experiences a feeling of "pure joy" in seeing the war films on television (25). Deprived of adequate guidance Sam turns to the media for reassurance. She allows her imagination to be usurped by the world of mass culture, especially that which resurrects the past. In so doing she relieves herself, in the words of Robert Warshow, "of the necessity of experiencing . . . life directly." Mass culture becomes "the screen through which she sees" reality and the mirror in which she sees herself. In the vision it provides, Sam accepts that its "ultimate tendency is to supersede reality."[20] For her the function of mind is the reproduction of picture, an act that involves the creation of environment through cinematic scenery. As she gets into bed with Tom, she is "aware that something was about to happen, like a familiar scene in a movie, the slow-motion sequence with the couple rolling in the sheets and time passing. She hoped there wouldn't be jump cuts. She didn't want to miss anything" (126). In pursuing Vietnam she sees the war as a film production in which line, set, and location are the grids for speculation. Vietnam is an act of picture making. She thinks "of tanks knocking down the jungle and tigers sitting under bushes. Her notions come from the movies" (210). In the concluding obscurity of Cawood's Pond she wishes upon herself the terror she feels, most strongly, in a film: "It would be like that scene in *Apocalypse Now* where the soldiers met a tiger, the last thing they expected in the guerrilla-infested jungle" (217). The sense of Vietnam that Sam responds to, the flashbacks, are not the "nice memories" but, as she tells Tom, the "scenes in a horror movie" (93). Where Vietnam is wilderness and wilderness is kudzu, Vietnam resembles "the thing on the late show" (165).

=   *Meditations in Green:*   =
The Eye of God

Those who search Vietnam for supernatural life behave in a manner consistent with the Puritan tendency to interpret the Book of Nature as a landscape in which God's mission in the wilderness is fully explained to observant spectators. In *Meditations in Green* the will of God, translated by the hand and eye of man, retains its purpose and shape even as the pursuit of truth is spiritually distorted. Film intercedes in our understanding of mission, and in the analysis of impersonally defined targets the American military announce their preoccupation with the work of the devil at the expense of spirituality. In order to avoid contamination the witness is forced to observe the wonders of the natural world through the cosmic lens of a military eye and to accept the loss of an intimate knowledge of divine theater. For James Griffin, who interprets the wonders of that world through an image enhancer, the picture is, symbolically, a negative. Griffin pretends to be the eye of God—"With his hand on the crank he could make the plane go fast, he could make the plane go slow" (57)—but he is empowered to observe the work of the devil. In his quonset hut Griffin aspires to be a social controller of landscape, to create a fiction of coherent activity out of the "florist's nightmare" (154) that the underground jungle activities imply. Nature is a commodity to be mined for evidence of evil intent: "Trees, trees, trees, trees, rocks, rocks, cloud, trees, trees, road, road, stream, stream, ford, trees, road, road. He stopped cranking. With a black grease pencil he carefully circled two blurry shadows beside the white thread of a road. . . . Wherever he put circles on the film there the air force would make holes on the ground" (43).

Griffin suffers from delusions of godliness, the boredom of impersonal control, and an excess of narrative authority in the making of a photographic text. He is an inventor of signs as well as an interpreter of images, and his use of power is excessive. In his "missions" Griffin becomes the mad scientist, measuring, reading, transposing, counting, "totally absorbed into the fascinating realm of carpet bombing, lost among the oddities of the weave." The games Griffin plays involve imaginary connections, "the bomb distribution games of connect-the-dots and see a smiling fish . . . a living organism of strength and guile, slithering among the damage" (57).

Photography is God's work; it contains the elements for the creation of composition, for defining the intention of malign and purposeful energies in the wilderness. On most occasions the Vietnamese are predictable. They conform to a plan. "There was no stopping these people, they took to craters like Americans took to shopping malls" (57–58). Godliness is supported when the work of the devil in nature is clarified. But when the devil disappears, whenever his intentions become obscure, Griffin's authority is diminished. Inaccuracy brings with it a loss of confidence in his congregation, the pilots who scan the photographic texts. Since the pilots cannot read and witness for themselves, they sometimes complain "about defaced negatives . . . indecipherable handwriting . . . mismarked targets on their flight maps" (295). In Vietnam meaning is a function of symmetry: the ability to read a "two-dimensional landscape . . . in neat black-and-white segmented squares" (57).

= A Theater of War =

The pursuit of pattern is an act of dedication to a Puritan mission. Wine-haven, who drops defoliant on the jungle, does so precisely and mathematically. "The tank holds a thousand gallons and at our speed we're laying down about three gallons per acre. Average coverage three hundred acres, elapsed mission time five minutes. Of course, in an emergency we can dump the whole thousand gallons in thirty seconds" (130). Winehaven likes to show the "results" of his work in the fields that the Viet Cong are "using for food." Winehaven defines what he does in precise, visual terms; his work "puts an interesting perspective on things, it's a glorious sight out there." The partnership established between the visionary and the "glorious" focuses on a religion of science and industry that Griffin understands. "I know," says Griffin, "I see the film." Winehaven, not surprisingly, is a "master of applied science." What he gives are "lessons in the detection and measurement of organic death. The physics of infrared, the chemistry of poisons" (131). The wine of his communion is an ester cocktail, "a jigger of 2,4,-0 to a jigger of 2,4,5-T" (131).

Winehaven is a prisoner of film who remakes the landscape in response to the negatives that Griffin inscribes. He is also conscious that his work should be looked on as theater, and aware of his role as performer. Here the inspiration for Winehaven is not Griffin but Weird Wendell Payne, the unit's movie director, who uses the base as the set for a film on the theater of war. Wendell shoots indiscriminately but knowingly, recognizing that the Vietnam conflict—under the influence of the camera—is a visual and egotistical affair: "Without a word of hesitation the pilot [Winehaven] squatted down, dipped his finger into one of the puddles growing on the ramp beneath the wing nozzles, and stuck it into his mouth. Incredulous, Griffin swung around to look behind him. About twenty-five feet away Weird Wendell, camera for a face, held up an arm, thumb and forefinger forming an O" (130). Even Griffin cannot resist the temptation to be filmed, to alter his role from a supplier of film to the film's subject. After a trip in a Mohawk he returns to base to confront Weird Wendell "aiming that obnoxious lens at his face." In an age where Vietnam, like Hollywood, is an integral part of the entertainment industry, Griffin cannot resist the urge to publicize his status and appearance. On the steps of the plane and in front of a "modest crowd" Griffin smiles and waves "cheerfully" and "appears absorbed in impersonating Charles Lindbergh or Errol Flynn" (212).

Wendell simulates a fantasy of escape that argues profoundly against social understanding. He is a promoter who transfers the solitary activity of filmmakers like Griffin and film actors like Winehaven onto a wider public canvas. His war cry, "I'll make you into a movie" (61), are buzzwords that allow him unlimited access to the 1069th where he is regarded as a "genius" (163), able to exercise "Svengali-like power over [his] immediate superiors" (162–63). Wendell's film projects are fraudulent stunts that rely heavily on extravagant action—death, suicide, riot, fire storms, blood-letting rituals at the O Club—to promote the idea of a dynamic theater of war in Vietnam. But the scenes are staged with an emphasis on violence. "I want controlled insane hysteria," he tells a group of soldiers who are "staging a minor ground attack" (161). His artifice alerts the reader to the potential for abuse that cinema verité sometimes creates. Wendell's quest for gratification—he is "having an exhilarating time" (163)—is masked by the pretense that his work is direct and objective, "unmeditated and real." Wendell, who is rarely to be "found on the set of the real war" (161), pretends to capture "the complete complexity of the American experience" (164) through a set of theatrical signs, each of which is derived from those cosmic signs God has chosen to present to his followers in the wilderness of Vietnam, wherein dwell the legions of the Antichrist.

Wendell exploits the tendency to play to the cameras. His technique is particularly successful because, as a documentarist, he is able to influence events. As a former Saigon bureau chief once pointed out, "It is considered standard for troops to fire their weapons for the benefit of cameramen. If our cameramen had to wait until a fire fight with the Viet Cong broke out, we'd have less footage—and perhaps cameramen."[21]

The point is supported by J. G. Ballard's short story, "Theater of War," in the book *Myths of the Near Future* (1982). Here, a futuristic Vietnam-like conflict is set in England and the action is scripted to suit the needs of the television crews who cover it. War has become entertainment, and the crews, ravenous for sensation, roam the country anxious to maintain their program ratings with stories of atrocity. In this context film is a medium of deception that encourages the soldiers to perform as if they were acting and that demeans their sense of personal safety.

Similarly, in *Apocalypse Now* Francis Ford Coppola enters the film—as a movie director—as an attack is in progress. Like Wendell Payne he issues a set of instructions to the soldiers who are told to act as if they are fighting. "Like you're fighting," he screams at the soldiers as they run for cover on the beachhead. "Just go through. It's TV. . . . Don't look at the camera. It's TV. Just go through. Like you're fighting." Where the dramatization of war is seen as an adequate substitute for the fact of war, theater has assumed a preeminent position in the minds of those who seek to promote it.

What television offered the soldier in Vietnam, as Rick Berg tells us, was "instant replay." The soldier "could fight in a battle and see it on the news that night."[22] As early as 1967, when the first field television network became operational, at least 85 percent of the American forces in Vietnam were able to receive AFVN television programs. As Lawrence Suid has said, "This marked the first time that any military command had provided full television service to its troops in the field." AFVN represented the logical extension of the mission of the Armed Forces Radio and Television Service to provide American troops in the field "with the same entertainment, news, sports, and information to which they had become accustomed at home."[23] This fact gives added resonance to the remark made by the narrator of *Dispatches*: "I keep thinking about all the kids who got wiped out by seventeen years of war movies before coming to Vietnam to get wiped out for good. We'd all seen too many movies, stayed too long in Television City" (169).

= A Prisoner of Film =

Visual images—photographic, cinematic, documentary, televisual—are a means of pacification in Wright's Vietnam. The intention of the 1069th is to find the enemy and obtain the correct visual information on the NVA. This is an "important mission," as Captain Raleigh tells the intelligence officer Claypool. People in America are eager for results. "We've got plenty of important eyes peeping over our shoulders, so don't fuck up" (44,45). In their quonset huts Griffin and Claypool observe the wilderness like secular priests, but their self-containment undermines their mission, and they pacify themselves, not the enemy. Their task of finding the Vietnamese—"the enemy in the negative"—confirms the catatonic state of modern American manners and the defunct imagination of the military. Viewing habits produce tedium.

Claypool, who has re-enlisted and joined intelligence, has "exchanged a year of his life for the security of a noncombat job" (147). In order to avoid both action and encounter, Claypool believes that "he wasn't supposed to carry a gun, to hump, to get shot, the army had promised" (147). Like Nathanael West's Homer Simpson in *The Day of the Locust* (1939), Claypool is a soldier in uterine flight, a shy and inarticulate émigré who spends his life in a comatose state. In the army, Claypool hides from the "organic inferno" (157) of the jungle. He is a devotee of film; the Book of Nature has no value to him. He sees it as an evil that conspires to smother American machines and American hopes and whose riotous potential can seriously damage the workings of the mind.

Claypool lives like a seer, a transparent eyeball in a quonset hut who scans the forest for signs of life. When he is forced to go on patrol in the jungle his devotion to print and picture offers no guidance: "He wasn't supposed to be here. He was punched from behind. Sprawled on his nose in the tanglewood. Flash. Boom. Wha' happened? 'I can't see, someone was crying, I can't fucking SEE!' Claypool shut his eyes and squeezed his asshole as tightly as he could. Here it was. The Big Scene" (158). The sensations of nature blur and confuse him. Without a negative to work from—a script for the big picture—Claypool stumbles into "a florist's nightmare," a "movie" of indeterminate form and sequence in which the natural world is "sinister" and alive" (154). He is a stranger in a strange land. "There should have been bats hanging down and flitting about. Vampire bats. . . . And the plants, the plants were all wrong. No movie had ever been made in here. Claypool recognized nothing" (157). Once he goes "beyond the perimeters" of the compound and enters into "open space" he is "nervous" (155) and sightless. Deprived of the sense-making mechanism of film and the capacity for mediation, Claypool is lost.

Claypool's problem reflects a general limitation of the American military in the field in Vietnam. Intelligence gathering was rarely the product of long-term cultural investigation or winning over the confidence of the Vietnamese villagers. The Special Forces units the army used for counterinsurgency "were hampered," says Andrew F. Krepinevich, "by a lack of familiarity with the language and culture of the people with whom they were working as well as by the absence of any army procedures for the procurement of such intelligence." Special Forces intelligence efforts were largely concerned with "supporting Army main-force units." To find and destroy the Viet Cong or the NVA on a nationwide basis "by conventional military methods took precedence over the more subtle tactic of rooting out the VCI." As Krepinevich argues, "the talents of the Special Forces in pacification were subordinated to the big-unit war" (230).

The absence of an undercover facility characterized the limitation of military intelligence in the more remote regions of Vietnam. Claypool's fear and loathing of the natural world is the extreme but logical conclusion of his efforts to minimize his involvement in the physical environment. Claypool is a tourist, a film buff reduced to the ultimate absurdity. He is also a function of the army's insular approach to war, and his limitations are the product of a strategic doctrine that holds that the enemy can be dealt with from a distance or that it can be overcome by the substitution of technological power for an intimate knowledge of location and terrain. When Sergeant Mars instructs Claypool to go on patrol, his response is a measure of his dependency on the narratives of film: "This wasn't supposed to be happening. . . . There was a guaranteed contract on file at St. Louis. He couldn't go. He didn't know what gear one packed to the field" (147). Claypool's mental containment is absolute. Like Griffin he spends his days "locked up" (131), trying to formulate a "big-unit strategy," encouraged to think, as Zecca advises in *A Flag for Sunrise*, "in terms of the larger scale . . . The Big Picture" (154).

= General Waste-More-Land =

The main objective of the 1069th is to try and locate the 5th NVA Regiment, and to this end all military intelligence activity is devoted. "Where from? Where to? How Big? How good? Find it! It was the mission of Research and Analysis to outline shapes, to colour in detail. . . . Shelves along all four walls were stacked with boxes, dates scrawled in black across the cardboard. Somewhere in those boxes was the enemy" (48). This obsession to detect the enemy's main unit means that "the weight of the intelligence effort" is "aimed at discovering how many divisions" they have, "not how many" are placed at the village level or the hamlet level. This preoccupation—according to Robert Komer—often occurred in Vietnam, "to the total neglect of the guerrillas and the so-called Viet Cong infrastructure, the political-military apparatus that was really running the war" (Krepinevich, 229).

Because of the army's refusal to make destroying the political infrastructure of the Viet Cong a priority, it failed to make counterinsurgency an issue of vital inquiry. Army intelligence, says Krepinevich, rarely offered anything more detailed than a basic estimate of military capacity. The reliance upon "armored formations," which "rarely operated at night, where the guerrillas were most active," and which "encouraged the infantry to operate 'buttoned up' inside their vehicles instead of out on patrol, was not appropriate to covert action and infiltration" (Krepinevich, 170). The emphasis on technology isolated the soldier from the people whose war he was supposed to be fighting. A soldier could discover only so much on a twelve-month tour there; for most of the time the people in Vietnam remained obscure.

In *Meditations in Green*, the beggar who sits at the gates of the 1069th is a figure of abuse: "Trucks loaded with laughing troops rumbled down the road and often a beer or soda can or even a gob of spit came flying toward the old man who did not move or speak" (41). If the Vietnamese won't speak, the Americans can't speak. The Vietnamese language—"gookese" (304)— taxes their brain too severely. Claypool's intelligence limits his knowledge of the spoken word to a few phrases in pidgin Vietnamese. His fear of the language is a fear of camouflage, since "too many of the words not only sounded alike but looked the same on paper, as if the Vietnamese would be quite content with just one word" (147). Claypool's situation is typical. The brief tours of duty by army officers in Vietnam "contributed to the attitude prevalent among many intelligence officers that familiarity with the culture, language, and society of Vietnam was not essential in the performance of their duty" (Krepinevich, 229). The preferred method was to rely on aerial reconnaissance and air mobility in order to achieve rapid analysis and rapid deployment. As a result the army lacked the will and the knowledge to intercept and engage the Vietnamese on their terms. Sir Robert Thompson put the criticism forcefully: "The major criticism I had tactically in Vietnam was that the one element in which you [the army] were never mobile was on your feet. You got landed from helicopters and the battle took place, but when the battle was over and you had won the battle, you even went out by helicopter. No one ever walked out. Now the enemy, who was mobile on his feet, could actually decide whether he was going to have a battle with you in the first place, and he could break it off whenever he wanted to" (Krepinevich, 170). When Claypool is lost in the jungle, "the sky" brings "helicopters" (160); within a few minutes the tormented pilgrim has returned to base.

In Vietnam, the role of technology undermined the value of counter-insurgency. Except for the occasional use of Combined Action Platoons and special operations (small-unit) strike teams (a low priority for the military), the United States never adequately informed itself about the rural environment it sought to subdue. So complete is the isolation of the 1069th that Trips believes he is not even in Vietnam: "Sensory evidence provided no clues to contradict his theory that they had not in fact left the United States at all but were simply prisoners in a bizarre behavioral study somewhere in Utah!" (251).

On the edge of the "perimeter" the 1069th is suspended between god-liness and voyeurism. Their cause represents the climax of Puritan history as well as the negation of its Christian purpose. The errand to spiritualize the people has collapsed. Nature provides clues to His errand in the wilder-ness, but each is a sign of wrongdoing by the enemy. The landscape is energetic but polluted. The unrighteous forest needs to be shorn of its un-healthy growth. The conspiracy of hidden vegetation and the malign will of primitive society renders cleansing a rational undertaking. With their earthy wisdom and aura of paganism the Vietnamese are involved in an attempt to rewrite history, to revert to devil worship in that very wilderness subdued by Puritan emigrants. Land that is poisoned, plowed, and cratered no longer affords protection to the enemy, nor can it demonstrate, for his benefit, the potential for insurgent growth. Holly, who wonders why there is "always haze in the sky" and if the land emits "its own organic pollution," suggests a program of regulation and reform. " 'I was just thinking that if we put a dome over it, dehumidified and air-conditioned the atmosphere, then ploughed the earth, and treated the water we might have a fairly decent prison farm' " (307).

As Winehaven says, "it's not as if the bushes were innocent." Beyond the perimeter the ecology of the wilderness is a direct threat. For those who "stare at the tree line for a while" the "movement" of nature is progressively forward, "slow but inexorable, irresistible, maybe finally unstoppable." Those who are puzzled like Griffin—"What movement, what are you talking about?"—are quickly put in their place: "The trees, of course, the fucking shrubs. And one day we'll look up and there they'll be, branches reaching in, jamming our M-60's, curling around our waists" (132). Sexual paralysis comes to those who stray too near the tree line. This is a sickness the Vietnamese are able to transmit. When Kraft goes missing in the forest, he too becomes paralyzed, full of "helpless amazement," "obviously useless" (321).

In *Meditations in Green* the Puritan mission is depraved. In the 1069th John Winthrop reappears as the lusty general, an oversexed militant whose search for the army of the devil, the 5th NVA Regiment, preempts the possibility of spiritual conversion. Inside the quonset huts, barricaded with wire, intelligence gathering has become a profession for the paranoid: a Puritan military who lust for the devil on rolls of film. In Wright's novel the old God of Israel is dead and the new God—science and technology—is the source of all providences. The camera eye of the Mohawk is an absolute deity, able to see and to know—like the ubiquitous Dr. T. J. Eckleburg in Scott Fitzgerald's *The Great Gatsby*—all that happens on the floor of the jungle. If the source of faith is the revelation of film, then the function of faith is the natural world: what Sacvan Bercovitch calls the "savage domain awaiting liberation."[24] But nature in Vietnam is not wholly what it was to the Puritans in New England, an ambiguous realm of promise and possibility, a place both sacred and secular, pagan yet sublime. The jungle is a spiritual slough, a wasteland that cannot easily be cultivated or brought within the confines of the "Hedge." If the men of the 1069th undertake "a redemptive errand for mankind," they seek to establish a community of the dead, a place where devastation precedes renewal and genocide reveals "the dim anaemic wonder" of the age.

The roots of American arrogance lie in the memory of colonial ownership. In New England, says Bercovitch, the Puritans believed that "the land belonged" to them before they "belonged to the land." In valuing possession of the land they first imposed "their own image upon it, and then [saw] themselves reflected back in the image they had imposed."[25] In the wilderness of Asia the Christian ministry of the faithful is obscure. What the 1069th see in Vietnam is the prevalence of the devil and their own obsession with ungodliness. Where the New England colonists were once devoted to the righteous purpose of an errand in the wilderness, the latter-day saints on their errand to Vietnam are now fixated by Satan's triumph.

The act of surrogate witness and the devotional world of film imagery condemn the veteran to a life that is passive and unsatisfactory. The deterioration in the quality of his vision confirms the problem of visual experience in the contemporary age. In *Meditations in Green* the relentless activity of scanning the natural world for signs and portents creates, inevitably, a buildup of energy that requires release. Deprived of space, vitality, and hope, those who aspire to godliness are overwhelmed by boredom. For the 1069th the war has already "gone on too long," the tedium is backed up. In the catatonic world of military intelligence "erosion" is "general" (91). Observing the enemy in the negative provokes unrest. The experience that begins with the "dim anaemic wonder" of witness generates, in *Meditations in Green* and other novels, an expectation of dramatic involvement that finally concludes in the pursuit of violence.

= Puritan Leadership =

For Stephen Wright, war is a matter of "incredible boredom punctuated by exclamation marks of orgiastic horror." Those who negotiate the boredom on behalf of others are described as "creative" (96). A "superior leader" like Wendell Payne understands the limits of passive activity. His films allow the soldier to console himself with vigorous gestures of expression, yet they relieve him of the necessity of coping directly with his environment. As "the very embodiment" (130) of intelligence, Wendell leads from the front, acting out in life what he offers in art. Wendell models himself on the archetypal movie director, Scott Fitzgerald's Monroe Stahr, a man whose love of film, like Wendell's, is "obsessive" (161). In the final sequence of his documentary film *The Movie*, Wendell arranges for his own death to be recorded. Wendell's life concludes with the "finish" of the "picture," with the heroic finish—for him at least—of the Vietnam War. As Wendell talks to Griffin, the fear of death is displaced by the vanity of the photogenic performer: "Shoot, you mangy cocksucker, shoot me, shoot them, shoot the whole fucking compound. The War: In Vietnam: The Final Hours, Huh?" (333).

There is a climactic release in self-annihilation. The lure of committing one's death to film, of securing one's role in history in a violent outburst of cathartic energy, also drives "the Old Man" to take his own life on a rain-spattered airstrip. Griffin, who has "witnessed the crash" like the good Puritan he is, sees it as "a spectacular feature of moving parts" (24). The C.O., "confident, expansive," goes to his death in a stage-managed takeoff in which the plane, "landing gear squeaking . . . lifted . . . like a flat pebble skipping off a lake as the low rhythmic thrum of engines drastically changed pitch, unreeling into a frantic shriek of steel under torque and still battling to sustain each desperate inch of altitude banked on a long aching arc down into a foul marsh not five hundred feet off the end of the asphalt and exited behind a mushroomy ball of ignited fuel" (24). Later we learn that such "flashy stunts for Hollywood" have been filmed by Wendell for a "movie" that "needed a finish." With Wendell in need of "a grand finale to his war flick" the pilot takes his plane "under the nose of the lens" and becomes "immortalized" (53).

The movie as stunt involves a variety of "orgiastic" horrors. Around the camp, ideas for action are deposited by Wendell who tears out pages from Ayn Rand's *Atlas Shrugged* and leaves them strategically placed "in modest piles." The gesture is an "antidote against the boredom" (166) and inspires a variety of fantastic incidents. At the O Club, pilots line up each evening, "once a proper altitude of intoxication had been achieved, to take turns leaping, chest thrust defiantly forward, arms spread defenseless as wings, from the top of the bar onto the unit emblem, that screaming woman's head painted in garish color on the hard tile floor." The ritual is an "insane business" in which the injured are "honored with an aluminum heart" (135). On different hallucinogens "Spaceman" Wurlitzer, "white scarf gaily streaming from his neck," flies his plane like "the Red Baron" celebrating "his latest kill, brazenly taunting the enemy and boosting Junker morale with an aerial victory dance" (55–56).

For James Griffin the fantasy of flight and the need to escape the limitations of the desk job undermine his work as an image interpreter. Winehaven sees it as a tension that comes from being grounded too long. "No feedback. Too much frustration" (131). Deprived of seeing for himself the results of his work, or of sharing in the exhilaration of "a load going down," Griffin becomes imprisoned in a silent and unresponsive movie. In the conjectural theater of military intelligence Griffin inherits John Winthrop's belief in the ocular nature of colonial errand, but he is denied the satisfaction of participating in it. He is both a receiver of texts and a maker of texts, an editor as well as a military director, but the scope of his work remains ambiguous. Unlike Wendell, he does not supervise the making of a film or the angle of the camera as it "shoots" the jungle from the belly of a Mohawk. As an intelligence officer who works inside "a Quonset hut surrounded by a high chain-link fence topped with coils of barbed wire behind a door marked RESTRICTED" (42), Griffin only plays at being God. As an elevated gossip, an interpreter of signs, his work contributes to that myth-making tendency of the Puritan mind. It is the work of a God who is not on-site, a watchtower God, a spectatorial God who seeks a piece of the action he creates.

Muller takes Griffin "away" (210) from the "exceptionally tedious world" (166) of godliness. On a scenic flight over Vietnam, Griffin turns his back on a humdrum technology to witness, with his own eyes, "the simple beauty of the land" (212). As the runway rolls up "on a reel beneath the nose" (212) he looks down at the base. The prisoner of war sees himself as the prisoner of film. "Arranged in such precise straight lines and right angles, the 1069th resembled a concentration camp or a movie lot, the Quonset huts housing sound studios" (212). In the air Griffin transcends his limitations. The "trip" is shocking and inspirational. It allows him a moment of colorful, "breathtaking" (215) release from that "dreary film buff's" (26) world in which he is imprisoned. Returning to base he is "bored" (229), and on a subsequent journey to find Quimby and Kraft, he volunteers to walk through the jungle to effect "a purge, a flushing out of the corners, primitive sacrament if necessary" (275).

As he enters the "prison of those he had condemned" (276) Griffin feels threatened. His desire for intimacy is a tourist's delusion. Old habits die hard, and without "the interdiction of a lens" (276), his sense of nature proves no more resolute than that of Claypool's. As he wanders, off-camera, through the triple canopy jungle, he is overcome by a feeling of stifling enclosure. In a world "perpetually pregnant" with organic matter, the trauma of a history that is "Gothic" (277) reappears. There is "no end" (276) to the vegetation; its stench and aggression do not allow Griffin the comfort of "distance" that the tourist requires. Nature belittles him, possessing a force "the camera could never record," a botanical power with an ability to convert "flesh and dreams into plant food." The absence of crater or cultivated land produces a "painful sense of isolation," of loss and deprivation (277). Panic gives way to anger and revolt. The profligate forest that the Puritans considered a manifestation of moral anarchy produces in Griffin "a chlorophyll freakout"; he becomes "mad, indignant" (278). The unsupervised horror of a world that is pre-Christian is confirmed with the discovery of Quimby's mutilated body and the dismembered corpses of the helicopter crew. There is general agreement that the people who inhabit the forest "ain't even human" (280). The only thing to do is to "fuck this fucking shithole of a country into a fucking parking lot" (280). Griffin, purged of all waywardness and unorthodox habits, returns to his desk in the quonset hut and rededicates himself to "shading" in the areas on his herbicide map.

The "orgiastic horror" becomes the new movie in which Griffin seeks satisfaction. In a state of "stoned devotion" he dreams annihilation, the creation of "bright wastelands" with the earth smoothed out. "Like an impotent king locked in a tower, Griffin sat on his stool and watched the land die around him" (294). On his wall maps he creates a "landscape of delights" with tinted squares and rectangles of orange and blue and white; on the negatives he invents cartoons with colored pencils. Griffin is a "god" of black humor and parody: "with a grease pencil he drew in comical glasses, moustaches on the mountains, black rainbows, silver lining inside the clouds." But he is also a Jeremiah who imposes retribution without love or mercy. In Griffin's desire to "complete the picture" he dreams "of chemical showers, of winged nozzles sweeping over the provinces from end to end, of 100 per cent coverage" (295).

In the yearned-for apocalypse Griffin ruins Vietnam with total color. In his work we reenter the landscape of an earlier painting, *The Burning of Los Angeles*, in Nathanael West's *The Day of the Locust*. Tod Hackett's painting provides a release for sexual frustration and anticipates the artwork of James Griffin. In both novels the western artist is a landlocked émigré who avenges himself in a Puritan crusade. Like the torch-bearing hordes who descend on Los Angeles in Hackett's cartoon, Griffin concludes his time in Vietnam as a joyful performer, a witch hunter who vindictively de-creates his world into an ash-choked, burnt-over mess.

9

The Profit of Godliness

== The God of Israel ==

"A MAN HAS NOTHING TO FEAR, HE THOUGHT TO HIMSELF, WHO understands history": This observation from Frank Holliwell concludes Robert Stone's *A Flag for Sunrise* (404), a novel that anticipates the recent history of U.S. political involvement in Central America and that presses insistently on the corrupting influence of the Vietnam War. Vietnam is a continuous point of reference in *A Flag for Sunrise*—the messianic fervor that took the nation on a moral and economic mission to Indochina has survived with undiminished energy in the Central American republics of Compostela and Tecan. The sense of shabby economic dependence and of American support for a worthless regime is strong throughout. So, too, is the moral cafard that afflicts those who live in countries with the time and money to cultivate their own expatriate needs. These themes were first introduced by Robert Stone in the novel *Dog Soldiers*, a book that dealt more immediately and more directly with the Vietnam War and its cultural effects on American life.

History continues at a relentless pace in Stone's novels. From Indochina to Latin America surviving colonial myths and aspirations appear to dominate the American way of life and the American way of war. But the continuity of history has little to do with the understanding of history. Neither in Vietnam nor in its aftermath has the country shown the slightest willingness to alter its belief in imperial mission. The mythology behind the Vietnam War remains an idée fixe in American life.[1] For Robert Stone a principal American requirement—and arguably the most destructive—is the imposition of the imperial American self: to provide the preindustrial world with a public demonstration of its own inferiority, as Ralph Heath says in *A Flag for Sunrise*, and to teach it "to be ashamed of being poor" (245). In *Dog Soldiers* and *A Flag for Sunrise* the American government and its citizens appear largely ignorant of the sins of history, and they prefer to speculate on the personal and public gain that is available through the exploitation of third world markets. America, says Marty Nolan, is "at a very primitive stage of mankind." The country is Darwinistic, its behavior is "apelike." Political morality exists on the basis of "what one pack of chimpanzees [can do] to another" (23). As an imperial power, the United States preys on the weak and explains its mission by denouncing the enemies of God. Stone's theme is salvation through cannibalism—a cannibalism generated by overproduction and a surfeit of capital, which is, for the Puritan, the profit of godliness.

Stone's novels are particularly interesting in the light of Puritan history, as they observe a direct correlation between the sense of mission in New England and the faith that sustains recent adventures in Southeast Asia and Central America. For Stone the confrontational language of the elect is a consequence of moral and economic ambition and a statement on the manners that have underpinned that ambition for 350 years. In *Dog Soldiers* and *A Flag for Sunrise* the American way of war is congruent with the American way of life: those who go abroad "in search of monsters to destroy"[2] have a clear, historical vision of the Antichrist.

The classic definition of colonial purpose and colonial militancy was first provided by John Winthrop in 1630 on the deck of the *Arbella*. He told the band of Puritans he was leading to a new and dangerous life that they were engaged upon a voyage that God not only approved but in which He participated. As he said, "We shall find that the God of Israel is among us, when ten of us shall make us a praise and glory, that men shall say of succeeding plantations; the Lord make it like that of New England: for we must consider that we shall be as a City on a Hill, the eyes of all people are upon us." The myth of a city on a hill—the idea that America provided a moral example to the rest of the world—became a basic doctrine of thought for later generations of Americans. As Loren Baritz puts it: "This myth helped to establish nationalist orthodoxy in America. It began to set an American dogma, to fix the limits of thought for Americans about themselves and about the rest of the world, and offered a choice about the appropriate relationship between us and them."[3]

It was certainly present in many of the speeches that provided a formative influence on a generation of Americans in the run-up to the Vietnam War, and it gave that engagement—as later presidents have struggled to give the American engagement in Central America—a spiritual dimension as well as a sense of moral principle. Where Winthrop talked of the colonists' need to defend themselves as a moral duty, John F. Kennedy, in his inaugural address, defined as "God's work" America's defense of the rights of others. Since America, as Woodrow Wilson had once put it, "was born a Christian nation," its spheres of influence were morally limitless. This belief—that the American Revolution was, in a sense, intended for all mankind—was something Kennedy aggressively romanticized. As he announced to the world in 1961, "We shall pay any price, bear any burden, meet any hardship, support any friend, oppose any foe to assure the survival and the success of liberty."[4]

The idea that America was the moral savior of humanity and was ready to carry the burden of idealism into the battlefield echoes through much of the political rhetoric of the sixties. During his term of office President Johnson had a vastly ambitious plan to create a "Great Society for Asia," and Vice President Hubert Humphrey in 1966 proclaimed that the Great Society would be brought to all of Asia. Humphrey's call reminded the American people of those Christian missionaries who had gone to China at the turn of the century "to win the hearts and minds of Asians" for Christ. Robert Kennedy, in declaring his candidacy for president, offered a classic restatement of this particular myth. "At stake," he said, "is not simply the leadership of our party, and even our country, it is our right to the moral leadership of this planet."[5]

The advantage of using a morally weighty and declaratory language in order to justify American involvement in the Vietnam War was that it tended to obscure the more commonplace and venal issues of American foreign policy. The rhetoric of the elect served to create the impression that the United States was entirely benevolent in its national motives and that it lacked any desire for economic advantage in the goals it strived to achieve abroad. Few novelists have been more critical of this assumption—that the country has both a divine right and a public duty to the moral leadership of the free world—and more willing to expose the commercial considerations on which American adventurism has rested than Robert Stone.

=== A Satanic Wilderness ===

In Stone's fictions the legacy of bearing what Herman Melville described in *White Jacket* as "the ark of the liberties of the world" has proved too severe a burden.[6] In South Vietnam and Central America, America has formed a

secular theology that expresses itself in cultural prejudice and the confrontational language of the elect. In *Dog Soldiers* an American missionary from
Ngoc Linh Province, whom John Converse meets in Saigon, describes how
the wilderness region of the country is a place of moral corruption and moral
challenge. On the face of it the conversation is hopeful. "I think our work's
been blessed," says the woman, "though we've certainly had our trials." As
the conversation progresses it becomes apparent that the woman's hope, such
as it is, has been blighted by the dogma of insular faith and that her sense
of Christian mission has evolved beyond its legitimate history. Decay has set
in, both physically and spiritually. There are "faded freckles in the grey skin
under the lady's eyes" (5). Converse wonders "if all the flesh of her body
were the same dingy grey as the skin of her face and if there were any more
faded freckles in it." Living "in God's Country" (which is what she calls Ngoc
Linh Province), the missionary seeks to create a city upon a hill—not through
love for the people whom she seeks to convert but through the doctrines of
Puritan survivalism.

Converse, who has flown over the region, knows it to be "thoroughly
frightening, a deep green maze of iron-spine mountains" where "the clouds
were full of rocks. No one went there, not even to bomb it, since the Green
Berets had left" (5). The woman who has lived there for fourteen years
believes that the wilderness is full of devils "who worship Satan" (8). In her
green print dress and canvas hat she reads a copy of A. J. Cronin's *The Citadel*
and appears "strikingly confident" about her "adventure." In conversation
she describes the demon mythologies that lie in wait for her and the culture
of those whose life she sees as a spiritual slough. With her "formidable
strength" she is able to resist the devils of the forest, the Puritan black men
who came in the night "into our village and took Bill [her husband] and a
fine young fella named Jim Hately and just tied their hands and took them
away and killed them" (6, 7).

Although the woman, like Faulkner's Joanna Burden, has the strength
to accept "God's will with adoration," her mission has failed in its obligation
to Christianize the savage and eliminate his hostile will. Consumed with a
sense of the evil that surrounds her in the woods, the woman has lost all
hope and succumbed to a vision of satanic will. "Time's short. . . . We're in
the last days now. If you do know your Bible, you'll realise that all the signs
in Revelations have been fulfilled. The rise of Communism, the return of
Israel" (7). The apocalyptic fate that awaits the world and the decline of
Christian values is explained by her failure to subjugate the hinterland. The
Puritan mission is incomplete. What has been achieved through colonization
in the Mekong Delta has yet to be realized in Ngoc Linh Province: the
transformation of wilderness into habitable settlement.

Whether or not they achieved success, colonial mythologies made sense
in Vietnam. Soldiers frequently refer to the Vietnamese as unchristian or
satanic or devilish ("Phantoms, I thought, we're fighting phantoms" or "Those

little babysans are devils, man, No Shit. Devils").[7] In the cities, Living Bibles International, an evangelical organization with strong right-wing political leanings, had teams of translators whose task it was to produce a copy of the Bible in Vietnamese. As long as the Viet Cong and the North Vietnamese Army received most of their support from the hinterland—the jungle, swamp, and hill-land regions—and American support lay primarily in the towns and cities of the Mekong Delta, it was possible to make an explicit equation between the territory of the Antichrist (in this case the Communist menace) and the world of the unreconstructed forest. In this typology the inhabitants of the forest, those who supported the North Vietnamese, could be seen as spiritual descendants of the Indian. Like him, they were imbued with the satanic power common to all native people who lived in the wilderness and had yet to receive the mercy of Christ's love. The correlation the missionary makes in *Dog Soldiers* between the spread of communism and the satanic power of the tribespeople of Ngoc Linh is in keeping with her own Puritan disposition. It is also in keeping with that of the typical American official in Vietnam who, according to Peer de Silva, would find himself "whether he realized it or not, standing solemnly before the Asians, his finger pointed skyward and the word 'repent' on his lips."[8]

Those who subscribed to the moral theology of settlement life in colonial New England would have well understood this particular conviction. The early Puritans of Massachusetts looked upon the Indian as a man who lived in a state of sin, a morally deficient being whose duty it was to confess himself in the presence of a Christian witness. The planting of religion in Massachusetts, therefore, meant more than simply importing good Christians into the wilderness; it also denoted the desire to convert the Indians from their sinful state. Although this was achieved with some success (especially by John Eliot), the Puritans were never properly able to abandon their distrust of the Indians, a "crafty . . . suttell people" whose natural domain was the land of darkness, or their view of the New England forest as the antithesis of civilization as they knew it. During the many skirmishes that took place between the Puritan colonists and the Indians of Massachusetts it was frequently claimed by New England commentators that the natives worshipped the devil. Despite the Puritans' conviction that they would ultimately defeat the forces of the antichrist, they were always wary of succumbing to the temptations concealed in the wilderness. The inhabitants of that world, the Indians, were regarded as "men transformed into beasts," the very "bondslaves of Sathan," who could rely upon the reprobates of the world to disrupt the transmission of the gospel into America.[9]

The essential problem with the Indian was not that he was morally treacherous but that he fought a guerrilla campaign in the forest and was therefore physically elusive. In King Philip's War of 1675 the Puritan troops were especially nervous about the difficulty of engaging an enemy they could not see to shoot at. The problem of tracking the Indian in the wilderness convinced many New Englanders that the war would be long and difficult. Shortly after the commencement of hostilities, one observer noted the significance of "the Leaves in the Wilderness" in concealing the enemy and recommended that the Puritan troops wait until the underbrush was "dried and burnt and the swamps frozen hard."[10] Since the presence of dense undergrowth played such a prominent role in both the Vietnam War and King Philip's War, the American soldier in Vietnam and the Puritan colonist in New England shared a tendency to resent that wilderness and to project his anger onto the inhospitable environment. In this scheme of things the use of defoliant in jungle warfare—the stripping away of the enemy's natural habitat—is an appropriate action that receives its sanction from the Puritan crusade in colonial New England where the Indian was seen as a creature that possessed powers "like wild Dear in the Wilderness . . . [so] that our soldiers can rarely find any of them." In 1676 Increase Mather urged the settlers to be grateful for the abrupt conclusion of King Philip's War. "For we expected," Mather suggested, "that when the summer was come on, and the bushes and leaves come forth, the enemy would do ten times more mischief than in the winter season."[11]

This fear of an enemy who becomes invisible in the forest has become, in the work of William Eastlake, an enduring and essentially American fear. In his Vietnam novel *The Bamboo Bed* (1969) he describes an infantry captain who has led his men into a restaging of Custer's last stand: "Clancy blundered. Clancy blundered by being in Vietnam. . . . Clancy had blundered by not holding the ridge. Clancy had blundered by being forced into a valley, a declivity in the hills. It was the classic American blunder in Vietnam of giving the Indians cover. The enemy was fighting from the protection of the jungle. You couldn't see them. Americans love the open. Americans do not trust the jungle. The first thing Americans did in America was clear a forest and plant the cities."[12] Eastlake's perception is entirely correct.

Throughout the seventeenth century New England commentators extolled the gradual transformation of the wilderness and praised the transition of New England from a refuge outpost to a settled land. Cotton Mather devoted large portions of his *Magnalia Christi Americana* to lauding the subjugation of the New England wilderness. He expressed little love for the "dismal thickets of America" prior to colonization and reserved his strongest accolades for the "immense toyl and charge [that] made a wilderness habitable."[13] For Cotton Mather and Increase Mather the taming of the land and the taming of the Indian were a necessary prelude to the urbanization of the American wilderness. The creation of habitable settlements was not only an effective "means of enlarging the pleasant gardens of Christ."[14] It was also a way of controlling the wastelands of Satan. As Peter Carroll says, "The Puritans articulated the sense of God's grace upon a country with the metaphor of the 'Hedge,' a protective wall which surrounded a people and assured them that the Lord would not forsake that nation."[15] The Hedge—whether it related to the fortifications that protected a town or the spiritual protection afforded the villagers by the Covenant of Grace—could not be breached except by those who threatened the safety of the entire community. For this reason the Puritan founders of New England discouraged the random dispersal of settlers and preferred instead a controlled program of wilderness expansion. Puritan ministers like Thomas Shepard and John Allin interpreted any unnecessary removals beyond the hearing of the Lord's ordinances as submission to wilderness temptations and criticized the existence of " 'a wandering disposition' among some of the colonists."[16] John Cotton, in a series of proposed statutes, suggested that "no man shall set his dwelling house" more than a "half a myle or a myle at the farthest, from the meeting house of the congregation."[17]

The Puritan failure to resolve the paradox between social cohesion and social dispersal is attested to by Nathaniel Hawthorne in *The Scarlet Letter*. Hester Prynne's tacit rejection of the moral dictates of the plantation is conveyed by her decision to live at the periphery of the town. We identify Hester Prynne with the untrained forest that tramples out to the west, that vacant area around the New England plantation that continually lured the colonists beyond the limits of the Hedge. The forest is the only place in which she and Dimmesdale can risk intimacy. Nature, the wild territory beyond the confines of Salem, is Hester's true orbit, the locus of the freedom and self-fulfillment of which she dreams. The moment she is released from prison, accordingly, she moves out of Boston to a comparatively remote cottage: "It had been built by an earlier settler, and . . . its comparative remoteness put it out of the sphere of that social activity which already marked the habits of the emigrants. It stood on the shore, looking across a basin of the sea at the forest covered hills toward the west."[18]

Hester's resistance to the established culture of Salem—her camouflage as a sister of mercy—becomes apparent only in the forest, en route to which the cottage is but a way station. When Hester loosens her hair for Dimmesdale she becomes a Viet Cong, a guerrilla, a razor-blade girl who plots to overthrow the moral community by ruining, through sex, its elected leadership. Hester wishes to defrock and emasculate Dimmesdale. She resists the imposition of Puritan confinement and spiritual quarantine and enters the devil's space, inviting her lover to enter and penetrate the space within her.

= Separatism in Massachusetts and Vietnam =

In punishing those who chose to "act out their latest daydream in the forest" the Puritan divines expressed their firm belief that "unsanctioned plantations were beyond the pale of God's protection." In the Puritan colonies the model for the true plantation of Christ was that of the organic Christian corporation. That the Puritan divines viewed the political corporation as an organic whole is proved by their refusal to admit the moral right of men to leave the colony once they had accepted its jurisdiction. For men like John Winthrop "any individual who attacked properly constituted authority sought a natural liberty whose reward must be danger and death"—banishment to the untamed wilderness.[19]

The separatist energy of those exiled by the Puritans reappears in Vietnam, where authority, insofar as it is exercised by the United States, is cast in terms of a corporate mission, which is to say, through military and technological power. In the literature and film those who reject the wisdom of the settlements are punished by the righteous. In Stone's *Dog Soldiers* these are leftists with "Movement sideburns and Movement voices" (33), Harvard lawyers from the Military Legal Defense Committee whom Converse meets en route to My Lat. In their eagerness to court-martial a black marine they appear out of the darkness at Tansonhut like latter-day magistrates from colonial New England. However, their job is not to banish disobedient soldiers to the wilderness but to retrieve them from it.

In Francis Ford Coppola's *Apocalypse Now* the magistrates reconvene as an informal tribunal for the purpose of capturing Colonel Kurtz. Kurtz is reminiscent of the antinomian preacher John Wheelright, a military version of the renegade minister who rejected the sanctified corporate mission for a charismatic vision of God's cause in the wilderness. Kurtz, who has been "groomed for one of the top slots in the corporation," has "split from the whole program." A West Point colonel with impeccable credentials, he has had conferred on him all the privileges available to the military establishment. Kurtz is a member of the elect who "could have gone for general but went for himself instead." As a Puritan who has broken his covenant with the magistrates, Kurtz has become God's disobedient servant in the wilderness, his garden the kingdom of the devil in Cambodia. ("They wanted to bring him into the fold," says Willard, "and it would all have been forgotten. But he kept winning it his way.") Kurtz no longer needs the protection of the Hedge. Nor does he need that particular authority which his office and his work are a means of conveying. Because he rejects the demonology of the forest Kurtz is a twofold embarrassment. Both his sense of liberty and his sense of style are incompatible with that Winthrop described as "the most just authority."[20] What Kurtz does is to abandon his corporate mission for a charismatic one. He defects from the gang.

Kurtz is the camouflaged man who ignores his Americanness and the need for physical identification through insignia, uniform, decorum, language. He is a nativist. His followers are Montagnard, his weapons un-American, his tactics Vietnamese. He disfigures himself and disables the symbolism of the American cause, so that the military are unable to identify where he is or even who he is. Kurtz has lived too long in the territory of the Antichrist. Where soldiers like Killgore punish the Viet Cong with the weapons the technocracy places at their disposal—helicopters, napalm, missiles, loudspeakers—Kurtz punishes by utilizing "primordial instincts" and conducting a campaign of "moral terror." Kurtz believes in the theater of war as a stylized mode of expression, as something that demands a private aesthetic: a painted face, a primitive implement, an antinomian identity.

Kurtz rejects technocracy and the city—the corporate energy of Puritan history—and becomes a polluted minister who celebrates filth, who renounces the spatial separateness of the city and the fire base. There is something of the mixed-up hippie in the way he conducts himself, the flawed and extravagant poseur, the demonic Puritan in search of power—like Charles Manson, for whom violence was both creative and liberating. Kurtz reminds America of its fear of the woods, its deep suspicion of those who renounce the protection of the Hedge and the sanctified wisdoms of the urban community. In choosing to ignore the rewards that accompany colonial exploration, Kurtz displays a ruthlessly anticolonial spirit. His life in the forest is prelapsarian. It provides us with a specific rejection of the material impetus behind American foreign policy that, in the past, has determined the broad thrust of American colonial adventure.

=== An Expansion of Markets ===

It is often forgotten that the Puritan missions of 1620 and 1630 were not just expressions of spiritual idealism. They were also economically motivated. Throughout the seventeenth century economic self-interest played a large part in attracting immigrants to the New World. W. A. Speck has said that "the mass of colonists who settled both areas of North America (New England and the Chesapeake) were probably prompted to do so by the hope of improving their material conditions across the Atlantic."[21] Most of the colonial settlers, especially in the regions south of New England, wanted the economic success that had previously eluded their grasp in the Old World, where many had actually managed the estates they could never hope to acquire. Once in the new world, many of the colonists attempted "to tap the natural wealth of the wilderness."[22] The agricultural laborer knew that land was plentiful and easily acquired, and tradesmen and day laborers built their hopes around the prospect of the high wages that were a natural consequence of the scarcity of labor. In a land where achievement was more important than titles of nobility there was always the possibility that a nobody could become a man of consequence if he worked hard and kept his eye on the main chance.

The passion for wealth was one that enjoyed the sanction of religion, especially in New England, where Puritan clergymen assured their congregations that God approved business callings and rewarded virtue with wealth. Cotton Mather, in *Essays to Do Good* (1710), argued that prosperity was the gift of God and that men of wealth were God's stewards, charged with the responsibility of doing good to their fellows. Such doctrines as these, inherited from seventeenth-century New England, came to occupy a central place in the American market-enterprise rationale. In other words, the concept of progress and social power, as Sacvan Bercovitch tells us, has its origins in the concept of commercial ownership and a property-owning class:

> In all fundamental ideological aspects, New England was from the start an outpost of the modern world. It evolved from its own origins, as it were, into a middle-class culture—a commercially oriented economy battered by the decline of European feudalism, unhampered by lingering traditions of aristocracy and crown, and sustained by the prospect (if not always the fact) of personal advancement—a relatively homogeneous society whose enterprise was consecrated, according to its civic and clerical leadership, by a divine plan of progress.[23]

Moral idealism, though it may have furnished many of the slogans for the rhetoric of the elect, is not on its own capable of explaining the link that exists between twentieth-century American foreign policy and the ambitions that sustained the Puritans in New England. Economic considerations have also played a large part in determining the course of colonial policy. Any argument to the contrary is difficult to sustain. If the American people, as James C. Thompson has argued, are "sentimental imperialists," they have not been so sentimental or so benevolent as to ignore the need to protect their investments or to fail to seek the expansion of markets abroad. This view of American imperialism is borne out in the novels of Robert Stone.

In *Dog Soldiers* and *A Flag for Sunrise* America's legitimate sphere of interest is now defined as an economic market. *Dog Soldiers* is set in a private landscape where the dream of mission has deteriorated into the cynical opportunism of the heroin trade and the task of raising one's spiritual powers has expended itself in a desperate pursuit of sex and drugs. In Stone's California the impetus that took the colonists to Massachusetts has created "mooches," Chinese voyeurs who go to the movies to watch pornography: their "fingers laboring over their damp half-erections, burrowing in the moldy subsoil of their trousers like arachnids on a decomposing log" (71–72). Outside, the streets are littered with the angry, burnt-out victims of the culture, wasted pilgrims like "the kind they call Broadway Joe," a "rabbit-mouthed longhair" with eyes that "were nearly sky blue with touches of amphetamine pink at the corners" (85, 87). In the post-Puritan landscape of California, the dreams of youth have given way to chemical dependencies, a helpless addiction to Laotian Red that Converse buys on the streets of Saigon. These are the fag-end days of the counterculture where the Puritan Hedge has become a device for protecting the fantasies of men like Hicks or the cop Antheil. For June, the "speed-hardened, straw-coloured junkie stewardess" whose "eyes are fouled with smog and propane spray," security is provided

by the San Franciscan prison-hotel, a structure of pastel metal blocks built
in the form of a wedge with "grids" and "minimal windows" (175). June,
who once carried drugs from Bangkok, lives under the visceral impact of
television images and too much dope. When Converse visits her she is watching a Giants game and smoking a joint: "She seemed slightly drunk or fa-
tigued. . . . She watched the television set for a while; the camera was passing
over the stands as the fans in Candlestick Park took their seventh inning
stretch. 'That's what this country needs is protection' " (179). What dope
offers at the end of the sixties is a dream of protection, a final release of
Puritan faith into "desperate emptiness" (25). What Vietnam provides
through the heroin market in which Converse deals is the dream's realization.

It is not quite clear what June wishes to be protected from, except perhaps
the reawakened memories of her own dubious history. ("The way dealing
is—scag for sure—you have to be ready to fuck people. You have to sort of
like it. Somebody goes down on you, does you—you walk on their face" [182].)
She could also be reacting to the indiscriminate violence of the streets, the
revolutionary warfare waged on America by the Motherfuckers and Weath-
ermen and SDSers or the Puritan zeal of West Coast groups like the San
Francisco Diggers, worker priests who, at the end of the sixties, conducted
a religious war against those who preyed on the victims of dope. What June
requires is not retribution, the cathartic violence of guerrilla warfare, but the
promise of a comatose future, a way of preserving a dream of salvation when
faced with the loss of what the sixties had promised. June, who wishes to
forget both the menacing environment of the drug ring and the sinister,
dessicated energies of the counterculture, opts for a life of feeble enclosure,
the security-conscious San Franciscan, in whose "airless immaculate" (176)
corridors no strangers are permitted to wander. Drugs, like Hollywood, provide protection and disguise. June's future is already clear. She will follow
in the footsteps of Converse's mother, a television addict who lives in the
lobby of the Hotel Montalvo and smells of "death" (151).

In *Dog Soldiers* the lovelorn must dream in order to bring some poetry
into their lives, either to escape the pain and rupture of experience or as a
means of endorsing positive action. Recreational films and recreational drugs
provide their followers with an image of the world they can accept as fact
and into which they might escape from everyday routine. Ray Hicks, who
reenacts a John Wayne fire fight on the side of a mountain in California,
appears to be "trapped in a samurai fantasy—an American one. He has to
be the Lone Ranger, the great desperado—he has to win all the epic battles
single-handed" (270). When Smitty and Danskin beat up Converse they do
so with the television set at full volume, as if their actions can be rendered
legitimate only through the words and music of the media. So persuasive are
the styles and energies of the screen that the need for fictional guidance
accompanies Smitty throughout the novel. He claims to have fought in Vietnam and "tells stories like you could never forget. Ears cut off. Balls cut off.

Little kiddies on bayonets. . . . That's his way of making out, you know what
I mean? He meets a chick and right away she's hearing about the atrocities.
And then I machine gunned all the kids, and then I strangled all their
grannies. And then we set the mayor on fire" (238). What Vietnam offers to
a redundant hippie is the promise of an audience: what Smitty yearns for,
in his fantasies as a soldier, is the winning of that audience.

Smitty is a wish-fulfillment veteran of the war; like the blond Spec 4
that Morgan bumps into in Jack Fuller's *Fragments* he is full of "bullshit,"
a put-together vet who talks like a grunt when he chases the girls only
because, as Fuentes says, "he's afraid they wouldn't listen to the truth"
(224–25). Smitty learns his lines by reading from the tabloids and by remembering the lines of tough guys in the slammer. In this he is helped by
Converse's friend Elmer Bender who puts together a strange confection of
stories and pictures on *Nightbeat* magazine. *Nightbeat* is a "weekly tabloid
with a heavy emphasis on sex" (23) in which pictures of the dead are used
to illustrate stories about scuba-diving rapists, killer hermits, or skydivers
devoured by starving birds. Elmer's revelations, from his office on Mission
Street, combine the weight of a sermon on the danger of the wilderness with
the medieval folklorism of a gossip sheet. Elmer appeals to ancient fantasies
with headlines that announce the presence of forces, either primitive or
supernatural, which seek to undermine the stability of the community. Elmer's imagination stimulates a craving for protection. It provides a "marvelous" linkage for a people whose history is attuned to the menace of external
threats and a war being fought, ostensibly, against the forces of the Antichrist
in Indochina.

The belief that underwrites the breakdown is shared by others with a
sense of mission. Dieter's refuge in the Mexican hills is necessary because,
as he says, "The world is breaking down into degeneracy and murder. We
have to make islands for ourselves like the ninth-century monks. We're in
the dark ages" (272). Similarly, when the missionary from Ngoc Linh talks
of corruption and the decline of the West, she does so in terms of an extrinsic
threat: the evil of the forest, the worship of Satan among those who are hostile
to the moral community. What Dieter and the missionary fail to anticipate
is the corruption within: the degenerate consumerism that governs the settlements that America has made in remote places. In Robert Stone's Vietnam
the Puritan mentality has created My Lat, a place "the color of ashes" (45)
with no observable life, an insane fire base guarded by marines who smile
constantly and have "crazy dopers' eyes" (46). In the city the confusion is
equally intense. Saigon, with its indeterminate style and polygot culture,
embodies the same cultural chaos as the West. Saigon is the kind of city the
Diggers of San Francisco reviled, its soul usurped by commerce and violence.

In *Dog Soldiers* the search for sensation mangles history, fragments and
rearranges the human character and concepts of order. Saigon is awash with
displaced persons, strange and androgynous hobos who seek recognition

through ingenious performance and self-abuse. There are the beggars whom Converse associates with leprosy at the Beach of Cap St. Jacques, the Filipino rock musicians with pachuco haircuts, the stonehead Dutchman who wears marigold chains and listens to Bob Dylan, the Honda salesmen and their Japanese girlfriends, and the Koreans who read the collected works of Saint-Exupéry and Zap comics.

Here is the city that Mary McCarthy saw dominated by Californians, space cadets whose presence only heightens the prevailing "unreality of the streets." In her book *Vietnam*, Saigon is a Western city. "As we drove into downtown Saigon, through a traffic jam," she says, "I had the fresh shock of being in what looked like an American city, a very shoddy West Coast one, with a Chinatown and a slant-eyed Asiatic minority."[24] The cultural confusion of life in Vietnam is intimately related to the cultural confusion America has chosen to inflict upon it. "After the war," says Converse, "they should fly over the Ia Drang valley dropping comic books and French dip sandwiches for all the G.I. Ma" (30–31). The novel provides few moments of release from this confusion. When Converse discovers a thermos flask it is a rare event. He treasures the moment and the flask, which is "an actual Vietnamese artifact" (22), as if to distance himself from the spiritually corrupt military liaison. More typically, those who come from the West, or are disposed favorably toward it, act as if they "invented the country" (31). The visiting salesmen or "contractors" are secure in the knowledge that their products are familiar to the Vietnamese. The values of the West have proved irresistible in the East; native culture has not sustained native aspirations. In the opening pages of *Dog Soldiers* Saigon seems plugged straight into a Western consumer goods invasion, in which the loss of native art and culture is a direct response to the overwhelming presence of an imported one.

= Everywhere It's Chicago =

In their works on mass communications and cultural imperialism Herbert Schiller and Alan Wells have discussed the ideological and economic benefits the United States has derived over the last thirty years as a result of the penetration of underdeveloped and third world countries by cultural agencies such as multinational film corporations and government-funded media agencies.[25] The Department of Defense, for example, has a worldwide network of thirty-eight television and over two hundred radio transmitters, and the great majority of its audience is non-American. The U.S. Information Agency, established in 1953, also has transmitters and prepares and distributes television programs for use in foreign countries, especially in Latin America and Indochina and in American-controlled or American-sponsored stations. American governmental intervention in the cultural life of other countries is supported "by the dynamic export policies of the broadcasting corporations"—ABC, NBC, and to a lesser extent, CBS—"from equipment and management to program sales."[26] Through the use of subsidiaries, stations, and networking contracts, the leading American film corporations have been able to penetrate the social structure of countries through the medium of television, particularly in Latin America, "the internationally recognized sphere of influence for the United States."[27]

The American media not only stimulate the social, cultural, and economic market of the countries they penetrate but also channel and specify the aspirations of the market. Certainly the purchase of advertising time is one way of "facilitating the distribution of commodities, broadening the market, and making people aware of commodities with which they would not otherwise be familiar."[28] The almost monopolistic control that North American film companies have in the screening of television programs and the overwhelming influence they have exercised in the purchase of advertising time has changed the outlook of entire economies in Latin America and Indochina from "producerism" to "consumerism." Through their close connection with American advertising agencies and other international corporations, American film companies have acted as the spearhead for an American consumer goods invasion. "This export boom," says Jeremy Tunstall, sometimes known as "Cocacolonization," has had "the effect of muting political protest in much of the world; local and authentic culture in many countries is driven onto the defensive by homogenized American Culture. Traditional drama and folk music retreat before *Peyton Place* and *Bonanza*. So powerful is the thirst of American commercial television that few nations can resist."[29]

American economic imperialism is related to American cultural imperialism, and both activities intersect in the use of mass advertising on television and promotion of American consumer commodities and "relevant" news. In Latin America, says Elizabeth de Cardona, the "primary influence of U.S. culture and commerce is now through the sales of T.V. programs" and the buying of prime slots by American advertising agencies.[30] The link between program advertising and U.S. consumer manufacture makes television a powerful medium for the export of American products. As Raymond Williams says, "the 'commercial' character of television has then to be seen at several levels: as the making of programmes for profit in a known market, as a channel for advertising, and as a cultural and political form directly shaped by and dependent on the makings of a capitalist society, selling both consumer goods and a 'way of life' based on them, in an ethos that is at once locally generated, by domestic capitalist interests and authorities, and internationally organised, as a political project, by the dominant capitalist power."[31]

In the work of Robert Stone the process of control appears absolute. Provincial resistance movements are forced to compete for the hearts and minds of the native people with the imperialist energies of the American film industry. Political desire comes into conflict with consumer desire. Film and television are now the main agents of secular mission, and the object of that mission is the stimulation of mass markets, the conferring of grace on those who support the ideology of what Alan Wells has termed "picture tube imperialism."

In *A Flag for Sunrise* American style has penetrated even the most remote hinterlands of Latin America. In Zalteca, Frank Holliwell and Tom Zecca leave their car in the company of boys who exude "a movie-hoodlum confidence." They await the appearance of the consul in a parlor where "prosperous-looking children were watching dubbed Yogi Bear cartoons on a color television set" (134). Throughout the novel there is a constant demand "to get the big picture pieced together" (366). The tragedy of a country like Tecan is that it proves the undoing of those who do. The revolt against the right-wing regime is led by brigade commanders whose "only prior experience of massed weaponry and its effects had been at the cinema" (378).

In *Dog Soldiers* the television battles screened in Vietnam offer a scenario in which conflict is perceived as a fantasy. In the Hotel Coligny, M. Colletti watches "Bonanza" on MACV where "handsome" cowboys defeat "ugly ones" in a Cinderella firefight. "It's the same in Saigon," says Converse. M. Colletti, who has been everywhere, replies, "Here, sure. Everywhere it's the same now. Everywhere it's Chicago" (38). Simplistic scenarios are what the culture exports. Cultural imperialism underpins economic imperialism; cultural diplomacy, which is often conducted through the work of multinationals, lies at the heart of American foreign policy. As Marty Nolan says in *A Flag for Sunrise*: "See, it's all a movie in this country and if you wait long enough you get your happy ending. Until somebody else's movie starts. In many ways it's a very stupid country" (23). What America has created, as Colletti has realized, is a protection racket, a racket that protects the particular images and particular values of the dominant culture. A good-looking American who defends his patch against wilderness energies and maverick guns can fortify the soul. But the soul is America's, not Vietnam's.

= War and Profit =

In *Dog Soldiers* John Converse has taken to smuggling dope as a means of avoiding the emptiness of the soul. In Vietnam Converse exploits the marketplace complicity that exists, through economic transaction, between the culture he comes from and the culture he now finds himself in. What Converse senses is the contractual nature of American political activity abroad, those business deals that govern the nature of third world relationships. It is for this reason that Converse dispenses with whatever moral objections he once might have had to trafficking in heroin. In a place of such dubious conduct as the Saigon marketplace Converse is no more immoral than the "red-necked contractors" (9) of Tu Do Street or the money changers and "merchant adventurers who paid the Indian currency sharks to hold their contraband in strong boxes that were as secure as anything there could be" (21). Converse is an opportunist who takes advantage of a business atmosphere and a buoyant international market to set up a scheme in which he provides the finance, Colonel Tho the heroin, and Charmian the outlets in the United States. "There would be no risk of misunderstanding because everybody was friends. . . . The thing had come together" (25).

For Robert Stone public sanction for American private enterprise derives from the economic considerations that govern the making of American foreign policy. In *Dog Soldiers* the heroin trade, the private culture of economic exchange, takes its lead from the corporate culture that American military activity protects. Public and private aspirations are mutually supportive. According to Mary McCarthy, "all wars have had their profiteers, but it has not usually been so manifest, so inescapable" as it was in Vietnam. McCarthy identifies Saigon as a particular problem, "middle-aged, inert, listless, bored. That, I suppose, is because everyone's principal interest there is money, the only currency that is circulating, like the stale air moved by ceiling fans and air conditioners in hotels and offices."[32]

Converse's trafficking in drugs is a covert economic activity that gains its legitimacy from the CIA. In American foreign policy, crime pays. Drug-running played a central role in financing both the Vietnam War and the CIA's operations in Central America. In *The Politics of Heroin in Southeast Asia* Alfred McCoy documents how the CIA assisted the tribesmen in Laos to sell opium as a cash crop in order to get fast money to finance the war against the Communist Pathet Lao in the 1960s. In the early sixties, Diem's brother, Nhu, organized the opium trade and relied on a covert CIA transport company for shipping the opium. Later, in 1965, the CIA's Air America flew Meo opium out of Laos for refining inside South Vietnam. According to McCoy, the organizers of the illicit drug operation were CIA operatives Theodore Shackley, Felix Rodrigues, General Singlaub, and Richard Secord.[33] These four men, says Roger Bowen, were also closely involved in the Iran-contra affair and worked "for Ollie North during the two-year period when the Boland Amendment forbade U.S. aid to the contras." Since the contras have been connected with trafficking in drugs in exchange for cash, it seems altogether reasonable to assume, says Bowen, that what happened in Vietnam has repeated itself in Central America and that the use of drugs as an economic resource has now become an acceptable mechanism for defending American national security interests.[34]

Stone's work supports the argument that economic self-interest and the protection of markets has been one of the cornerstones of American foreign policy. The need to ensure that American capital could operate without hindrance in key areas of influence and strategy has determined the shape of

American diplomacy since World War II. The Vietnam War, as Stone suggests, was of vital economic concern to a variety of interest groups within the United States during the sixties and seventies. Industrial and economic growth was stimulated in many of the key political states, and enormous benefits were derived by industries that specialized in capital-intensive, high-technology and consumer products. Andy Stapp once suggested that "the war was generated on the need for U.S. capital to expand or die,"[35] and an editorial in I. F. Stone's *Weekly* during the 1960s suggested that if the main concern of the American government was the Vietnam War, then "the main beneficiary of its vast expenditure" was "the military bureaucracy and its Siamese twin, the armaments industry."[36]

For an overproducing domestic economy Vietnam in the sixties was the new frontier, the space where man could boldly go. The chain of command stretched downward from a Californian president who committed Congress to an inflationary program of defense spending to the California defense industries that received the contracts, the finance capital that underwrote those contracts, and the Washington politicians who were rewarded for securing the appropriations. Although it is probably untrue to claim that "the Vietnam War fuelled a surge in economic growth and material well-being, across the entire class spectrum of American society,"[37] it did stimulate massive investment across a range of industries from construction to consumer to defense. In Robert Stone's novels the seediest characters are always "the contractors," salesmen who live on the fringes of criminality and enterprise and who make money by racketeering in the war zones and exploiting the corrupt political economies of South Vietnam and Central America.

War was big business in South Vietnam. William Gibson tells us that the massive port facility at Cam Ranh Bay was constructed entirely from materials that were brought in from the United States. The prefabricated piers, fuel tank farms, warehouses, barracks, hospitals, and runways were all constructed from American imports. Allied to this was the Commodity Import Program, or the PX system, which resulted in the mass importation "of thousands of tons of consumer goods." Says Gibson, "All U.S. military personnel, U.S. civilians, and foreign civilians and military personnel directly hired by the U.S. government were entitled to purchase each year 'one television set, two radios, two still cameras, one movie camera, one movie projector, one slide projector, one stereo tape recorder, one refrigerator, one washing machine, one spin dryer, two watches. . . .' "[38]

The sale of American consumer products was also strongly encouraged outside the bases in South Vietnam. One of the main doctrines in the American counterinsurgency thesis was the "pacification" of the Vietnamese middle class by conferring on them many of the benefits of American consumerism. This was achieved, suggests Gibson, by "importing thousands upon thousands of cars, motorcycles, televisions, stereos, refrigerators and

other modern consumer goods for a more or less affluent class of Vietnamese."
Consumerism was promoted "as a major source of psychological satisfaction
in Vietnam. Just as the military had appropriated the logic of advanced capitalist production for reorganizing its internal structure and concept of war,
so leading civilian and military officials came to conceive of pacification in
terms of establishing and promoting American-style mass media, advertising
and consumerism."[39] Outside the cities the attempt to restructure South
Vietnam from a largely peasant society into an urban-based, American dependency was based on the idea of destroying the traditional, rural, Vietnamese community. What Gibson has called "the ravaging of Vietnam"[40] was the
principle that underwrote a national policy of forced resettlement and the
urbanization of the provinces. Through the use of a materialist approach—
"often measured in terms of bulgar wheat, cement, schoolbooks and
aspirins"[41]—the Vietnamese resettlement program came to be regarded as a
capitalist crusade, an attempt to devise artificial communities by stimulating
a craving for "consumer goods."[42]

Economic considerations of a more institutionalized nature defined the
course of American foreign policy in the immediate post–World War II era.
U.S. interests in Indochina were always tied up with the fate of Japan. Here,
the logic of protectionism was based on the threat of Communist political
and economic influence and the assumption that the fall of South Vietnam
and Laos to the Communists would be profoundly damaging to the U.S.
sphere of influence in Indochina. Given that Japan was a trading nation,
wholly dependent on the Asian market for its raw materials and foodstuffs
and the export of consumer products, the fear arose that it might be persuaded
out of economic necessity to develop an alliance with regimes that were not
politically acceptable to the West. The goal of Stalinist domination in the Far
East and the economic and strategic potential of Japan formed the basis of
the domino theory. As a National Security Council report of December 1949
indicated, "the industrial plant of Japan would be the richest strategic prize
in the Far East for the U.S.S.R."[43] Throughout the 1950s and early 1960s
the United States suspected a Communist plot to dominate Japan. A National
Security Council staff study of February 1952 warned that "the fall of Southeast Asia would underline the apparent economic advantages to Japan of
association with the communist-dominated Asian sphere. Exclusion of Japan
from trade with Southeast Asia would seriously affect the Japanese economy
and increase Japan's dependence on United States aid."[44] In the 1960s the
United States selected Vietnam as the place in which to prove to Beijing and
Moscow that Communist-inspired wars of liberation were both dangerous
and unpromising. For John F. Kennedy, Vietnam represented "the corner-
stone of the Free World in Southeast Asia." The country's "economy" was
"essential to the economy of Southeast Asia" and its "political liberty" was
regarded as "an inspiration to those seeking to obtain or maintain their liberty
in all parts of Asia—and indeed the world."[45]

= Protectionism =

Protectionist influences and tendencies determine the course of civilian thinking in *Dog Soldiers* and *A Flag for Sunrise*, in which the offer of protection to the weak (who accept it but may not require it) meets their request for protection (which they may not really need). For Stone, the dream of mutual need is destroyed by its own believers; the mythology of care deteriorates into corporate racketeering. In *Dog Soldiers* the fear of those who lack protection in their private lives is matched only by the desperation of those who have gained protection. In their lives we see the American people frightened not only of themselves, and of what they can do to themselves, but of what they can do to others when their missionary zeal goes awry. Hiding out, the search for a haven, is a recurrent motif—whether it be drugs (June), television (Mrs. Converse), communes (Dieter), war stories (Smitty), or the samurai fantasy of the "desperado" Ray Hicks (270). *Dog Soldiers* reeks with the odor of escape and shelter, the fear of those who must run for cover in cities that are overrun with suspicion.

The metaphor of protectionism has remained a key political concern for Robert Stone. In *A Flag for Sunrise* it is clear that he does not accept that the Vietnam War resulted in a change in the American national character or that the war undermined the country's faith in American governmental authority. In *A Flag for Sunrise* the morality of interventionism in Central America not only is accepted as a political reality by those who work there but also determines the private morality and covert activities of those who invest there. When, at the conclusion of the novel, Frank Holliwell gives in to the intimidation of corporate interests (and their affiliates), the value of accepting protection is demonstrated. As a Cuban agent tells him, the logic is simple: "You're in danger. We protect our friends. You are our friend, sir" (356). To survive, Holliwell must do what is asked of him (report on the activities of a suspected subversive, Sister Justin Feeney) by those who represent the corporate interests the U.S. government supports in Tecan. What is true for individuals is true for the banana republics Holliwell visits, those countries whose existence is also guaranteed on the basis of an offer that cannot be refused. The offer is designed to encourage American business enterprise, to protect and promote American investment in a political and economic environment regarded by the United States as a legitimate sphere of influence. In order to establish a sound economic base from which to market American consumer products it is necessary to have a supportive political leadership and a stable electorate. This may be achieved by the planning and financing of an armed coup and the overthrow of the elected government, as occurred in Guatemala in 1954, when the interests of the United Fruit Company of America were jeopardized by the socialist land policies of Jacobo Arbenz.

Equally spectacular results may be achieved by the use of dollar diplomacy and American aid programs and by flooding the market with cultural images—through radio, television, cinema, newspapers, and magazines— that promote the interests of the United States.[46] In return for aid and the monitoring of insurrectionist movements, the host country can give preferential treatment and tax concessions to American companies who wish to invest or who require a stable market for their exports. If those investment companies promote tourism (as is the case with Investors Security International in *A Flag for Sunrise*), this will bring foreign revenue to the country and further enhance the corporate American base. "Such factors," which "produce a fairly stable system to support the basic imperial drive," are used as a model of "imperial" conduct in *A Flag for Sunrise*.[47] In the novel, America's overseas empire in Latin America functions "as a device for internal consolidation of power and wealth. At the same time, it provides markets, sources of raw material, a cheap labor market and investment opportunities."[48]

In rooting out the self-interest of American corporations and their quest for Latin American assets, Stone returns us in *A Flag for Sunrise* to the socialist conviction that "American corporations exercise very extensive autority, and even commanding power in the political economy of third world nations."[49] The novel demonstrates that the United States will, with a reasonably high degree of probability, tend to support those countries that offer the best hope of guaranteeing American capital the freedom to move unhindered and the opportunity to make use of human and material resources at minimal cost. The United States will also tend to support resistance movements in countries where this does not obtain (such as the contras in Nicaragua), and who, if they gained political power, would support interventionism by the United States. In Tecan and Compostela, Stone is keen to show that "in the face of well-entrenched commercial pressures and the widespread co-option of their population to modern life styles . . . effective development imperatives can be implemented only by imposing strong political controls."[50] Through its support of local assets, like Heath and Soyer, the United States is able to keep the "development imperatives" of Tecan in alignment with American corporate imperatives.

The intention is to build a city modeled on the business and entertainment centers of Latin America—a society, in other words, whose economic progress is strictly controlled according to the needs of visiting American consumers and the export needs of American leisure and recreational industries. In Tecan, diversification away from land and into tourism is actively encouraged as a means of redirecting corporate investment, regardless of the damage to the social and cultural traditions of the country or the economic infrastructure of the rural regions. What happened in Cuba, where the United States dominated the economic life of the island by controlling, directly and indirectly, the sugar industry and by overtly and covertly preventing any dynamic modification of the island's one-crop economy, is here reversed.

Nevertheless, as William Appleman Williams suggests, the principle of corporate profit still determines the manner in which the United States behaves. Tecan and Cuba are alike, for in both places the United States sets "clear and narrow limits" on the country's political aspirations. It tolerates the use "of torture and terror, of fraud and force," by those who rule in its name. But it intervenes "with economic and diplomatic pressure and with force of arms" when the people threaten "to transgress the economic and political restrictions set by American leaders."[51]

= Native Species =

To move from *Dog Soldiers* to *A Flag for Sunrise* is to move from a world of picaresque criminality and a worm's-eye view of economic corruption to the more visible public corruption of the state. Stone subscribes to a belief that American foreign policy is guided by an insistence, as Williams puts it, "that other people cannot really solve their problems and improve their lives unless they go about it in the same way as the United States."[52] Although Vietnam has been regained by the devil, the Puritan missionaries retain a hope that Central America may be more easily redeemed. What America defines as acceptable in Central America is conveyed at an early moment in the novel when a Catholic nun, who has gotten mixed up in "subversive activities," is told by a friend to obey the wishes of the Mother Provincial in New Orleans and go back home. Just as the church wishes to withdraw its mission from the Republic of Tecan because the political climate of the country is unstable, so the government in Washington wishes to eliminate the forces of unrest. For this reason Marty Nolan of the CIA asks Frank Holliwell to help with information on a visit he is about to make to the neighboring country of Compostela. "Information is a positive force," Nolan explains. "It furthers communication. It reduces isolation and clarifies motive. The more everybody knows about what everybody is doing, the less misunderstanding there is in the world" (21).

The scope for misunderstanding what happens in Tecan has already been reduced by the presence of "American-style hardware stores and the President [who] speaks English just like we do here on Court Street" (21). In Tecan, American styles of life and art and the presence of American consumer commodities have visibly transformed the country's social and cultural identity. What Nolan strives to preserve is the cultural homogeneity of the region and the interests of American consumer capitalism. Karl Jaspers defines the effect of this in the following way in *Man in the Modern Age*:

> With the unification of our planet, there has begun a process of levelling-down which people contemplate with horror. That which has today become general to our species is always the most superficial,

the most trivial, and the most indifferent of human possibilities. Yet
men strive to effect the levelling-down as if, in that way, the unification of mankind could be brought about. On tropical plantations
and in the fishing villages of the Far North, the films of the great
capitals are thrown on the screen. People dress alike. The conven-
tionalities of daily intercourse are cosmopolitan; the same dances, the
same types of thought, and the same catch-words . . . are making
their way all over the world.[53]

The striking similarity between Jaspers and Stone underlines not merely
a shared apprehension of the changes wrought by economic imperialism and
its resultant social dislocation but also the cultural impact of so fundamental
an alteration in the relationship between the individual and his native environment. On the streets of the nation's capital, Puerto Alvarado, "men of
property stood . . . with transistor radios pressed against their ears, [and]
teenaged parents in cheap cotton dress-up clothes clung to their several tiny
children." On the festival streets there are "girls in hip-huggers and 'Kiss
Me, Stupid' tee shirts and girls whose fancy dress was their school uniforms.
There were nearly white boys who wore Italian-style print shirts and looked
bored, stiff self-conscious mestizos in starchy white sport shirts, blacks who
broke their Spanish phrases with 'mon' and 'bruddah,' practiced karate moves,
swayed, danced with themselves in a flurry of loose wrists and flashing palms"
(40). The spirit of the dance and the intensity of the light show with which
the festival climaxes partake of the same energies. The light that flashes
around the plaza "electrifies the posters of *Death Wish* in front of the cinema"
and transforms the figure of Christ in a glass and mahogany coffin on the
steps of the church. The captive audience is entertained by a spectacle that
derives its stimulus from the world of cinema and the illusory properties of
a Hollywood film set. "See, it's all done with light," says Father Godoy. "Like
the movies." Later, Godoy condemns the trickery of an art form that has
ruined the native culture of the region: "A fair was a great thing once. . . .
There were a great many tents and tricks. Today it's not so much because
the movies come here now" (49). The irony of the remark is that it is made
by a priest who is himself culturally corrupt: a man who speaks the language
of the tribe and commits himself to its political battles but dresses like a
tourist. "Father Godoy," we are told, wears "creased chino pants, a blue plaid
shirt and expensive sunglasses" (34) and drives a Toyota.

The penetration of Latin America by the corporate culture of the United
States appears irresistible. Compostela may live under the illusion that it
enjoys "a reputation for progressive politics," but it has all but succumbed
to American styles of self-expression. The Compostelans, who are "always
picking up North American–type public relations notions and getting them
slightly wrong" (66), have outdone themselves in the Panamerican-Plaza.
"The lobby . . . had a fine banana tree at the foot of its mezzanine stairway

and a fetching interior waterfall. Beyond that, it was a spiritual extension of Miami Airport" (69). The hotel guide is Oscar Ocampo, a friend of Holliwell's from Vietnam, and a one-time left-wing political activist. Ocampo has recently been bought off (granted protection) by the American government, and he now acts as an informer on subversive activities for the CIA. Ocampo's home is cluttered with stone Mayan artifacts which he sells to the tourists, many of whom arrive in Compostela under the auspices of Global Fishfinders, Houston, Texas.

Global Fishfinders, "a bunch of rich Texas doctors," are the owners of Lago Azul Lodge, a Bavarian-style holiday resort built initially by an American airline in the 1930s. The lodge is situated by a lake stocked with large-mouthed bass from Louisiana, which, like the corporate investment that created the resort, has "killed every native species" in the vicinity. Holliwell visits the lodge en route for Zalteca and eats in a "tropical-Bavarian" restaurant surrounded by "the mounted carcasses of outsized large mouths, some of them bigger than sand sharks" (131, 132). The suspicions he has held about the predatory nature of American private enterprise are now fully confirmed by what he sees. The lecture he has given at the National University of Compostela—in which he attacks the principle of American cultural and economic imperialism—takes on an added significance.

What lurks behind Holliwell's fear of mass culture and the postliterate forces that culture exploits is a restatement of Matthew Arnold's complaint in *Culture and Anarchy*. What Arnold saw as Americanization Holliwell sees as the rapid approach of cultural barbarism. In both cases American culture has led to the growth of a form of expression that lacks the redeeming structure of tradition, that is brash and unsubtle, that makes a virtue of its own ephemerality, and that appeals to the lowest common denominators of taste and expression. For Holliwell, as for Arnold, the pursuit of the trivial is confirmed in a society whose cultural identity was forged in an industrial age. The country lacks an established tradition. It has evidenced none of the structures necessary for the validation of such a tradition. It has also been deprived of all those resources necessary to counter what might be regarded as a pernicious democratic mediocrity. Holliwell's attack on the urban industrial spirit concludes with a drunken denunciation of Mickey Mouse America. The language lacks both the high-mindedness of Arnold and the critical exuberance of a Dwight Macdonald. Artistically it doesn't work, but the argument is nevertheless forcibly stated.

The "debasement" continues with help from "assets" (351) of the CIA: Tecanecan stooges like Miguel Soyer and "sinister" contractors of the Hotel Paradise in Puerto Alvarado who talk in whispers "about coke or emeralds" (311). The controlling figure is Ralph Heath, an employee of Investors Security International and the spokesman for an international fruit company. The fruit company wishes to develop the land it owns in the coastal region of Tecan for tourism, especially package tourism where, as Heath says, "the profits are" (244). The fruit company also owns the land on which stands the ancient and ruined village plantation where Father Egan ministers to the hippies who have journeyed there under the impulse of an obscure spiritual mission. If the standing stones in a plantation settlement attract the disaffected youth of America—those for whom the myth of creating a city on a hill remains a durable faith—they also attract men like Heath for whom the purpose of a mission is best represented not by the stelae but by a hotel building. Heath abhors the "very rubbishy sort of American" (249) who wanders abroad and with whom he must contend. By this he means not just the hippies but the "psalm-singing" Communists like Father Egan and Sister Justin Feeney in their devotionist missions, "bastards" who "turn the people against us and against the government" (619, 170).

Although Holliwell calls Heath a "missionary," what Heath would like to do is "teach" the people "contempt" and humiliation, to replace the politics of nativism with servility, and to airlift the fruit workers to the Pacific coast where the land is not required for corporate development. "We're going to have tourists coming down here at the rate of a few thousand a month. We're going to have me spying through key-holes so the hotel staff doesn't pinch their Minoxes. We're going to teach the people to steal" (245). Ralph Heath is one of those "strong-arm philosophers" (248) who believe in the mythology of corporate mission and who reduce the idea of a city on a hill to a secular obsession. Like his coconspirators, he is driven by a dream of economic opportunism. He is a member of a culture for whom foreign relations is defined by the maximization of corporate profit. He embodies the ideals and aspirations that characterized American attitudes in Cuba during the 1950s, and his greed anticipates the revolutionary struggle that follows as a consequence.

If Heath is one of the "cowboys" then, not surprisingly, those who oppose him are referred to as "Indians" (351, 352). Although Holliwell remembers the distinction between these adversaries from the time he spent in Vietnam, his attachment to nativism is purely sentimental. Although his sympathies are pulled in the direction of those who wear "braids and native dress," by the end of the novel Holliwell has abandoned the resistance movement and implicated Justin Feeney in the uprising against the government. Just as Jake Barnes in *The Sun Also Rises* loses his aficion by betraying the trust of Montoya, so Frank Holliwell succumbs to the menace of a later generation of American tourists whom the government of Tecan wishes to protect. Behind the government is the CIA, and behind the CIA is Investors Security International. As Heath says, "It's a very large investment that's under consideration on this coast, converting to tourism and so forth. Lot of money's been paid out. They want to know what's going on, eh?" (369).

When faced with the problem of resisting the reductionist culture that Heath wishes to establish, Holliwell also converts to tourism. At a crucial moment he suffers from a failure of radical will. He becomes, as Soyer anticipates, a member of "a nation of betrayers . . . without pride" (368). Holliwell retains some sympathy for the oppressed, but he does not share their political convictions. Like Converse, he is haunted by Indochina and the memory of its arbitrary violence. What remains is that "potent mixture of nostalgia and dread," the sight of soldiers in M.P.s' helmets, "the empty stares, the demented traffic," the beggars "clustered about" the doors of the newly built bus station as they were in Danang or Hue, or any of those places in "the pre-industrial" world in which America has declared an interest (128).

= The Return of the Native =

The Americanized world pretends control but invites collapse. For Stone the energies of the West are Spenglerian; there are no shelters, the lodges are breached, the Viet Cong are "everywhere" (368). In *Dog Soldiers* the sanctuaries are not adequate to withstand the anger of the natives. When John Converse turns on the air-conditioner back in his room at the Hotel Coligny, it provides "a busy and, to the American ear, vaguely reassuring sound which drowned out the sounds from the street" (38). For a moment the Hotel Coligny (Saigon) anticipates the environment of the San Franciscan (California). For most of the time Saigon is unsafe. Violence is imminent and "murder" haunts the room Converse sleeps in. In such an atmosphere the United States demands subservience but cannot command respect or gratitude. Saigon is "a city of close watchers" (19); it houses a race of people who bide their time. Those who stare do not do so in a spirit of affection but simply endure the belittling rewards of the patronized. Mme Colletti, patronesse of the Hotel Coligny, looks at Converse "with suspicion and loathing" (20), and the girls at the Crazy Horse "turn their eyes on him with identical expressions of bland, fathomless contempt." The enemies are everywhere. The girls in the bar may be "war widows or refugee country girls or serving officers of the Viet Cong." Converse cannot tell the difference. He is "an American with a stupid expression and pockets stuffed with green money, and there was no way they could get it off him short of turning him upside down and shaking him. It must make them want to cry, he thought. He was sympathetic" (26–27). Converse senses the hatred of the people but cannot control it. Nor is he able to enlarge the scope of his immediate sympathy to accommodate a program of political action. He is left with a feeling of "vague dissatisfaction" (39), the knowledge that eventually a price must be paid.

In South Vietnam life exists in a state of siege on the terms established by the settlement as fortress. Here is the fire base where journalists print the *Gulf Gazette*, collect pornography, and protect their horde of Laotian Red in movie cannisters. Here are the enlisted men's clubs "where marines and Seabees [sit] in the fading twilight drinking beer from pitchers" and blot out the world with Johnny Cash "at full volume" (50).

The American settlements live under the threat of physical attack from without and moral collapse from within. The dinginess of My Lat—the anemic and featureless landscape, the ramshackle buildings, the ash-colored compound, the weeds and warped metal that fringe the town—provide an indication of the moral drabness of Puritanism. In My Lat and Saigon the language of mission has been effaced by greed and lethargy. The Puritan enthusiasm for spiritual endeavor has finally collapsed into whispered obscenities at the Tempura House. Insofar as the punishment received is a sign from God, the resentment felt by the Vietnamese has a moral as well as an economic basis. The "incoming" that Converse is treated to as he finishes his meal in a Japanese restaurant does not discriminate: it announces the victory of the Antichrist.

CHRONOLOGY

1954   The Viet Minh defeat the French at Dien Bien Phu. Defeat signals the end of French military involvement in Indochina. France offers 25,000 French Vietnamese safe passage to France and citizenship at eighteen. The Geneva Accords partition Vietnam and conclude on 21 July. The call for joint elections on reunification within two years is rejected by the United States, which fears the popularity of Ho Chi Minh. The elected government of Jacobo Arbenz in Guatemala is overthrown in a CIA-backed coup. Head of the CIA is Allen Dulles, brother of John Foster Dulles, U.S. secretary of state. Both men are directors of the United Fruit Company, which owns land in Guatemala, some of which the Arbenz government wishes to expropriate.

1955   The United States arms the South Vietnamese under Ngo Dinh Diem who declares himself president of the Republic of Vietnam. North of the seventeenth parallel the Communists, under Ho Chi Minh, accept military aid from the Soviet Union. Graham Greene publishes *The Quiet American*, after living and working as a journalist in Vietnam since the early fifties.

1956   France withdraws its remaining troops from Vietnam.

1957   Viet Cong units become increasingly active in South Vietnam. The Soviets launch Sputnik. Eisenhower announces a reexamination of America's defense capability.

1958   William J. Lederer and Eugene Burdick publish *The Ugly American*; the novel warns of the complacency and incompetence of American diplomats in Southeast Asia.

1959   Castro comes to power in Cuba. Two American advisers are killed by guerrilla soldiers in South Vietnam.

1960   North Vietnam announces a call for the unification of South Vietnam by force. The number of U.S. military advisers in Vietnam increases.

1961   The Bay of Pigs invasion of Cuba fails. The Berlin wall is erected. Viet Cong units mount attacks throughout Vietnam. U.S. Special Forces are sent by President Kennedy to Vietnam and accompany ARVN troops in battle.

1962   The U.S. Military Assistance Command Vietnam is established in Saigon. Diem's presidential palace is bombed by South Vietnamese Air Force pilots. North Vietnamese troops build up along the Ho Chi Minh Trail. Soviet missile crisis in Cuba.

1963   Diem assassinated in a military coup and replaced by a military junta. Prince Sihanouk denounces U.S. aid to Cambodia. The North Vietnamese are allowed to use Cambodia as a supply base. Kennedy is assassinated. There are now 16,000 military advisers in Vietnam.

1964   The Gulf of Tonkin Resolution in Congress allows President Johnson to use force to combat North Vietnam after USS *Maddox* is destroyed by North Vietnamese torpedo boats. Leonid Brezhnev succeeds Khrushchev.

1965   Operation Rolling Thunder—aerial bombardment of military targets in North Vietnam—authorized by President Johnson. American infantry arrive in Danang. Nguyen Cao Ky becomes premier of South Vietnam. First major ground action fought solely by U.S. troops result in defeat of North Vietnamese in Ia Drang Valley. CIA's Air America flies Meo opium out of Laos to finance war against the Communist Pathet Lao. Draft protests and the burning of draft cards start as more soldiers are sent to Vietnam. Student antiwar protests mount, especially at the Berkeley campus. Protest songs become popular: Phil Ochs, "Draft Dodger Rag" and "I Ain't Marching Anymore"; Tom Paxton, "Lyndon Johnson Told the Nation"; Malvina Reynolds, "Napalm."

1966   U.S. troop levels exceed 200,000. Armed Forces Vietnam Network begins screening television programs; permanent broadcast studios are constructed in Saigon.

1967 Nguyen Van Thieu is elected president of South Vietnam. Mary McCarthy becomes first American writer to go to Hanoi; publishes *Vietnam*. Two billion dollars of public and private money is invested in the creation of think tanks for the purpose of developing scientific research and technology, much of which finds its way into Vietnam. So does Jimi Hendrix. "Foxy Lady" and "Purple Haze" are popular with troops. At home, folk-rock antiwar song, "I-Feel-Like-I'm-Fixin'-to-Die-Rag" is released by Country Joe and the Fish. Pentagon besieged by a motley army of 50,000 antiwar demonstrators including New Left pacifist-ideologists, artists, shamans, troubadours, and hobos, described in Norman Mailer's *Armies of the Night*. Mailer also publishes *Why Are We in Vietnam?*

1968 John Wayne directs and stars in *The Green Berets*. Eddie Adams photographs Nguyen Ngoc Loan, South Vietnam's chief of police, as he executes a captured Viet Cong suspect. Crew of USS *Pueblo* captured by North Korea. William Westmoreland appointed army chief of staff. Battle of Khe Sanh. Communist forces launch Tet offensive in thirty-six of South Vietnam's forty-four provincial capitals. Johnson announces he will not seek reelection as Tet is perceived as a military defeat for the United States. Students protest at Columbia University and occupy the campus for eight days. Street protests and violent clashes occur at the Democratic National Convention in Chicago. Takeshi Kaiko's *Into a Black Sun* is published.

1969 Nixon announces the policy of Vietnamization and begins the first withdrawal of U.S. troops from Vietnam. My Lai massacre of 1968 is publicized. Ho Chi Minh dies. Massive antiwar demonstrations are mounted in the United States, especially Washington. The problem of the returning veteran is dealt with in *Sticks and Bones*, a play of outstanding quality by David Rabe. William Eastlake's *The Bamboo Bed* is published.

1970 Sihanouk is deposed as ruler of Cambodia. U.S. and ARVN forces invade North Vietnamese bases in Cambodia. Protests in the United States lead to killing of four students at Kent State and Jackson State University. "Give Peace a Chance" by John Lennon is released.

1971 Le Duan's *The Vietnamese Revolution*, a classic document on revolutionary conflict, appears. The *New York Times* publishes *The Pentagon Papers*. Veterans throw their medals outside White House in protest.

1972 President Nixon visits China. After the breakdown of the Paris peace negotiations, he orders the mining of Haiphong Harbor. Vietnam veterans march on the Republican National Convention in Miami. Veterans are portrayed in films like Elia Kazan's *The Visitors* and *Dead of Night* as sadistic and sociopathic. David Morrell publishes *First Blood*, a novel that deals with the alienation of the returned veteran. The first anthology of Vietnam veterans' poetry appears:

Winning Hearts and Minds. Frances Fitzgerald argues for a greater understanding of Vietnamese life and culture in *Fire in the Lake*, as does Jeffrey Race in *War Comes to Long An.*

1973   The peace agreement is signed in Paris by Henry Kissinger and Le Duc Tho. A cease-fire is announced. The United States stops bombing Cambodia. Khmer Rouge advance into the urban centers of Cambodia. Last U.S. combat troops leave in March. Estimated cost of military expenditures in previous eight years was $120 billion. Approximately 58,000 American soldiers and 600,000 Vietnamese soldiers were killed. Fourteen million tons of explosives were dropped on Vietnam—the most heavily bombed country in the history of the world. One out of 30 people in all of Indochina killed; 1 out of 12 wounded; 1 out of 5 made a refugee. U.S. Senate forbids any aid to North Vietnam without prior specific approval by the Congress. Robert Stone's *Dog Soldiers* appears.

1974   North Vietnamese army begins the spring offensive with 285,000 men based in the South. The U.S. National Academy of Sciences reports that the use of chemical herbicides did irreparable damage to the ecology of South Vietnam. John Balaban's *After Our War* receives the Lamont Award from the Academy of American Poets.

1975   The North Vietnamese army launches major attacks. Ban Me Thuot, Kontum, Pleiku, Hue, and Danang are quickly captured by Communists. ARVN troops are overwhelmed and pull back to Saigon. On 30 April Saigon is captured by Communists.

1976   Vietnam is officially unified as the Socialist Republic of Vietnam. Northern party members dominate the new administration. Vietnam plants less rice than it did in 1940. Jimmy Carter is elected president. Ron Kovic's *Born on the Fourth of July* is published.

1977   United Nations reports that 10,000 hamlets were damaged in Vietnam, 1.5 million oxen and buffalo killed, and 900,000 children orphaned. Vietnam is admitted to the United Nations at the Thirty-second General Assembly. Carter declares a full, complete, and unconditional pardon for those who evaded the draft. Michael Herr's *Dispatches* and Philip Caputo's *A Rumor of War* appear.

1978   Soviet Union and Vietnam sign a friendship treaty granting Soviet forces free access to Vietnam's harbors and rivers. Currency reforms abolish private savings and businesses. Reeducation of and hostility toward the ethnic Chinese intensify. Boat-person exodus gathers momentum. In 1978 more than 205,000 refugees survive the ordeal of escape. Vietnam invades Cambodia and forces Khmer Rouge toward the Thailand border. Establishes the People's Republic of Kampuchea. Vietnam veteran still portrayed as murderous psychotic (*Taxi Driver*) but also as an innocent victim in *The Deer Hunter. Coming Home* offers a more saccharine treatment of veterans' disabilities. Tim O'Brien's *Going after Cacciato* is published.

1979   The U.S. General Accounting Office reports that thousands of U.S. troops deployed in Vietnam were exposed to Agent Orange herbicide, contrary to previous Defense Department denials. China attacks Vietnam, and 260,000 Sino-Vietnamese flee overland into China. Refugees reach peak numbers. *Apocalypse Now*, directed by Francis Coppola, the most spectacular and ambitious of Vietnam war films, is released. Nicaraguans rise up and oust the Somoza dictatorship. Honduras shelters the fallen dictator's cronies.

1980   Ronald Reagan is elected president. Donald E. McQuinn's *Targets* appears.

1981   Archbishop Oscar Arnulfo Romero and four American churchwomen are murdered in El Salvador. CIA begins to recruit former members of Somoza's National Guard to destabilize the Nicaraguan government and plans to use Argentine intelligence and paramilitary operatives to train Nicaraguan exiles. Argentina withdraws after U.S. supports Britain over the Falklands. American soldiers take over as advisers in Honduras where the contras are based and trained. Robert Stone's *A Flag for Sunrise* is published. Vietnam establishes an army of one million, fourth largest in the world, with 47 percent of its GNP going toward defense. Tens of thousands of Vietnamese are encouraged to settle in New Economic Zones.

1982   Vietnam Veterans' Memorial is erected in Washington, D.C. First ever visit of U.S. veterans to Hanoi is led by Robert Muller, founder and president of Vietnam Veterans of America. The Reagan administration accepts some Amerasian children through a U.N. refugee program. Through the Orderly Departure Program one flight a month brings Amerasians from Ho Chi Minh City to Bangkok. John Del Vecchio's *The Thirteenth Valley* is published.

1983   Laos, Kampuchea, and Vietnam agree to link their banking and economic systems. Elite force of 7,000 contras is trained and equipped by the United States in Honduras. Joint military exercises between U.S. and Honduran soldiers are conducted near Nicaraguan border. Tran Van Dinh's *Blue Dragon—White Tiger: A Tet Story*, Robert Mason's *Chickenhawk*, and Stephen Wright's *Meditations in Green* are published.

1984   Continued reports from South Vietnam tell of religious persecution and the repression of cultural and religious leaders. Hanoi announces that 100,000 people were sent to New Economic Zone labor camps during the early part of 1984. Refugees from Laos, Vietnam, and Cambodia continue as a major problem for Hong Kong and Thailand. Vietnamese propose a joint U.S.-Vietnam search for MIA's. Boland Amendment cuts off all aid to contras unless specifically authorized.

1985   In a seminal work Col. Harry Summers suggests that the United States could have won in Vietnam had its military strategy been different. Excavation teams including eleven American military specialists and Vietnamese workers discover downed American planes and bodies north of Hanoi at Yen Thuong. *Rambo: First Blood Part II*, a glossy, jingoistic climax to earlier missing-in-action films—*Uncommon Valor* (1983) and *Missing in Action* (1984)—appears. Triggers "Rambomania" and "Namstalgia" across the United States. Revisionism in popular culture is big box office and leads to a spate of attacks against Asian-Americans in the United States. Mark Frankland's *The Mother-of-Pearl Men* is published, as is Bobbie Ann Mason's *In Country*, a novel set in Kentucky in which the Vietnam veteran is neither the central character nor the author. Gorbachev succeeds Chernenko.

1986   Larry Heinemann's *Paco's Story* is published. Oliver North takes over responsibility for negotiating the release of hostages in Iran and arranges profits from arms sales to go to the contras. Oliver Stone's film *Salvador* suggests that Central America may become a new war zone in America's backyard unless the American public wakes up and challenges the country's foreign policy. Reagan, in support of insurgency against the Ortega government, says, "I'm a contra, too."

1987   The Tower report, first official investigation of the Iran-contra affair, is issued. Oliver Stone's *Platoon* wins Golden Globe and Academy awards. Combat films—*Full Metal Jacket* and *Hamburger Hill*—appeal to both liberals and conservatives. Vietnam's annual inflation is 700 percent and foreign debt in nonconvertible currencies is estimated at $6 billion. Vietnam opens up to tourism, free markets, and more self-criticism. Nguyen Van Linh, general secretary of the Communist party, professes his admiration for Soviet glasnost and admits in an interview published in the *Observer* disastrous mistakes and economic mismanagement of the country since 1975 caused by bureaucratic centralism and state subsidy.

1988   Russia begins the withdrawal of its troops from Afghanistan. Russian and American veterans meet in Moscow. Congress continues to block presidential attempts to provide contra aid. George Bush is elected president. The United States becomes more willing to admit Vietnamese refugees, especially Amerasian children. Neil Sheehan's *A Bright Shining Lie* is published.

1989   Families of American servicemen missing in Indochina sail to the Vietnamese coast and release helium-filled balloons carrying offers of $2.4 million to anyone who can deliver a missing serviceman to the Red Cross. Massive unrest and repression in China. Vietnam withdraws its troops from Cambodia. Oliver Stone films Ron Kovic's memoir, *Born on the Fourth of July*. Brian DePalma's film, *Casualties of War*, details a rape/murder committed by American recruits in Vietnam. U.S. invasion of Panama and the overthrow of General Noriega.

1990   Tim O'Brien publishes another war narrative, *The Things They Carried*. Defeat at the polls for the Ortega government in Nicaragua.

NOTES AND
REFERENCES

Introduction

1. Quoted by Phillip Knightley in *The First Casualty* (New York: Harcourt Brace Jovanovich, 1975), 423.

2. James C. Wilson, *Vietnam in Prose and Film* (Jefferson, N.C.: McFarland, 1982), 53, 54.

3. Patricia Caldwell, *The Puritan Conversion Narrative: The Beginnings of American Expression* (Cambridge: Cambridge University Press, 1983). Subsequent page references follow in the text.

4. Robert Warshow, *The Immediate Experience: Movies, Comics, Theater and Other Aspects of Popular Culture* (New York: Atheneum, 1975), 35. In spite of the high number of black and Hispanic soldiers who served in Vietnam, especially in combat units, the literary output of these groups has been relatively low. The prominence of Puritan testimony and the dominating influence of Puritan myth may have had something to do with the inhibited response of nonwhite Americans to the war.

5. For a more detailed discussion of the American literary response to Viet-

nam in the 1960s and 1970s and for an appreciation of the range of writing from the 1950s to the 1980s, see the books by Beidler, Walsh, Klinkowitz, Myers, Lomperis, and Pratt listed in the Bibliography. Pratt's essay, "From the Fiction, Some Truths," argues the importance of providing the reader with a chronological order that reflects both the time period in which the novel is set and the date it is published. "Only then," says Pratt, "can a reader appreciate the maximum relevance of any given work" (Timothy Lomperis and John Clark Pratt, *Reading the Wind: The Literature of the Vietnam War* [Durham: Duke University Press, 1987], 124).

6. Malcolm Bradbury, preface to Malcolm Bradbury and Sigmund Ro, eds., *Contemporary American Fiction* (London: Edward Arnold, 1987), xvi.

7. Nancy Anisfield, ed., *Vietnam Anthology: American War Literature* (Bowling Green, Ohio: Bowling Green State University Popular Press, 1987), 7.

Chapter 1

1. Lloyd B. Lewis, *The Tainted War: Culture and Identity in Vietnam War Narratives* (Westport, Conn.: Greenwood Press, 1985), 71.

2. Ibid., 72, 78.

3. Jerome Klinkowitz, *The American 1960s: Imaginative Acts in a Decade of Change* (Ames: Iowa State University Press, 1980), 76. The discussion of Vietnam literature reappears as "Writing under Fire: Postmodern Fiction and the Vietnam War," in Larry McCafferty, ed., *Postmodern Fiction: A Bio-Bibliographical Guide* (Westport, Conn.: Greenwood Press, 1986), 79–92.

4. Lewis, *The Tainted War*, 71.

5. *Newsweek*, 15 April 1985, 35.

6. Lewis, *The Tainted War*, 72.

7. Philip Caputo, *A Rumor of War* (New York: Ballantine Books, 1984), xiv. Subsequent page references follow in the text.

8. Lewis, *The Tainted War*, 98, 76.

9. Bradbury, *Contemporary American Fiction*, viii.

10. Pratt, "From the Fiction, Some Truths," 152–53.

11. Lewis, *The Tainted War*, 79.

12. Herman Rapaport, "The Thousand Plateaus," in Sohnya Sayres, ed., *The 60s without Apology* (Minneapolis: University of Minnesota Press, 1984), 139, 140.

13. Wilson, *Vietnam in Prose and Film*, 51.

14. Mark Baker, *Nam: The Vietnam War in the Words of the Men and Women Who Fought There* (London: Abacus, Sphere Books, 1982), 24.

15. Rapaport, "Thousand Plateaus," 140.

16. Michael Herr, *Dispatches* (London: Picador, Pan Books, 1982), 42. Subsequent page references follow in the text.

17. Klinkowitz, *The American 1960s*, 75.

18. Gustav Hasford, *The Short-Timers* (London: Bantam, 1985), 38. Subsequent page references follow in the text.

19. Takeshi Kaiko, *Into a Black Sun* (Tokyo: Kodansha International, 1983), 176. Subsequent page references follow in the text.

20. Joan Didion, *Slouching towards Bethlehem* (Harmondsworth: Penguin, 1974), 38, 39.

21. Klinkowitz, *The American 1960s*, 78.

22. Ibid., 76, 88, 78, 79, 82.

23. Saul Bellow, *Humboldt's Gift* (Harmondsworth: Penguin, 1976), 9.

24. Klinkowitz, *The American 1960s*, 31.

25. Michiko Kakutani, "Novelists and Vietnam: The War Goes On," *New York Times Book Review* 15 April 1984, 1, 39–40.

26. Paul Fussell, *The Great War and Modern Memory* (Oxford: Oxford University Press, 1977), ix.

27. Robert Mason, *Chickenhawk* (London: Corgi, 1983), 378. Subsequent page references follow in the text.

28. Baker, *Nam*, 378.

29. Loren Baritz, *Backfire: A History of How American Culture Led Us into Vietnam and Made Us Fight the Way We Did* (New York: Morrow, 1985), 321.

30. No one has yet provided a sustained analysis of the relationship between the Vietnam experience and the colonial experience in New England. However, there are indications from some critics that such a study ought to be undertaken. Noam Chomsky's essay "Visions of Righteousness" (*Cultural Critique*, no. 3 [Spring 1986]: 10–43) links the craft of Indian fighting in the New England colonies with the destruction of native culture and society in America's sporadic adventures overseas. In *Backfire*, Loren Baritz develops the idea of the Vietnam War as a spiritual mission, one that reminds us of the errand undertaken by the Pilgrim Fathers in seventeenth-century New England. William Appleman Williams discusses the importance of the phrase "the City on a Hill" as a guiding principle of American civilization and one that reveals, in American foreign policy, an underlying belief in demonology (Williams, "The City on a Hill on an Errand into the Wilderness," in Harrison E. Salisbury, ed., *Vietnam Reconsidered* [New York: Harper & Row, 1984], 11–15). The assumption commonly made by soldiers that Vietnam's hinterland was a place of savagery and "Indian" menace is discussed in John Hellmann's *American Myth and the Legacy of Vietnam* (New York: Columbia University Press, 1986) and Frances Fitzgerald's *Fire in the Lake: The Vietnamese and the Americans in Vietnam* (New York: Random House, 1972). For Thomas Myers the most definitive experience in Vietnam is that encountered by the point man, the soldier who sacrifices personal safety in order to explore "the thick undergrowth of mythic space" where "the enemy" is hidden (Myers, *Walking Point: American Narratives of Vietnam* [Oxford: Oxford University Press, 1988], 7). For many writers the undergrowth is both a moral wilderness and a war zone, a place that threatens spiritual destruction through sexual attack—capture, mutilation, sodomy, and buggery. The danger of sexual abuse in the wilderness also informs the Puritan captivity narratives and the diaries and sermons of the New England saints (Alden T. Vaughan and Edward W. Clark, eds., *Puritans among the Indians: Accounts of Captivity and Redemption, 1676–1724* [Cambridge: Harvard University Press, 1986]). Perhaps the closest that any critic has yet come to suggesting a direct parallel between the Indian wars in New England and the Vietnam War is the Austrian critic Walter Holbling. Vietnam writers, says Holbling, have consciously looked back to the past for

"adequate fictional models" and cultural paradigms they might use to make sense of the conflict. Some of these "central American myths" are embodied in the religiously motivated Indian-war narratives of the seventeenth and eighteenth centuries. From these myth-generating narratives, says Holbling, the writer is able to perceive the components of mission, "the conviction of being engaged in a just war in a unique historical situation, and racial warfare" (Holbling, "Literary Sense-Making: American Vietnam Fiction," in Jeffrey Walsh and James Aulich, eds., *Vietnam Images: War and Representation* [London: Macmillan, Lumiere, 1989], 125). For other useful discussions of Puritan history, see Richard Slotkin, *Regeneration through Violence: The Mythology of the American Frontier: 1600 –1860* (Middletown, Conn.: Wesleyan University Press, 1973); Roy Harvey Pearce, *Savagism and Civilization: A Study of the Indian and the American Mind* (Baltimore: Johns Hopkins University Press, 1953); Louise K. Barnett, *The Ignoble Savage: American Literary Racism, 1790–1890* (Westport, Conn.: Greenwood Press, 1985).

31. For example, Hellmann's *American Myth and the Legacy of Vietnam*; Philip Beidler's *American Literature and the Experience of Vietnam* (Athens: University of Georgia Press, 1982); and John Clark Pratt's paper, "The Lost Frontier: American Myth in the Literature of the Vietnam War" (presented at the Vietnam and the West conference at the University of Swansea, Wales, March 23–26, 1988).

Chapter 2

1. Hellmann, *American Myth and the Legacy of Vietnam*, 17. Subsequent page references follow in the text.

2. Slotkin, *Regeneration through Violence*, 562–63.

3. Andrew F. Krepinevich, Jr., *The Army and Vietnam* (Baltimore: Johns Hopkins University Press, 1986), 266. Subsequent page references follow in the text.

4. Loren Baritz, *City on a Hill: A History of Ideas and Myths in America* (New York: Wiley, 1964), 19.

5. Richard Slotkin and James K. Folsom, eds., *So Dreadful a Judgement: Puritan Responses to King Philip's War, 1676–1677* (Middletown, Conn.: Wesleyan University Press, 1978) 381.

6. Slotkin, *Regeneration through Violence*, 38.

7. Ibid., 77.

8. Daniel J. Boorstin, *The Americans: The Colonial Experience* (Harmondsworth, England: Penguin, 1965), 386.

9. Slotkin, *Regeneration through Violence*, 55.

10. Boorstin, *The Americans*, 381.

11. Stephen Wright, *Meditations in Green* (London: Abacus, Sphere Books, 1985), 78, 137. Subsequent page references follow in the text.

12. Ronald J. Glasser, *365 Days* (New York: George Braziller, 1980), 8. Subsequent page references follow in the text.

13. Slotkin, *Regeneration through Violence*, 47.

14. Ibid., 126.

15. Winston Groom and Duncan Spencer, *Conversations with the Enemy* (New York: Viking Penguin, 1983), 429, 430.

16. Rick Berg, "Losing Vietnam: Covering the War in an Age of Technology," *Cultural Critique*, no. 3 (Spring 1986): 93.

17. Boorstin, *The Americans*, 380, 378, 379.

18. Lewis, *The Tainted War*, 93, 94.

19. James Fenton, "The Fall of Saigon," *Granta* 15 (Spring 1985).

20. Ibid., 33, 38–39, 40.

21. Nathaniel Hawthorne, *The Scarlet Letter* (New York: Signet, 1959), 125.

22. Don Luce and John Sommer, *Viet Nam: The Unheard Voices* (Ithaca, N.Y.: Cornell University Press, 1969).

23. Ibid., 33.

24. David Gelman, "Vietnam Marches Home," *Newsweek*, 13 February 1978, 86.

25. Peter Marin, "Coming to Terms with Vietnam," *Harper's*, December 1980, 53.

26. Ross McGregor, "A Terrible Irony: American Response to the Vietnam War in Fiction," (Ph.D. diss., Ruhr. Universitat Bochum, 1987).

27. Marin, "Coming to Terms with Vietnam."

28. Peter McInerney, " 'Straight' and 'Secret' History in Vietnam War Literature," *Contemporary Literature* 22, no. 2 (Spring 1981): 190; and Peter Rollins, "The Vietnam War: Perceptions through Literature, Film and Television," *American Quarterly* 36, no. 3 (1984): 422.

29. C. D. B. Bryan, "The Different War," *New York Times Book Review*, 20 November 1977, 1.

30. Graham Greene, *The Quiet American* (Harmondsworth, England: Penguin, 1988), 36. Subsequent page references follow in the text.

31. Slotkin, *Regeneration through Violence*, 38.

32. Luce and Sommer, *The Unheard Voices*, 146.

33. Boorstin, *The Americans*, 357.

34. Slotkin, *Regeneration through Violence*, 56. The same principle may be observed in Vietnam. Although the spiritual phase came during the French occupation, after Dien Bien Phu it was assumed that only military action could rid the land of its Communist devils.

35. Perry Miller, *The New England Mind from Colony to Province* (Cambridge: Harvard University Press, 1953), 229.

36. Larry Berman, *Planning a Tragedy: The Americanization of the War in Vietnam* (New York: W. W. Norton, 1982), 43.

37. Ross McGregor, *A Terrible Irony*, 62–63.

38. Ibid., 55.

39. Peter Marin, "Coming to Terms with Vietnam," 53.

40. Baker, *Nam*, 289.

41. *Time*, 15 April 1985, 23.

42. James Webb, *Fields of Fire* (New York: Bantam, 1981), 210.

43. Peter N. Carroll, *It Seemed Like Nothing Happened: The Tragedy and Promise of America in the 1970s* (New York: Holt, Rinehart & Winston, 1984), 314.

44. Slotkin, *Regeneration through Violence*, 39.

45. Baker, *Nam*, 289.

46. Al Santoli, *Everything We Had: An Oral History of the Vietnam War by Thirty-three American Soldiers Who Fought It* (New York: Ballantine, 1984), 259–60.

47. Ellman Crasnow, "New Founde Land," in Malcolm Bradbury and Howard Temperley, eds., *An Introduction To American Studies* (Harlow: Longman, 1981), 34.

48. Sacvan Bercovitch, *The Puritan Origins of the American Self* (New Haven: Yale University Press, 1975), 118.

49. Michiko Kakutani, "Novelists and Vietnam," 39.

50. Ellman Crasnow, "New Founde Land," 33.

51. Martha Gellhorn, *The Face of War* (London: Virago Press, 1986), 215, 250.

52. Ibid., 254, xi.

53. Mary McCarthy, "How It Went," in *The Seventeenth Degree* (London: Weidenfeld & Nicolson, 1974), 27.

54. Ibid., 103.

55. Mary McCarthy, *Hanoi* (London: Weidenfeld & Nicolson, 1968), 90.

56. Gellhorn, *The Face of War*, 243.

57. McCarthy, *Hanoi*, 103, 104.

58. Norman Podhoretz, *Why We Were in Vietnam* (New York: Simon & Schuster, 1983), 93.

59. McCarthy, "How It Went," 4.

60. Ibid., 5.

61. Carol Gelderman, *Mary McCarthy: A Life* (London: Sidgewick & Jackson, 1989), 350.

62. McCarthy, *Hanoi*, 102–5, 130.

63. Ibid., 26, 28–29.

64. Slotkin, *Regeneration through Violence*, 51.

65. Baritz, *City on a Hill*, 27.

66. Everett W. Knight, *Literature Considered as Philosophy: The French Example* (London: Routledge, Kegan Paul, 1957) 40.

67. Larzer Ziff, "Literary Culture in Colonial America," in *Sphere History of Literature in the English Language*, vol. 8, *American Literature to 1900* (London: Sphere, 1975), 55.

68. Alfred Kazin, "The Self as History: Reflections on Autobiography," in Marc Pachter, ed., *Telling Lives: The Biographer's Art* (Washington, D.C.: New Republic Books, 1979), 89.

69. Ernest Hemingway, *Death in the Afternoon* (Harmondsworth: Penguin, 1966), 6.

70. Raymond Olderman, *Beyond the Waste Land: A Study of the American Novel in the Nineteen Sixties* (New Haven: Yale University Press, 1972), 1, 3.

71. Lewis, *The Tainted War*, 79.

Chapter 3

1. Ellman Crasnow, "New Founde Land," 64.
2. Adi Wimmer, "The Vietnam Veteran in American Literature and Popular Art" (presented at the Vietnam and the West conference).
3. Ibid., 3–4.
4. Berg, "Losing Vietnam," 114–15.
5. Ibid., 116.
6. *Time*, 23.
7. Raymond J. Bakke, "The Urban Church," in Mark A. Noll, et al., eds., *Christianity in America: A Handbook* (Grand Rapids, Mich.: Lion, 1983), 454.
8. Ibid., 454–55.
9. Ibid., 473.
10. Claude-Jean Bertrand, "Surfing for Christ on the Airwaves: The Electronic Church in the U.S.," in Maurice Gonnaud, et al., eds., *Cultural Change in the United States since World War II* (Amsterdam: Free University Press, 1986), 95.
11. Ibid., 94. Also Ronald M. Enroth, "The Christian Counterculture," in *Christianity in America*, 471.
12. Carroll, *It Seemed Like Nothing Happened*, 187.
13. Ibid., 235.
14. James Reston, Jr., *Sherman's March and Vietnam* (New York: Macmillan, 1984), 244.
15. Ibid., 187, 245.
16. In spite of Carter's pardon severe problems remained. Carter, for example, showed no compassion for the 500,000 military deserters or the 400,000 veterans who were cashiered out of the service with dishonorable discharges. Those veterans, who were disproportionately black and Hispanic, were disqualified from all G.I. benefits. Even the establishment of a Special Discharge Review Board did little to alleviate the suffering and hardship that a bad discharge brought about. See Reston, 260–63.
17. Baker, *Nam*, 206.
18. Daniel Snowman and Malcolm Bradbury, "The Sixties and Seventies," in *An Introduction to American Studies*, 289.
19. Carroll, *It Seemed Like Nothing Happened*, 299.
20. Ibid., 300.
21. Richard E. Ogden, *Green Knight, Red Mourning* (New York: Zebra Books, 1985), Foreword.
22. Bobbie Ann Mason, *In Country* (London: Flamingo, Fontana Paperbacks, 1985), 230. Subsequent page references follow in the text.
23. Ron Kovic, *Born on the Fourth of July* (New York: Pocket Books, 1977), 167. Subsequent page references follow in the text.
24. Thomas Couser, *American Autobiography: The Prophetic Mode* (Amherst: University of Massachusetts, 1979), 5.
25. Nathanael West, "Some Notes on Miss Lonelyhearts," *Contempo* 3, no. 9 (15 May, 1933): 1–2.
26. Alf Louvre and Jeffrey Walsh, eds., *Tell Me Lies about Vietnam: Cultural*

Battles for the Meaning of the War (Milton Keynes: Open University Press, 1988), 20.

27. John Carlos Rowe, "Eye-Witness: Documentary Styles in the American Representation of Vietnam," *Cultural Critique*, no. 3 (Spring 1986): 134–35.

28. Pratt, "From the Fiction, Some Truths," 153.

29. Ibid., 141.

30. Norman Mailer, *Why Are We In Vietnam?* (New York: Holt, Rinehart & Winston, 1982), 157, 114, 160, 8, 133.

31. Philip Caputo, *A Rumor of War* (New York: Ballantine, 1984), 272. Subsequent page references follow in the text.

32. Rowe, "Eye-Witness," 135.

33. Berg, "Losing Vietnam," 43.

34. Boorstin, *The Americans*, 27.

35. Advertising circular, 1988, from Jo-Ely Publishing Company, P.O. Box 26453, Raleigh, NC 27611.

Chapter 4

1. Boorstin, *The Americans*, 24.

2. Jac L. Tharpe, "Homemade Soap: The Sudsy Autobios of the Linsey Crowd," *Southern Quarterly* 22, no. 3 (Spring 1984): 146.

3. Bertrand, "Surfing for Christ," 96.

4. Barret Mandel, "Full of Life Now," in James Olney, ed., *Autobiography: Essays Theoretical and Critical* (Princeton: Princeton University Press, 1980), 56.

5. Cedric Watts, *The Deceptive Text* (Hemel Hempstead: Harvester, 1984), 176.

6. Fussell, *The Great War*, 207.

7. Anisfield, *Vietnam Anthology*, 7.

8. Fussell, *The Great War*, 207.

9. Ernest Hemingway, *The Sun Also Rises* (London: Pan, 1958), 5.

10. Kakutani, "Novelists and Vietnam," 39.

11. Joan Didion, *The White Album* (Harmondsworth, England: Penguin, 1979), 11, 88.

12. Didion, *Slouching towards Bethlehem*, 11.

13. Philip Roth, "Writing American Fiction," *Commentary* 31 (March 1961): 224.

14. Didion, *The White Album*, 48.

15. Dwight Macdonald, "T. Wolfe and His Magic Writing Machine," *New York Review of Books*, 26 August, 1965, 3–5.

16. Guido Carboni, "The Necessary Fiction: Notes toward a Definition of the Postmodern Novel," in *Cultural Change in the United States*, 35.

17. Kakutani, "Novelists and Vietnam," 40.

18. James Fenimore Cooper, *The Last of the Mohicans* (Harmondsworth, England: Penguin, 1986), 1.

19. Carboni, "The Necessary Fiction," 35, 36.

20. Walt Whitman, "Slang in America," in *Complete Prose Works* (New York: D. Appleton, 1909), 406.

21. Robert Stone, *Dog Soldiers* (New York: Ballantine, 1978), 242. Subsequent page references follow in the text.

22. Peter Rollins, "Television's Vietnam: The Visual Language of Television News," *Journal of American Culture* 4, no. 2 (1981): 115.

23. Ibid., 123.

24. See J. Fred MacDonald, *Television and the Red Menace: The Video Road to Vietnam* (New York: Praeger, 1985).

25. Leslie A. Fiedler, *Love and Death in the American Novel* (London: Paladin, 1970), 26.

26. Johan Huizinga, *Homo Ludens* (London: Routledge and Kegan Paul 1944), 3.

27. Fussell, *The Great War*, 192.

28. Chapter title in Constance Rourke, *Native American Humor* (New York: Doubleday Anchor, 1953).

Chapter 5

1. Marin, "Coming to Terms with Vietnam," 51.

2. Chomsky, "Visions of Righteousness," 23.

3. Chomsky, "Visions of Righteousness," 10.

4. McGregor, "A Terrible Irony," 54.

5. Anne Malone, "Once Having Marched: American Narratives of the Vietnam War" (Ph.D diss., Indiana University, 1983 University Microfilms International, Ann Arbor, Mich., 1985), 94.

6. Robert Muller, "Vietnam and America," in *Vietnam Reconsidered*, 269.

7. Chomsky, "Visions of Righteousness," 31.

8. John McAulif, "Vietnam Today: An American View: II," in *Vietnam Reconsidered*, 259.

9. McGregor, *A Terrible Irony*, 62; "A Bloody Rite of Passage," *Time*, 15 April, 1985, 22; McInerney, " 'Straight' and 'Secret' History," 195.

10. Wilson, *Vietnam in Prose and Film*, 81.

11. Quoted in Richard Corliss, "Stone Age Battles," *Observer*, 8 March 1987, 24.

12. *Time Out*, 25 March–1 April 1987.

13. Max Hastings, "America at War with Itself," *Daily Telegraph*, 25 March 1987, 8.

14. See David Dunn, "Cultural Stereotyping and Representations of the Vietnam War in Marvel, DC and Power Comics," in *Vietnam and the West*, 1–30: David Huxley, "The 'Real' Thing: New Images of Vietnam in the American Comic Book," in *Vietnam Images*, 160–70.

15. Lomperis, and Pratt, *Reading the Wind*, 66.

16. Gordon O. Taylor, "American Personal Narratives of the War in Vietnam," *American Literature* 52 (1980): 294. Subsequent page references follow in the text.

17. Beidler, *American Literature and the Experience of Vietnam*, 16.

18. Myers, *Walking Point*, 7–8. Subsequent page references follow in the text.

19. W. D. Ehrhart, "Vietnam War Poetry," in *Vietnam and the West*, 1.

20. Jeff Walsh, "Poetic Representations of Vietnamese Women by American Soldier Poets," in *Vietnam and the West*, 2.

21. Jeff Walsh, " 'After Our War': John Balaban's Poetic Images of Vietnam," in *Vietnam Images*, 145, 147.

22. Mark Frankland, "The Forgotten South," in *Vietnam and the West*, 1–2.

23. Mark Frankland, *The Mother-of-Pearl Men* (London: John Murray, 1985). Subsequent page references follow in the text.

24. Lucy Nguyen, Introduction to *Pham Van Ky, Blood Brother's*, Lac-Viet Series no 7 (New Haven: Council on Southeast Asia Studies, Yale University, 1987), ix.

25. David James, "Presence of Discourse/Discourse of Presence: Representing Vietnam," *Wide Angle* 7, no. 4 (1985), 47.

26. See Scott McConnell, *Leftward Journey: The Education of Vietnamese Students in France* (Reading, Berkshire: Transaction, 1980).

27. Ernest Hemingway, "Hills Like White Elephants," in *Men and Women* (Harmondsworth, England: Penguin, 1963, 1963), 52.

Chapter 6

1. Beidler, *American Literature*, 5.

2. Eric James Schroeder, "Two Interviews: Talks with Tim O'Brien and Robert Stone," *Modern Fiction Studies* 30 (Spring 1984): 146.

3. Beidler, *American Literature*, 5.

4. James Park Sloan, *War Games* (New York: Avon, 1973), 150.

5. Jean-Paul Sartre, "American Novelists in French Eyes," *Atlantic Monthly*, August 1946, 114.

6. Larry Heinemann, *Paco's Story* (Harmondsworth, England: Penguin, 1987), 209, 210.

7. Jerome Klinkowitz, *Literary Disruptions* (Urbana: University of Illinois Press, 1975), 28.

8. John Hellmann, "The New Journalism and Vietnam: Memory as Structure in Michael Herr's *Dispatches*," *South Atlantic Quarterly* 79 (Spring 1980): 142.

9. Alfred Kazin, *Bright Book of Life* (Boston: Little, Brown, 1973), 91.

10. Donald Ringnalda, "Fighting and Writing: America's Vietnam War Literature," *Journal of American Studies* 22, no. 1 (April 1988): 26, 33, 37.

11. Kakutani, "Novelists and Vietnam," 40.

12. W. L. Webb, "The End of the Word Is Nigh," *Guardian*, 2 December 1986, 24.

13. Bradbury, *Contemporary American Fiction*, viii.

14. Kakutani, "Novelists and Vietnam," 39, 40.

15. Ibid.

16. Webb, "The End of the Word," 24.

17. Klinkowitz, *The American 1960s*, 183. Interestingly this article is reprinted verbatim as "Writing Under Fire: Postmodern Fiction and the Vietnam War" in Larry McCafferty, ed., *Postmodern Fiction: A Bio-Bibliographical Guide* (Westport, Conn.: Greenwood Press, 1986), 79–92.

18. Jean Baudrillard, "How the West Was Lost," *Guardian*, 21 October 1988, 27.

19. Webb, "The End of the Word," 24.

20. William Broyles, Jr., "The Road to Hill 10," *Atlantic Monthly*, April 1985, 99.

21. Webb, "The End of the Word," 24.

22. Kakutani, "Novelists and Vietnam," 40.

23. Olderman, *Beyond the Waste Land*, 21.

Chapter 7

1. Reyner Banham, "Europe and American Design," in Richard Rose, ed., *Lessons from America: An Exploration* (London: Macmillan, 1974), 79.

2. Ibid., 79–80.

3. Ibid., 80.

4. Baritz, *Backfire*, 200. The need to civilize the peasants of Third World countries remains a guiding principle behind the American evangelical mission in Latin America. The current work of the New Tribes Mission with the Ayoreo Indians of Paraguay is that of bringing capitalism and Christianity to the peasant and of winning his allegiance with the offer of limited material reward.

5. Malcolm W. Browne, *The New Face of War* (New York: Bantam, 1986), 42.

6. Jeffrey Race, *War Comes to Long An: Revolutionary Conflict in a Vietnamese Province* (Berkeley: University of California Press, 1972), 6.

7. Banham, "Europe and American Design," 81.

8. William Gibson, *The Perfect War: Technowar in Vietnam* (Boston: Atlantic Monthly Press, 1986), 226.

9. Luce and Sommer, *Viet Nam: The Unheard Voices*, 147. An obsession with product solutions and an ignorance of the social repercussions of the product also characterized the use of defoliant. See Krepinevich, *The Army and Vietnam*, 210–14.

10. Baritz, *Backfire*, 327.

11. Browne, *The New Face of War*, 64, 65.

12. Gibson, *The Perfect War*, 83.

13. Jeffrey M. Schevitz, *The Weaponsmakers: Personal and Professional Crisis during the Vietnam War* (Cambridge: Schenkman, 1979), 7. For additional information see Dale Carter, *The Final Frontier: The Rise and Fall of the American Rocket State* (London: Verso, 1988), 232–3.

14. Ibid., 13.

15. Browne, *The New Face of War*, 41.

16. "Blacks in the Nam," in *Nam: The Vietnam Experience* (London: Orbis, 1987), 308–13.

17. Ibid., 57.

18. Rapaport, "Vietnam: The Thousand Plateaus," 143.

19. Luce and Sommer, *Viet Nam: The Unheard Voices*, 143.

20. Ibid., 194.

21. Ibid.

22. Browne, *The New Face of War*, 47.

23. Alvin Kernan, "The Mob Tendency in Satire: *The Day of the Locust*," *Satire Newsletter* 1 (1963): 16.

24. Jonas Spatz, *Hollywood in Fiction* (The Hague: Mouton, 1969), 9.

25. McCarthy, *Vietnam*, 14.

26. Morris Dickstein, *Gates of Eden: Remembering the Sixties, Surviving the Seventies* (New York: Basic Books, 1977), 274.

27. Tom Wolfe, "Clean Fun at Riverhead," in *The Kandy-Kolored Tangerine-Flake Streamline Baby* (London: Mayflower, 1968), 35.

28. Ibid., introduction, 12.

29. Michael Clark, "Remembering Vietnam," *Cultural Critique*, no. 3 (Spring 1986): 62.

30. Anisfield, *Vietnam Anthology*, 3.

31. Baker, *Nam*, 56.

32. F. Scott Fitzgerald, *The Crack-Up and Other Pieces and Stories* (Harmondsworth, England: Penguin, 1965), 39.

33. Mark Twain, *Life on the Mississippi* (New York: Bantam, 1963), 86.

34. Tom Wolfe, "The Last American Hero," in *The Kandy-Kolored . . . Baby*, 100.

35. Alasdair Spark, "Flight Control: The Social History of the Helicopter as a Symbol of Vietnam," in *Vietnam Images*, 88. I am indebted to Alisdair Spark for much of my information on the helicopter's role in Vietnam.

36. Ibid.

37. Ibid., 88.

38. Ibid., 89, 88.

39. Jack Fuller, *Fragments* (Sevenoaks: Coronet, 1985), 142. Subsequent page references follow in the text.

40. Herman Rapaport, "Vietnam: The Thousand Plateaus," 138.

41. Ibid., 143–44, 145, 138.

42. Baker, *Nam*, 105.

43. Eric Mottram, "Blood on the Nash Ambassador: Cars in American films," in Philip Davies and Brian Neve, eds., *Cinema Politics and Society in America* (Manchester: Manchester University Press, 1981), 242.

44. Luce and Sommer, *Viet Nam*, 188; Baker, *Nam*, 135.

45. Sloan, *War Games*, 12–13.

46. J. G. Ballard, *Hello America* (London: Triad Granada, 1983), 150.

47. Ibid., 151.

48. Joe Haldeman, *The Forever War* (London: Futura, 1984), 67.

49. Philip E. Slater, *The Pursuit of Loneliness* (Boston: Beacon Press, 1970), 48. According to Slater, "A wilderness-survival expert once pointed out to me that army training in hand-to-hand combat virtually ignores the body's own weaponry: ripping out the windpipe or jugular of one's opponent with one's teeth, for example, might be in many situations the most simple and expedient way of disabling him, but well-brought-up Americans shun such intimate contact with the victims of their mutilations."

Chapter 8

1. Lawrence Ferlinghetti, "Where is Vietnam?" in Walter Lowenfels, ed., *Where is Vietnam?* (Garden City, N.Y.: Doubleday, 1967), 36.

2. John Aldridge, *After the Lost Generation* (New York: McGraw-Hill, 1951), 10.

3. George Creel, *How We Advertised America* (New York: Harper & Bros., 1920).

4. Ernest Hemingway, "Soldier's Home," in *The Essential Hemingway* (Harmondsworth, England: Penguin, 1972), 312.

5. F. Scott Fitzgerald, *The Diamond as Big as the Ritz and Other Stories* (Harmondsworth; England: Penguin, 1972), 11.

6. McCarthy, *Vietnam*, 31.

7. Rowe, "Eye-Witness," *Cultural Critique*, 131.

8. John Calvin, *Institutes of the Christian Religion*, trans. John Allen (London: Thomas Tegg, 1844), 143.

9. F. Scott Fitzgerald, *The Diamond as Big as the Ritz*, 96.

10. John Lahr, *Acting Out America: Essays on Modern Theatre* (Harmondsworth, England: Penguin, 1972), 11.

11. Ibid., 12.

12. Percy H. Tannenbaum, ed., *The Entertainment Functions of Television* (Hillsdale, N.J.: Lawrence Erlbaum, 1980); George Comstock, *Television in America*, vol. 1 (London: Sage, 1980).

13. John Dos Passos, *The Big Money, U.S.A.* (New York: Modern Library, 1937), 462.

14. Lewis, *The Tainted War*, 227.

15. Didion, *The White Album*, 86–89.

16. Gloria Emerson, *Winners and Losers* (New York: Harcourt Brace Jovanovich, 1972), 11.

17. C. W. E. Bigsby, ed., *Superculture: American Popular Culture and Europe* (London: Elek, 1975), 15.

18. Marshall McLuhan, *Understanding Media: The Extensions of Man* (New York: McGraw-Hill, 1964), 65–73.

19. Didion, *The White Album*, 11.

20. Warshow, *The Immediate Experience*, 39.

21. Edward J. Epstein, *News from Nowhere: Television and the News* (New York: Vintage Books, 1974), 152–53.

22. Berg, "Losing Vietnam," 102.

23. Lawrence H. Suid, "Armed Forces Vietnam Network," in *Vietnam and the West*, 16.

24. Sacvan Bercovitch, *The American Jeremiad* (London: University of Wisconsin Press, 1978), 164.

25. Ibid., 163, 162.

Chapter 9

1. This is also the thesis of Robert J. McKeever. In "American Myths and the Impact of the Vietnam War: Revisionism in Foreign Policy and Popular Cinema in the 1980s" (*Vietnam Images*, 43–56).

2. John Quincy Adams, Oration, 4 July 1821. As William Gibson has shown: "Calls for new intervention in the Third World came before the Vietnam war ended" (Gibson, *The Perfect War*, 454).

3. Baritz, *Backfire*, 26.

4. Ibid., 42.

5. Ibid., 30.

6. Ibid., 30.

7. Caputo, *A Rumor of War*, 55; James C. Webb, *Fields of Fire* (New York: Bantam, 1981), 91.

8. Baritz, *Backfire*.

9. Peter N. Carroll, *Puritanism and the Wilderness: The Intellectual Significance of the New England Frontier, 1629–1700* (New York: Columbia University Press, 1969), 11.

10. Ibid., 207.

11. Ibid., 208.

12. William Eastlake, *The Bamboo Bed* (New York: Simon & Schuster, 1969), 24–25.

13. Carroll, *Puritanism and the Wilderness*, 220.

14. Ibid., 125.

15. Ibid., 17.

16. Ibid., 76.

17. Ibid., 121.

18. Nathaniel Hawthorne, *The Scarlet Letter* (New York: Signet, 1959), 84.

19. Baritz, *City On a Hill*, 20.

20. Ibid., 19.

21. W. A. Speck, *British America, 1607–1763*, BAAS Pamphlets in American Studies 15 (Brighton: British Association for American Studies, 1985), 20.

22. Carroll, *Puritanism and the Wilderness*, 191.

23. Bercovitch, *The American Jeremiad*, 20.

24. McCarthy, *Vietnam*, 72, 12, 14.

25. Alan Wells, *Picture-Tube Imperialism? The Impact of U.S. Television on Latin America* (Maryknoll, N.Y.: Orbis, 1972); Herbert J. Schiller, *Mass Communications and American Empire* (New York: A. M. Kelley, 1970).

26. Raymond Williams, *Television: Technology and Cultural Form* (Glasgow: Fontana Collins, 1979), 41. "In more than ninety foreign countries," writes Williams, "the three leading corporations have subsidiaries, stations and networking contracts; they are particularly strong in Latin America, the Caribbean, Africa, Asia and the Middle East."

27. Wells, *Picture-Tube Imperialism?* 94.

28. Ibid., 76–77.

29. Jeremy Tunstall, *The Media Are American* (London: Constable, 1977), 39.

30. Elizabeth De Cardona, "American Television in Latin America," in

George Gerbner, ed., *Mass Media Policies in Changing Cultures* (Chichester, Sussex: John Wiley & Sons, 1977), 60.

31. Williams, *Television*, 41.

32. McCarthy, *Vietnam*, 19.

33. Alfred McCoy, *The Politics of Heroin in Southeast Asia* (New York: Harper & Row, 1972).

34. Roger Bowen, "Create Two, Three, Many Vietnams: Vietnam as Antecedent to the American War in Central America, or Why the Left Is Right," in *Vietnam and the West*, 7–8.

35. Abe Peck, *Undercovering the Sixties: The Life and Times of the Underground Press* (New York: Pantheon, 1985), 322.

36. Albert E. Kahn, *The Unholy Hymnal* (London: Wolfe, 1971), 110–11.

37. Lewis, *The Tainted War*, 154.

38. Gibson, *The Perfect War*, 254.

39. Ibid., 226. For an extended discussion of American participation in the black market economy of South Vietnam, see "Forced Draft: Urbanization and the Consumer Society Come to Vietnam," in *The Perfect War*.

40. Ibid., 216.

41. Luce and Sommer, *Viet Nam*, 152.

42. Mary McCarthy, *Medina* (London: Wildwood House, 1973), 60.

43. Noam Chomsky, Hans Morgenthau, and others, "The National Interest and the Pentagon Papers," *Partisan Review* 39 (Summer 1972): 341. See also William Appleman Williams, ed., *America in Vietnam: A Documentary History*, (Garden City, N.Y.: Anchor Press, 1989).

44. Chomsky, 342.

45. Ibid., 343.

46. Bob Ostertag, " 'Saint Rambo' Inspires the War Where Boy Shoots Boy," *Guardian*, 19 January 1988.

47. Chomsky, "The National Interest and the Pentagon Papers," 355.

48. Ibid., 345.

49. William Appleman Williams, *The Tragedy of American Diplomacy* (New York: Dell, 1960), 11.

50. Wells, *Picture-Tube Imperialism?* 149.

51. Williams, *Tragedy*, 11.

52. Ibid., 9.

53. Bigsby, *Superculture*, 11–12.

SELECTED
BIBLIOGRAPHY

PRIMARY WORKS

Full publication data is given for the editions quoted in the text. Original publication dates, if different, are listed immediately following the title.

Baber, Asa. *Land of a Million Elephants*. London: Hutchinson, 1970.

Baker, Mark. *Nam: The Vietnam War in the Words of the Men and Women Who
   Fought There*. 1981. London: Abacus, Sphere Books, 1982.

Balaban, John. *After Our War*. Pittsburgh: University of Pittsburgh Press, 1972.

———. *Blue Mountain*. Greensboro: Unicorn Press, 1982.

———. *Co Dao Vietnam: A Bilingual Anthology of Vietnamese Folk Poetry*.
   Greensboro: Unicorn Press, 1980.

Ballard, J. G. *Hello America*. London: Triad/Granada, 1981.

Berry, D. C. *Saigon Cemetery*. Athens: University of Georgia Press, 1972.

Bosse, M. J. *The Journey of Tao Kim Nam*. London: F. Muller, 1959.

Bunting, Josiah. *The Lionheads*. New York: George Braziller, 1972.

Burdick, Eugene, and William Lederer. *The Ugly American*. Greenwich, Conn.:
   Fawcett Publications, 1967.

Butler, Robert Olen. *The Alleys of Eden*. New York: Horizon Press, 1981.

Caputo, Philip. *A Rumor of War*. 1977. New York: Ballantine Books, 1984.

Crumley, James. *One to Count Cadence*. New York: Random House, 1969.

Dann, Jean Van Buren, and Jack Dann, eds. *In the Field of Fire*. New York:
   TOR, 1987.

Del Vecchio, John. *The 13th Valley*. 1982. London: Sphere Books, 1985.

Donovan, David. *Once a Warrior King*. London: Corgi, 1987.

Downs, Frederick. *The Killing Zone: My Life in the Vietnam War*. New York:
   W. W. Norton, 1978.

Eastlake, William. *The Bamboo Bed*. New York: Simon & Schuster, 1969.

Ehrhart, W. D., ed. *Carrying the Darkness: the Poetry of the Vietnam War.* Lubbock, Texas: Texas Tech University Press, 1989.

Emerson, Gloria. *Winners and Losers.* New York: Harcourt Brace Jovanovich, 1976.

Frankland, Mark. *The Mother-of-Pearl Men.* London: John Murray, 1985.

Fuller, Jack. *Fragments.* 1984. Sevenoaks: Coronet, 1985.

Garson, Barbara. *MacBird.* New York: Grove Press, 1967.

Gellhorn, Martha. *The Face of War.* London: Virago, 1986.

Glasser, Ronald J. *365 Days.* 1971. New York: George Braziller, 1980.

Goff, Stanley. *Brothers: Black Soldiers in the Nam.* New York: Berkley Books, 1985.

Greene, Graham. *The Quiet American.* 1955. Harmondsworth: Penguin, 1988.

Groom, Winston. *Better Times than These.* New York: Berkely, 1978.

Halberstam, David. *One Very Hot Day.* Boston: Houghton Mifflin, 1967.

Haldeman, Joe. *The Forever War.* London: Futura, 1984.

Hasford, Gustav. *The Short-Timers.* 1979. London: Bantam, 1985.

Heinemann, Larry. *Close Quarters.* New York: Farrar, Straus & Giroux, 1974.

———. *Paco's Story.* 1986. Harmondsworth: Penguin, 1987.

Herr, Michael. *Dispatches.* 1977. London: Picador, Pan Books, 1982.

Just, Ward. *Stringer.* 1974. Port Townsend, Wash.: Graywolf Press, 1984.

Kaiko, Takeshi. *Into a Black Sun.* 1968. Tokyo: Kodansha International, 1983.

Kolpacoff, Victor. *The Prisoners of Quai Dong.* New York: New American Library, 1967.

Kopit, Arthur. *Indians.* New York: Bantam, 1971.

Kovic, Ron. *Born on the Fourth of July.* 1976. New York: Pocket Books, 1977.

Larsen, Wendy Wilder, and Tran Thi Nga, *Shallow Graves, Two Women and Vietnam.* New York: Harper & Row, 1986.

Little, Loyd. *Parthian Shot.* New York: Ivy Books, 1975.

Mai, Huu. *The Last Stronghold.* Hanoi: Foreign Languages Publishing House, 1963.

Mailer, Norman. *Why Are We in Vietnam?* New York: Putnam's, 1967.

Marshall, Kathryn. *In the Combat Zone.* Boston: Little, Brown, 1987.

Mason, Bobbie Ann. *In Country.* London: Flamingo, Fontana Paperbacks, 1985.

Mason, Robert. *Chickenhawk.* 1983. London: Corgi, Transworld Publishers, 1983.

McCarthy, Mary. *Hanoi.* London: Weidenfeld & Nicolson, 1968.

———. *Vietnam.* London: Weidenfeld & Nicolson, 1967.

———. *Medina.* London: Wildwood House, 1972.

McQuinn, Donald E. *Targets.* New York: Tom Doherty Associates, 1980.

Mooney, Ted. *Easy Travel to Other Planets.* New York: Ballantine Books, 1983.

Moore, Robin. *The Green Berets.* New York: Crown Publishers, 1965.

Nhu Tang, Truong, and David Chanoff. *A Vietcong Memoir.* New York: Random, 1986.

O'Brien, Tim. *Going after Cacciato.* New York: Delacorte, 1978.

———. *If I Die in a Combat Zone.* New York: Delacorte, 1973.

———. *The Things They Carried.* Boston: Houghton Mifflin, 1990.

Pelfrey, William. *The Big V.* New York: Liveright, 1972.

Phillips, Jayne Anne. *Machine Dreams.* New York: E. P. Dutton, 1984.

Rabe, David W. *The Basic Training of Pavlo Hummel/Sticks and Bones*. New York: Viking Press, 1973.

———. *Streamers*. New York: Alfred A. Knopf, 1982.

Ray, Michele. *The Two Shores of Hell*. London: John Murray, 1967.

Ribman, Ronald. *The Final War of Ollie Winter*. In *Great Television Plays*. New York: Dell Publishing, 1975.

Roth, Robert. *Sand in the Wind*. Boston: Little, Brown, 1973.

Rottman, Larry, Jan Barry, and Basil T. Paquet, eds. *Winning Hearts and Minds*. New York: McGraw-Hill, 1972.

Santoli, Al, *Everything We Had: An Oral History of the Vietnam War by Thirty-three American Soldiers Who Fought It*. New York: Ballantine, 1984.

———. *To Bear Any Burden: The Vietnam War and Its Aftermath in the Words of Americans and Southeast Asians*. New York: E. P. Dutton, 1985.

Schell, Jonathan. *The Real War*. New York: Pantheon, 1987.

Sontag, Susan. "Trip to Hanoi." In *Styles of Radical Will*. New York: Farrar, Straus & Giroux, 1969.

Stone, Robert. *Dog Soldiers*. 1973. New York: Ballantine, 1978.

———. *A Flag for Sunrise*. 1981. London: Picador, Pan Books, 1983.

Terry, Megan. *Viet Rock*. New York: Simon & Schuster, 1967.

Terry, Wallace. *Bloods: An Oral History of the Vietnam War by Black Veterans*. New York: Random House, 1984.

Thi, Nguyen. *A Village Called Faithfulness*. Hanoi: Foreign Languages Publishing House, 1976.

Trinh, Minh Duc Hoai. *This Side . . . The Other Side*. Washington, D.C.: Occidental Press, 1980.

Van Dinh, Tran. *Blue Dragon—White Tiger: A Tet Story*. Philadelphia: TriAm, 1983.

Van Ky, Pham. *Blood Brothers*. 1947. Trans. Margaret Mauldon. Lac-Viet Series no. 7. New Haven: Council on Southeast Asia Studies, Yale University, 1987.

Van Lien, Che. *The Fire Blazes*. Hanoi: Foreign Languages Publishing House, 1965.

Webb, James. *Fields of Fire*. New York: Bantam, 1981.

Webb, Kate. *On the Other Side*. New York: Quadrangle, 1972.

Weigl, Bruce. *The Monkey Wars*. Athens: University of Georgia Press, 1985.

West, Morris. *The Ambassador*. New York: William Morrow, 1965.

Winn, David. *Gangland*. New York: Alfred A. Knopf, 1982.

Wright, Stephen. *Meditations in Green*. 1983. London: Abacus, Sphere Books, 1985.

SECONDARY WORKS

Bibliography and literary criticism are so intermingled in books about Vietnam that it is often impossible to make satisfactory distinctions between them, and so this listing combines both types of research publication. Useful articles that appear in special collections are not listed individually as they are in the Notes but under the general titles of the texts.

Adair, Gilbert. *Vietnam on Film*. New York: Proteus Books, 1981.

Anisfield, Nancy, ed. *Vietnam Anthology: American War Literature*. Bowling Green, Ohio: Bowling Green State University Popular Press, 1988.

Baritz, Loren. *Backfire: A History of How American Culture Led Us into Vietnam and Made Us Fight the Way We Did*. New York: Morrow, 1985.

Beidler, Philip. *American Literature and the Experience of Vietnam*. Athens: University of Georgia Press, 1982.

Bercovitch, Sacvan. *The American Jeremiad*. London: University of Wisconsin Press, 1978.

———. *The Puritan Origins of the American Self*. New Haven: Yale University Press, 1975.

Berg, Richard, and John Carlos Rowe, eds. *Cultural Critique*, no. 3 (Spring 1986).

Bergonzi, Bernard. "Vietnam Novels: First Draft." *Commonweal* 27 (October 1972): 84–88.

Boorstin, Daniel. *The Americans: The Colonial Experience*. New York: Random House, 1965.

Braestrup, Peter. *Big Story: How the American Press and Television Reported and Interpreted the Crisis of Tet in 1968 in Vietnam and Washington*. New Haven: Yale University Press, 1983.

Browne, Malcolm W. *The New Face of War*. New York: Bantam, 1986.

Broyles, William, Jr. "The Road to Hill 10." *Atlantic Monthly*, April 1985, 90–118.

Butterfield, Fox. "The New Vietnam Scholarship." *New York Times Magazine*, 13 February 1983.

Caldwell, Patricia. *The Puritan Conversion Narrative: The Beginnings of American Expression*. Cambridge: Cambridge University Press, 1983.

Carroll, Peter N. *Puritanism and the Wilderness: The Intellectual Significance of the New England Frontier, 1629–1700*. New York: Columbia University Press, 1969.

———. *It Seemed Like Nothing Happened: The Tragedy and Promise of America in the 1970s*. New York: Holt, Rinehart & Winston, 1984.

Christie, Clive J. *A Preliminary Survey of British Literature on South-East Asia in the Era of Colonial Decline and Decolonisation*. Bibliography and Literature no. 3. Hull: Center for South-East Asian Studies, University of Hull, 1986.

Clifton, Merrit, ed. *Those Who Were There: Eyewitness Accounts of the War in Southeast Asia, 1956–75, and Aftermath*. Paradise, Calif.: American Dust Series, Dustbooks, 1984.

Douglas, Mary. *Purity and Danger: An Analysis of Concepts of Pollution and Taboo*. New York: Praeger, 1966.

Durand, Maurice M., and Nguyen Tran Huan. *An Introduction to Vietnamese Literature*. Trans. D. M. Hawke. New York: Columbia University Press, 1985.

Erikson, Kai T. *Wayward Puritans*. New York: John Wiley, 1966.

Fenton, James. "The Fall of Saigon." In *Granta* 15. Harmondsworth, England: Penguin, Spring 1985.

Fifield, Russell H. *Southeast Asia in United States Policy*. New York: Frederick A. Praeger, 1963.

Fitzgerald, Frances. *Fire in the Lake: The Vietnamese and the Americans in Vietnam*. New York: Random House, 1972.

Gelman, David. "Vietnam Marches Home." *Newsweek*, February 13, 1978.

Gibson, James William. *The Perfect War: Technowar in Vietnam*. Boston: Atlantic Monthly Press, 1986.

Gonnaud, Maurice, Sergio Perosa, and Christopher W. E. Bigsby, eds. *Cultural Change in the United States since World War II*. Amsterdam: Free University Press, 1986.

Groom, Winston, and Duncan Spencer. *Conversations with the Enemy*. New York: Viking Penguin, 1983.

Hallin, Daniel C. *The Uncensored War: The Media and Vietnam*. Oxford: Oxford University Press, 1986.

Hellmann, John. *American Myth and the Legacy of Vietnam*. New York: Columbia University Press, 1986.

Herring, George C. *America's Longest War: The United States and Vietnam, 1950–1975*. New York; John Wiley, 1979.

Herzog, Tobey C. "Writing about Vietnam: A Heavy Heart-of-Darkness Trip. *College English* 41 (February 1980): 680–95.

The Indochina Institute Report, George Mason University, 4400 University Drive, Fairfax, VA 22030–4444.

Indochina Newsletter, P.O. Box 129, Dorchester, MA 02122.

James, David. "Discourse of Presence/Presence of Discourse: The Vietnam Documentary." *Wide Angle* 7, no. 4 (1985): 41–51.

Jameson, Fredric. "Postmodernism, or the Cultural Logic of Late Capitalism." *New Left Review* 146 (1984): 53–92.

Joiner Center Newsletter, William Joiner Center for the Study of War and Social Consequences, University of Massachusetts at Boston. Vol. 1, no. 1, June 1987.

Kakutani, Michiko. "Novelists and Vietnam: The War Goes On." *New York Times Book Review* 15 April 1984, 1, 38–41.

Karnow, Stanley. *Vietnam: A History*. New York: Viking, 1983.

Klinkowitz, Jerome. *The American 1960s: Imaginative Acts in a Decade of Change*. Ames: Iowa State University Press, 1980.

Kolko, Gabriel. *The Anatomy of a War: Vietnam, the United States and the Modern Historical Experience*. New York: Pantheon, 1985.

Krepinevich, Andrew F. Jr. *The Army and Vietnam*. Baltimore: Johns Hopkins University Press, 1986.

"The Legacy of Vietnam." *Newsweek*, April 15, 1985.

Leitenberg, Milton, and Richard Dean Burns. *The Vietnam Conflict: Its Geographical Dimensions, Political Traumas and Military Developments*. War/Peace Bibliography Series in cooperation with the Center for the Study of Armament and Disarmament, California State University, Los Angeles. ABC-CLIO, Oxford, England, 1973.

Lewis, Lloyd B. *The Tainted War: Culture and Identity in Vietnam War Narratives*. Westport, Conn.: Greenwood Press, 1985.

Lomperis, Timothy. *The War Everyone Lost—and Won: America's Intervention in Vietnam's Twin Struggles*. Baton Rouge: Louisiana State University Press, 1984.

Lomperis, Timothy, and John Clark Pratt. *Reading the Wind: The Literature of the Vietnam War.* Durham, N.C.: Duke University Press, 1987.

Louvre, Alf, and Jeffrey Walsh, eds. *Tell Me Lies about Vietnam: Cultural Battles for the Meaning of the War.* Milton Keynes: Open University Press, December 1988.

Luce, Don, and John Sommer. *Viet Nam: The Unheard Voices.* Ithaca,: N.Y. Cornell University Press, 1969.

MacDonald, J. Fred. *Television and the Red Menace: The Video Road to Vietnam.* New York: Praeger, 1985.

MacPherson, Myra. *Long Time Passing: Vietnam and the Haunted Generation.* New York: Doubleday, 1985.

Marin, Peter. "Coming to Terms with Vietnam." *Harper's,* December 1980, 41–56.

McInerney, Peter. "Apocalypse Then: Hollywood Looks Back at Vietnam." *Film Quarterly* 33 (Winter 1979–80): 21–32.

———. " 'Straight' and 'Secret' History in Vietnam War Literature." *Contemporary Literature* 22 (Spring 1981): 187–204.

Myers, Thomas. *Walking Point: American Narratives of Vietnam.* New York: Oxford University Press, 1988.

Nam: The Vietnam Experience, 1965–75. London: Orbis Publishing, 1987.

Newman, John. *Vietnam War Literature.* Metuchen, N.J.: Scarecrow Press, 1982. Second edition 1988.

Olney, James. *Authobiography: Essays Theoretical and Critical.* Princeton: Princeton University Press, 1980.

Peake, Louis A. *The United States in the Vietnam War, 1945–1975: A Selected Annotated Bibliography.* New York: Garland, 1986.

Podhoretz, Norman. *Why We Were in Vietnam.* New York: Simon & Schuster, 1983.

Pratt, John Clark. *Vietnam Voices: Perspectives on the War Years, 1941–1982.* Harmondsworth: Viking Penguin, 1984.

———. "Bibliographic Commentary: "From the Fiction, Some Truths." In Timothy J. Lomperis, *Reading the Wind: The Literature of the Vietnam War.* Durham, N.C.: Duke University Press, 1987.

Race, Jeffrey. *War Comes to Long An: Revolutionary Conflict in a Vietnamese Province.* Berkeley: University of California Press, 1972.

Rapaport, Herman. "Vietnam: The Thousand Plateaus." See Sohnya Sayred, ed., *The 60s without Apology.* Minneapolis: University of Minnesota Press, 1984.

Ringnalda, Donald. "Fighting and Writing: America's Vietnam War Literature." *Journal of American Studies* (Cambridge University Press) 22 no. 1 (April 1988): 25–43.

Rollins, Peter. "Television's Vietnam: The Visual Language of Television News." *Journal of American Culture* 4, no. 2 (1981): 114–35.

———. "The Vietnam War: Perceptions through Literature, Film, and Television." *American Quarterly* 36 no. 3 (1984): 419–32.

Salisbury, Harrison E., ed. *Vietnam Reconsidered: Lessons from a War.* New York: Harper & Row, 1984.

Schroeder, Eric James. "Two Interviews: Talks with Tim O'Brien and Robert Stone." *Modern Fiction Studies* 30 (1984): 135–64.

Sheehan, Neil, et al. *The Pentagon Papers. New York Times* ed. New York: Bantam Books, 1971.

Slotkin, Richard. *Regeneration through Violence: The Mythology of the American Frontier: 1600–1860.* Middletown, Conn.: Wesleyan University Press, 1973.

Slotkin, Richard, and James K. Folsom, eds. *So Dreadfull a Judgement: Puritan Responses to King Philip's War, 1676–1677.* Middletown, Conn.: Wesleyan University Press, 1986.

Smith, Julian. *Looking Away: Hollywood and Vietnam.* New York: Charles Scribner's Sons, 1975.

Sugnes, Christopher L., and John T. Hickey. *Vietnam War Bibliography.* Selected from Cornell University's Echol's Collection. Lexington, Mass.: Lexington Books, 1983.

Summers, Harry, Jr. *On Strategy: A Critical Analysis of the Vietnam War.* New York: Dell, 1982.

Taylor, Gordon O. "American Personal Narrative of the War in Vietnam." *American Literature* 52 (1980): 294–308.

Thompson, James C., Jr., Peter W. Stanley, and John Curtiss Perry. *Sentimental Imperialists: The American Experience in East Asia.* New York: Harper & Row, 1981.

Vietnam Generation. An academic journal devoted to publishing articles about the Vietnam War and the effect of the war upon American culture, politics, and society. Includes bibliographic database. American Studies Department, Yale University, January 1989–.

Walsh, Jeffrey, and James Aulich, eds. *Vietnam Images: War and Representation.* London: Lumiere Macmillan, 1988.

Wells, Alan. *Picture-Tube Imperialism? The Impact of U.S. Television on Latin America.* Maryknoll, N.Y.: Orbis, 1972.

Williams, William Appleman. *The Tragedy of American Diplomacy.* New York: Dell, 1960.

Wilson, James C. *Vietnam in Prose and Film.* Jefferson, N.C.: McFarland, 1982.

Wittman, Sandra. *Writing about Vietnam: A Bibliography of the Literature of the Vietnam Conflict* (Boston: G. K. Hall & Co., 1989).

INDEX

THE AUTHOR

Phil Melling graduated from the University of Manchester in 1969 with first class honours in American studies. In 1978 he became the first full-time member of the Board of American Studies at the University of Wales, Swansea. He has taught at the University of Keele, the University of Manchester, Louisiana State University, and the University of Wisconsin–La Crosse. In recent years he has been the recipient of a British Council award and an Indiana Council for the Humanities scholarship. In addition to publishing studies on culture and the literature and society of the 1930s, Melling is also a playwright. His *Hotel Vietnam* has had three productions in Britain and a run at the Gate Theatre, London. In 1988 he organized the second international conference on Vietnam and the West at the University of Wales. He is now working on a novel and two books of Vietnam essays.